Urban
Economics and
Land Use in
America

Urban
Economics and
Land Use in
America

—

The Transformation of Cities
in the Twentieth Century

ALAN RABINOWITZ

M.E.Sharpe
Armonk, New York
London, England

Library of Congress Cataloging-in-Publication Data

Rabinowitz, Alan.
    Urban economics and land use in America : the transformation of cities in the
twentieth century / Alan Rabinowitz.
        p. cm.
    Includes bibliographical references and index.
    ISBN 0-7656-1410-3 (hardcover : alk. paper) ISBN 0-7656-1411-1 (pbk. : alk. paper)
        1. Cities and towns—United States—History—20th century. 2. Urbanization—
United States—History—20th century. 3. Metropolitan areas—United States—History—
20th century. 4. Urban economics. I. Title.

HT1230.R22 2004
307.76′0973—dc22

                                                                    2003061448

Printed in the United States of America

The paper used in this publication meets the minimum requirements of
American National Standard for Information Sciences
Permanence of Paper for Printed Library Materials,
ANSI Z 39.48-1984.

BM (c)   10   9   8   7   6   5   4   3   2   1
BM (p)   10   9   8   7   6   5   4   3   2   1

For my children

Contents

V. Looking Onward

Tables and Figures

Tables

Figures

Acknowledgments

This book emerged from experience and education over much of the twentieth century. As a start, I must acknowledge the significance of place in my life, for love of cities was bred into my bones. I was born in the Manhattan of the late 1920s, where our milk was delivered by horse cart, ice for the icebox and coal for the boiler came by small trucks, a time long before air-conditioning and automatic washing machines, a town with trolley cars and elevated railroads. As the suburbs and metropolises across the nation transformed the urban landscape during the rest of the century and pretty much replaced the physical and social ambiance of the cities America knew at the beginning of the century, I was living and working in "BosWash," the great swath of geography that runs from the Washington, D.C., area past Baltimore, Philadelphia, New York City, and the industrial cities of New England, until we moved to the Pacific Northwest.

I want to acknowledge a father who loved Manhattan and, in his time, knew the story of every building in it. My ideas were shaped by meeting and talking with some of the great urbanists with whom he was associated at various times in his career, such as Lillian D. Wald, Abraham Kazan, Herbert Lehman, Charles F. Noyes, Austin Tobin, Charles Abrams, Robert Moses, George Gove, and Jacob Potofsky.

And then there were my teachers, bosses, mentors, and colleagues as the years went by: Charles Abbott, Charles Ascher, Edward Banfield, Kerry Brooks, Charles Boyce, Wilford J. Byrne, Henry Cohen, Margaret DePopolo, Joseph Eldredge, Henry Fagin, Ellen Feingold, Ernest Fisher, Aaron Fleisher, Harry Foden, Bernard Frieden, Justin Gray, Leo Grebler, Arthur Grey, Charles Haar, Chester Hartman, Ruth Knack, Norman Krumholz, Edward Logue, Jeanne Lowe, Kevin Lynch, Ann Markeson, Martin Meyerson, S.M. Miller, Leo Molinaro, Folke Nyberg,

Dennis O'Harrow, Lisa Peattie, Ira Robbins, I.D. Robbins, Lloyd Rodwin, Jerry Rothenberg, Ann Satterthwaite, Paul Sedway, Ann Sheehan, John Sirjamaki, Roger Starr, Victor Steinbreuck, Stanley Tankel, Walter Thabit, Stephen Thompson, Sam Bass Warner, Joseph A. Weinberger, Marc Weiss, William L.C. Wheaton, Louis Winnick, Adam Yarmolinsky, Philip Zeigler, and so many others.

Valuable in the writing of this book, in addition to all the authors cited in the text, were Alan Divack, Roger Waldon, Stephen Silha, Eric Swenson, Colin Greer, Ruth Stokes, Jessica Klein, and Peter Barnes. Eric Valentine, my editor, was strategic and effective, and I am grateful for the ensuing good work in publishing by Lynn Taylor, Henrietta Toth, Laurie Lieb, and Teri Grimwood. My wife, Andrea, was invaluable, not only as mate in the years during which this book actually got written but as helpmate in all the many decades as her profession of clinical social work and my work in community development and planning coalesced.

I

Introduction

1

Overview

The addition of 200 million people to the nation's 1900 population transformed the urban economy of twentieth century America and created the suburbanized society we know at the beginning of the twenty-first century. That transformation made the metropolis, composed of many suburbs and one or more central cities, into the place where most of the population lived and worked. As the work of rebuilding the America of 1900 proceeded, we made basic changes again and again to all of the institutions that affect our urban economy: banking and finance, commerce and industry, real estate and construction, and, especially, local, state, and federal government. On the whole, the nation did an impressive job of settling so many more people than we had in 1900, although we also made some poor choices along the way as we retooled our economic and legal systems to handle the work. I am not the only one who believes we could have done better than to end up with the kind of sprawly, inequitable metropolitan areas that are scattered across the nation.

The first half of this book provides context for understanding the urban development scene as it appeared to the generations of Americans who inhabited this country about the year 1900. The previous century had enabled the United States to establish its continental boundaries and to provide land for settlement by dispossessing most of the Native Americans. The frontier was seen as "closed" only at the end of the nineteenth century. As the twentieth century began, citizens were aware of the vast changes that automobiles, airplanes, telephones, and radios would bring, and I discovered a wonderful tract by the eminent economist Richard T. Ely to illustrate the impact that suburbanization would have on the city. Several of these early chapters contain statistics for the whole of the twentieth century that provide background for discussing the impact of population growth and migration from east to west, from central city to suburb, and from rural to urbanizing regions.

The middle part of the book chronicles the changes in the political and economic life of the nation. Here we see generational conflict, institutionalized racism, world wars and depression, the rise of the real estate industry, and the origins and work of city and regional planners, as well as the rise and fall of "social housing," the savings and loan industry, environmental controls, and various private, academic, and governmental urban programs. Shedding light on many of these phenomena are quotations from participants in the events, especially from unpublished retrospective memoranda by Louis Winnick found in the archives of the Ford Foundation. The last two chapters deal with globalization, terrorism, and governance as they apply to America's metropolises since the destruction of the World Trade Center in 2001.

One endemic pervasive theme that runs through all the various dimensions of urbanization in twentieth-century America is the garden city, conceived as an oasis of civilization not too far from a major urban center, connected to the center by some sort of congestion-free transportation system but separated from the center by a greenbelt. This concept was extracted from a famous book published in England in 1898 by Ebenezer Howard and presented in a new form in 1902 with all of his communitarian social theories excised. America's builders, bankers, and local officials, happily adopting this soft garden city approach, then began to produce the kinds of real estate developments and garden apartments that filled up our suburbs and metropolises for the rest of the century. Reflecting this truncated version of Howard's vision of the garden city on a large scale are America's "new communities" such as Reston, Virginia, and Columbia, Maryland, and Britain's New Towns; for the midrange there are large-scale real estate developments with acres of single-family detached houses, while rows of garden apartments constitute the small-scale version.

Following this overview, Chapter 2 is devoted to Howard's work in order to illustrate the difference between the kind of metropolises we got and what we might have had if Americans had implemented his main ideas. Howard advanced original notions for creating an integrated town-and-country society, with agricultural greenbelts providing much of the food and open space for the villages in the area where there would be the requisite houses, manufactories, and stores. Each of these settlements would be linked to countless others in the nation. The economics of Howard's system would allow low rents for all the residents. Howard saw his scheme as the answer to overcrowding and poverty in the cities in England. Even though he wrote more than a hundred years ago, I find his ideas for "social cities" still basic to the good society and worth reconsidering by our body politic.

Adoption of Howard's ideas in the United States might have diverted us from headlong immersion in an ocean of autonomous suburbs and strip developments along our congested arterial highways. It might have prevented us from creating a society with the enormous income disparities we typically see between parts of our metropolises. We might be enjoying far more green open spaces for recreation and agriculture in those same metropolises than have been left to us by a century of real estate development as practiced in our present form of capitalism. Unless we begin to act as comprehensively and as humanely as Ebenezer Howard would have us do, the sadly deficient social and economic conditions that now characterize our metropolitanized society will probably continue indefinitely.

This book emerged from my reflection on the ideas that influenced the institution-building work of the generations in power during those ten decades. My objective is to help change those conditions by encouraging readers to broaden and deepen their understanding of where we were at the beginning of the twentieth century, why and how so many new institutions came into being, and what happened to them over time. I wrote this book for the people, young and old, who ask about the processes that created our present circumstances and want ways to think about the future. I wrote to provide context and background for those who are studying in such fields as government, law, sociology, the natural and artificial environment, civil engineering, public health, business, and city planning and who expect to have careers dealing with metropolitan problems. And I wrote to explain my days and years to my grandchildren, for much of the work happened in my lifetime. And of course, in the process of doing all this, I found myself adding my personal perspectives to useful quotations from learned observers of the passing scene on scores of events, ideas, laws and judicial decisions, people and their professions, books, and research findings that came along in the varied circumstances of the century's decades. Some of these subjects and conclusions may be familiar, but I hope that they will be viewed in new and interesting ways hereafter.

To personalize the different proposals for changing the various institutions that constitute the urban economy, I invented two prototypical groups, the "Ebenezers" and the "Babbitts." In this book, Ebenezers are people who stand up for the kind of community values explicitly advanced in Ebenezer Howard's first book. In frequent opposition to Howard's philosophy are those I named the Babbitts (after George Babbitt, the protagonist of Sinclair Lewis's novel *Babbitt*), whom I define as people who see themselves as good enough citizens (even though some of them seem pretty venal to me) but who prefer to spend their time and money for the direct benefit of a community they know rather than for uncertain benefits for a general public outside the bounds of their own community. I assume my readers are familiar with both the Ebenezer and Babbitt types.

Most of the people who live in the suburbs are probably Babbitts but many are Ebenezers. According to polls, most of these suburbanites seem to enjoy working and shopping in a low-density environment, and nothing can get them away from the gasoline-powered vehicles they require for effective living; they enjoy their single-family houses on separate lots and the more recent gated condominium developments. Most of them are not against helping other people, and many of them are properly chagrined at the ecological damage they are collectively causing, but they are somewhat less apologetic about the social and economic consequences of their preferences for middle-class living in the suburbs, and practically all of them tell pollsters that they want a high-quality environment, good jobs, and great schools for their metropolis. Obtaining voting majorities for systemic changes to accomplish what the pollsters inquire about has not yet happened anywhere in America, however. One notable aspect of the presidential campaigns in 2000 was the agreement among all the major parties that, for the first time in history, "sprawl" was an important issue for voters and that the federal government should do something about it, but nothing was done in the months before the events of September 11, 2001.

The factors that produced sprawl were deeply influenced by the characteristics of the five or six generations that came to power one after another during the twentieth century. The decisions by legislators about our urban and urbanizing society are paramount among those factors that create the institutionalized forms of government and private enterprise that in turn determine how our system builds our metropolises. Many of our concepts about this system stem from the work of Richard T. Ely, one of the great institutional economists, concerning the urban economy of the United States, which may explain my delight in discovering the 1902 lecture that is quoted in Chapter 7 below.

And actually, as our population rose from 76 million in 1900 to 281 million in 2000, the many new systems of governance, public and private finance, and large-scale real estate development that were invented and established during that period did allow those additional people to get fairly well settled in hundreds of new and old metropolises. These systems can still be made to operate fairly effectively. What they often lack, and what will be increasingly needed as the nation gears up to ingest another 100 million more people in the next three or four decades, are ways to incorporate "heart" into the proceedings, not bleeding-heart sentimentality, but a keen sense of how this vast machinery of development, in the process of creating net benefits for the majority of people, generates all sorts of unwanted "disbenefits" for the community as a whole as well as for its less fortunate segments.[1] Unfortunately, at least in my opinion, proposals for "smart growth" and "new urbanism" are probably too late and certainly too little to accomplish changes on a significant scale without changes in the hearts and minds of the voters substantial enough to get the system restructured—never mind that it is also probably too late to create the world that Ebenezer Howard envisaged.

A major stumbling block is our nationwide difficulty in imagining what we want for our metropolises other than what we have. We spent the twentieth century transforming the world of 1900 into the metropolises of today. Now we seem to know only how to produce more of the same. My favorite word to describe the cumulative impact of the long succession of legislative, economic, and political choices we made during the twentieth century is "transmogrification"! My *Oxford Universal Dictionary* states that it is a somewhat jocular term dating from 1656: "To alter or change in form or appearance; to transform utterly, grotesquely, or strangely." Its significance, relative to our inability to imagine a different future is wonderfully illustrated in Bill Watterson's *Calvin and Hobbes* comic strip, when Calvin, the small boy, asks if Hobbes, his toy tiger, wants to see the new transmogrifier, which looks like a cardboard box and which Calvin has designed and built; Hobbes says he did not know that Calvin had a transmogrifier and then, finding it works amazingly well, asks what Calvin will do with it now; Calvin pensively replies, "good question."[2]

Calvin, quite properly, is not sure what to do with his transmogrifying machine, and Americans are not sure what kinds of changes they want to see in their metropolises, even though we do know a great deal about what it will take to improve life in a metropolis for all of its residents. We do know that every urban area is unique in some ways, similar to other metropolises in others. We do know the various institutional factors that promote racism and economic disparities in and among the autonomous cities and suburbs in the typical metropolis, and we know the trouble that we as a society will have to endure in order to eliminate such blights of the body politic. The problem, of course, is that all changes have some combination of heavy political, financial, sociological, or physical consequences. What group is paying the taxes and what group benefits? Who gets to live in affordable housing, and wouldn't it be cooler to use the funds for a new baseball stadium? Why should citizens in our sovereign suburbs who commute by automobile to the central city for their jobs have to contribute to a mass transit system they do not use? And so on. Transmogrification will continue to happen willy-nilly, as citizens and their elected representatives make their choices.

Some of the changes are just as the dictionary says—utter, grotesque, and strange—as in the destruction of the World Trade Center's towers on September 11, 2001. That event marks the end of the century in a more dramatic, profound way than did the mere passage into a new millennium in the year 2000, and it is changing many of our assumptions about how America might develop in the twenty-first century. As people are added to the population, the typical metropolis may become more densely settled (and, perhaps, fewer monumental skyscrapers will be erected), but the more important changes will be those affecting the laws, the state constitutions, and the implementing processes and procedures that emerged from the twentieth century.

The successive generations in power in America during those ten decades included individuals with widely different politics and interests, and America was well transmogrified in their time. The hundreds of metropolises in which we live in these early years of the new century are the raw material for the future, just as the cities of 1900 were the raw material for the post–Civil War generations who knew that America was on its way to becoming a Great Power. Not surprisingly, we find intense debates going on about how to improve the economic, social, and physical livability of each locality. One wonders whether the changes to come can match the changes that were wrought in the twentieth century.

Metropolitanization is so basic to our civilization that the changing ways we live in cities and suburbs involve almost all aspects of our culture, our political and social institutions, and, increasingly, our relations with the global economy. And during the last hundred years, those diverse pieces of land that constitute the United States have been so transformed, dug up and replanted, redeveloped, and argued over that a Rip Van Winkle gone to sleep in 1900 would have found little in 1999 that was familiar to the eye and much that was beyond comprehension as to function or operation. He would have to struggle to understand an unfamiliar set of cityscapes and countryscapes together with sea changes in the nature of jobs, income, housing, transportation, and communication. The prognostications of the pundits of 2000, however, are less visionary than those of 1900, for the current pundits, it seems to me, are more invested in their schemes for reducing sprawl or making localities competitive in world markets than in painting rosy pictures of life in the twenty-first century.

Because of the law of unintended consequences, many well-intentioned bits of legislation produced vaster changes than originally anticipated or hoped for as they got implemented by thousands of towns and cities, tens of thousands of business firms and financial institutions, and millions of individuals and families. As examples, consider how the first-ever federal program of assistance to state and local governments, which did not come until 1916 in the form of a rural roads program, blossomed into myriad federal categorical programs that in turn were bulldozed into block grants in the 1970s; or how the introduction of a simple form of land use zoning in the 1920s became the incredibly complex sets of controls that shape our urban regions; or how some simple deregulations led to the evaporation of three-quarters of a trillion dollars in the collapse of the savings and loan institutions in the 1980s (with hardly a murmur or public inquiry, much less outrage). And consider also the cumulative impact of such nongovernmental events as the publication in 1962 of Rachel Carson's *Silent Spring,* which energized the whole modern environmental movement.[3]

I have great respect for the environmentalists who devote their lives to protection and improvement of the nation's lands and our limited resources of air and water, and, even though many of the topics in this book are not directly applicable to their interests, I hope they will find in these pages some insight into why it is so hard to make progress in their field. As we changed the ways we operate our political economy, during the previous ten decades, we discovered that our nation's land had come under unbearably intense and constant pressure from both public and private agencies. Somewhat late in the great land-use game that enraptures Americans came the 1964 Wilderness Act (Public Law 88–577), which Congress enacted "in order to assure that an increasing population, accompanied by expanding settlement and growing mechanization, does not occupy and modify all areas within the United States . . . leaving no lands designated for preservation and protection in their natural condition. . . ."[4]

In fact, we have not only occupied and urbanized vast amounts of land that were open, forested, farmed, or otherwise untrammeled in 1900, but we have modified, developed, redeveloped, and reshaped the cities and towns of 1900 into the sprawling, congested metropolitan conglomerations of 2000. Although sordid political stories and embarrassingly poor developments accompanied some of those land conversions, others were done with the best of intentions and the highest level of professional skills so that the changes are lovely, beneficial, impressive, and far beyond the wildest imaginations of the pundits of 1900 who tried to look ahead.

We do well to celebrate the designers and builders of the truly fine projects; the nation's libraries are full of books detailing great civic design and architectural achievements and studies of particular localities, all far beyond the scope of this book. Nor is this volume on the scale of the wonderful studies, involving scores of researchers over extended periods, that portray the state of the nation at a particular moment in history, such as Lord Bryce's *The American Commonwealth,* published in 1888, and the massive report of President Herbert Hoover's Research Committee on Social Trends, *Recent Social Trends in the United States,* in 1933, just before President Roosevelt took office.[5] This book is simply my own interpretation of the America of my lifetime and worklife, since I have been alive through almost three-quarters of the twentieth century and participated directly and indirectly, as both innocent citizen and diligent professional, in many of the activities that transmogrified America. The book is as synoptic, historically accurate, anecdotally analytic, and grounded as I can manage.

Even though this book is more modest than those great studies, I want to convey the same sense they did of the historical continuity that underlies American society as we experience it daily. In 2004 we may have vast amounts of data and wonderful ways to manipulate them with computers, but many of us have lost or never had an understanding of our place in that history. What matters are the ideas and ideologies, as well as the motivations, of those who instituted or institutionalized those seminal pieces of legislation, investment, or publication in the past ten decades. It is the chain of these ideas and acts that makes this work interesting, sometimes inspirational, sometimes infuriating, always instructive. The fun of writing this kind of a book, of course, is to see, in retrospect, how one idea fed into the next until we collectively transformed—transmogrified—the America of 1900 into the America we call home today.

In the early drafts of this book, I tried to avoid the whole question of what Americans might now do to make their towns and cities more livable, with less traffic congestion and more physical beauty and safety. All I wanted to do was to show how, step by step for the past hundred years, we created these complicated and inequitable places. I hoped that a mere showing of the processes at work during that dynamic century would be enough to suggest to any reader that those processes would continue unabated unless we made some structural changes to our metropolitan-building systems despite the obvious political difficulties in making such changes. But even my friendly critics said I could not avoid the question, so, laying my professional reputation on the line at the very start, here is what I think can and should be done:

1. Because I believe that the fatal flaw was allowing suburbs for the well-to-do to have too much autonomy, too exclusive an access to taxable resources, and too little responsibility for the health, education, and welfare of less fortunate citizens of the metropolis, I have come to believe that it is imperative for each state legislature to exercise its unquestioned power to realign the powers it gives to local governments to correct that fatal flaw. No real progress can be made along these lines by local officials themselves or by citizens acting under existing laws and dealing with the scores, and sometimes hundreds, of autonomous governmental entities in a typical metropolis.

2. The best way for each state to ordain new governance for its metropolises is to institute its own brand of "metropolitan federalism," with each metropolis having its own elected legislature composed of a senate and house, its own elected chief executive, and its own elected judiciary, thus recognizing neighborhood values and needs as well as the need for metropolitan-wide activities.

3. Any new system for governance of the metropolis must be able to produce money for a long list of necessary public goods and services,

especially for education and care for children. I pray that the federal government will find a way to support local schools generously, but I do not think that either the U.S. Congress or the state legislatures will continue to send money to the metropolises of America for transportation and other forms of infrastructure. Each metropolis is going to have to figure out how to raise the funds necessary for such purposes from its own citizens.

4. Local governments (including metropolitan-wide ones) obviously need to have the power to regulate all sorts of activities, but flexibility and common sense should be the watchwords of the administrators. A wide variety of expert skills is required to make local governance effective. The circumstances of 1900 no longer apply, when a small group of experts, with the blessing of the city's leading citizens, could make and implement plans and projects to improve the locality. So we need to invent some new forms of metropolitan-wide planning that incorporate fairness, expertise, comprehensiveness, and good design into the search for efficiency and economy.

The list above is good enough for a start. I do believe that lots of little improvements can combine to solve very big problems. I do believe that many good ideas for improving life in the metropolis are worth implementing more fully. Those ideas include those under the rubric of smart growth and new urbanism. I do not really think that Very Large Ideas of the kind advanced by Ebenezer Howard or by his friend Henry George (who advocated a single-tax system) have any chance of being implemented, but I believe very deeply that the spirit that they represent is an essential ingredient for betterment of the metropolitan condition. In short, Ebenezer really does live on in the hearts of all those who want to see the metropolis serve the needs of all people rather than just those who can hide themselves away in wealthy enclaves or gated communities.

2

How Garden Cities Became the Standard for the Development of American Suburbs

What unsettled the propertied classes about Ebenezer Howard and what makes him of particular use as an icon for this book was his pioneering work, *To-morrow: A Peaceful Path to Real Reform*, published in England in 1898.[1] What made him famous a few years later was publication of his *Garden Cities of Tomorrow*, a truncated, bland revision of his original thought that allowed our movers and shakers to get away with talking only about "garden cities" rather than about social reform for society as a whole.[2] Scores of books have been written about the influence of the garden city on the building of suburbs in the United States but almost none of them recall the role that garden cities were intended to play in implementing Howard's vision of a rational and fair urban society.

Howard, an "obscure 48-year-old shorthand writer living in genteel poverty with a harassed wife and four children in a modest house in north London" in October 1898,[3] takes the prize, in my opinion, for providing the most feasible and fairest utopian concept of what urban life could have been like in the twentieth century (granted that implementation of his ideas now in the twenty-first century is only barely conceivable, and only if we begin to reconstruct the suburbs over a long period of time). Anyhow, for me, his ideas still constitute a high standard by which to evaluate the urban society that America made and remade in the twentieth century.

What Howard did was write a potentially revolutionary book dealing with the manifold problems of congested cities that were not able to provide healthy environments and decent livelihoods for their citizens. He was truly more interested in the economic welfare of people than in

Figure 2.1 **Portrait of Ebenezer Howard**

Source: Adapted from cover illustration by Clifford Harper for "One Hundred Years of *To-morrow.*" Special Supplement to *Town and Country Planning* (October 1998). Used by permission of TCPA.

the shrubbery in an upscale suburb, and so I have used the term "Ebenezer" throughout the rest of this book to refer to anyone who works to make urban life better for all people, the poor as well as the rich, in contrast to a "Babbitt" who is primarily interested in his or her own comforts in an urban, but more likely a suburban, setting.

As we shall see, *To-morrow*'s message was quickly suppressed and traduced, reemerging limply in that watered-down 1902 version entitled *Garden Cities of Tomorrow.* A politically neutered interpretation of the garden city became the model for the subsequent development of most of the housing and nonresidential areas of both the United States and Britain. The model helped our capitalist society to avoid many of the basic issues that Howard addressed in his first book, issues that persisted throughout the twentieth century (and still today) concerning social justice and economic fairness.

But to understand how dramatic Howard's original proposals were, we need to provide some background on both America and his native England. In America, the twentieth century was opening with a fair amount of attention paid to urban problems and slums, primarily in cities of the Northeast. Chicago had burned in 1871, the last accidental destruction of a major city. In earlier times such great conflagrations had burned overcrowded neighborhoods of wooden buildings down to the ground on a regular basis, automatically providing opportunities for rebuilding and upgrading, but the skills of the firefighters improved in the late nineteenth century even as brick and brownstone structures were replacing combustible wood, so that a much less combustible and more permanent form of city was being created.

The great Professor Ely (about whom we will talk later on) and his rather more conservative academic colleagues were happily constructing the economic theories of public utilities and public investment in growing cities and were not particularly concerned in their professional capacities with the actual messy conditions in what were being called Great Cities. The populations of Great Cities like London and New York had been expanding rapidly as they absorbed the enormous waves of migration from other countries, and from rural areas that were slowly losing population.[4]

The elite, educated businessmen and reformers in England and America that constituted the audience for the economists of the day had similar expectations about how their cities and fledgling suburbs should be developed. This was the age of new modes of rapid transit and a vast amount of what is often called "regularization" of the urban environment. Regularization covers the building of water and sewage systems; the creation of utility services for electric, gas, telegraph, and telephone; and the professionalization of police, fire, and sanitation departments.

As cities lost the battle to own their own public utilities so that they could profit from their natural monopolies on the sale of gas, electricity, and water and from franchises for use of city streets by privately owned "public" utilities, they were forced into greater and greater reliance on property taxes on land and buildings. Gradually business leaders, politicians, and academics learned to deal with the essential elements of state and local public finance, community economic development, and, later in the century, and for the more mathematically adept, policy analysis in the new field of urban economics.[5] At the same time, Ely and his fellow economists and political scientists were debating alternative fiscal and financial approaches to urban development, especially regarding public utilities and transit companies. At Harvard, for example, the primary roost of the leading economists was the university's Bureau of Municipal Affairs.

Over the years, professional economists became less involved with local problems and much more interested in keeping track of and understanding the national economy. By the 1920s, leaders such as Wesley Clair Mitchell at the new National Bureau of Economic Research were concocting national income and product accounts and generating data to explore concepts for managing the national economy such as were being advanced by John Maynard Keynes. In the aftermath of the worldwide depression of the 1930s and World War II, their attention shifted to monetary stability in the international community and economic development of underdeveloped nations. In the 1950s, Walter Isard began the Regional Science Association to allow the economics profession to deal with the spatial aspects of urban, regional, and transportation problems.

Cities have always needed revenues. In 1900, there were relatively few state sales taxes and no federal, state, or local taxes on income, for all monies an individual or firm received from whatever source were considered property under U.S. and state constitutions and could be taxed only at a flat rate rather than in a progressive way. In 1913, the states ratified the Sixteenth Amendment to the Constitution that permitted federal income taxes and changed forever the fiscal landscape of the nation.

Reformers in the central cities from 1900 on could not fail to hear the siren song of the autonomous suburbs, to which were moving well-to-do families who did not want to pay property taxes for inner-city services, such as public baths, beneficial to people not like themselves. The added costs of providing for immigrant populations in the cities were of no direct benefit to suburbanites. They simply removed themselves to the suburbs, away from the slummy, overcrowded buildings housing legions of immigrant and low-income people, a condition that had begun to trouble city leaders and health departments on both sides of the Atlantic. Not long before, in 1892, and for the first time in American history, the U.S. Congress had acknowledged the existence of cities, for the practice before had been to assume that, under the Constitution, federal officials could deal only with state government, not local governments that were wholly creatures of the states. The acknowledgement came in the form of a study commission to consider problems in slum areas of four major cities, but it was many decades before any significant urban legislation was forthcoming.

Enter Henry George and what became the single tax movement. His great work, *Progress and Poverty*, first published in 1881, is often seen as a precursor to Ebenezer Howard's reliance on municipal ownership of land. Here is one of Henry George's crisp comments on the subject of taxation:

> The elder Mirabeau, we are told, ranked the proposition of Quesnay, to substitute one single tax on rent (the *impôt unique*) for all other taxes, as a discovery equal in utility to the invention of writing or the substitution of the use of money for barter.
>
> To whomsoever will think over the matter, this saying will appear an evidence of penetration rather than of extravagance. The advantages which would be gained by substituting for the numerous taxes by which the public revenues are now raised, a single tax levied upon the value of land, will appear more and more important the more they are considered.[6]

George's idea was that the single tax would be placed only on the rental value of the land, and, of course, the rental value of any piece of land is mostly a reflection of the increase of population and the associated intensification of activities upon the land. He argued that municipal ownership of land is feasible and desirable, but clearly such an idea was not attractive to either the Americans of his day or of ours. Here is how he justified the idea of removing land from private ownership:

> The greater part of the land of Great Britain is cultivated by tenants, the greater part of the buildings of London are built upon leased ground, and even in the United States the same system prevails everywhere to a greater or lesser extent. Thus it is a common matter for use to be separated from ownership.
>
> Would not all this land be cultivated and improved just as well if the rent went to the State or municipality, as now, when it goes to private individuals? If no private ownership in land were acknowledged, but all land were held in this way, the occupier or user paying rent to the State, would not land be used and improved as well and as securely as now? There can be but one answer: Of course it would. Then would the resumption of land as common property in nowise interfere with the proper use and improvement of land.
>
> What is necessary for the use of land is not its private ownership but the security of improvements. It is not necessary to say to a man, "this

land is yours," in order to induce him to cultivate or improve it. It is only necessary to say to him, "whatever your labor or capital produces on this land shall be yours." Give a man security that he may reap, and he will sow; assure him of the possession of the house he wants to build, and he will build it. These are the natural rewards of labor. It is for the sake of the reaping that men sow; it is for the sake of possessing houses that men build. The ownership of land has nothing to do with it.[7]

Both George and Howard were willing to use land in order to create an industrial civilization and a firm agricultural base for the mass of people forced to live in poverty in unattractive settings while the fruits of their labor gravitated unfairly to landlords and other "rentiers," those who, in the language of Karl Marx, receive a share of the income created by the labor of others and who are not productive themselves. George, however, did not create the physical design of the community that would be implementing his notion of a proper political economy. That honor goes to Ebenezer Howard.

If twenty-first century media standards had been applicable in 1898, according to Ray Thomas in his *Town and Country Planning* article a century later, Ebenezer Howard would have been called "a tired-of-London suburbanite, the scourge of landlords, a communist utopian, the enemy of property-owning democracy, a transmogrified land-taxer, a greenhorn developer, and, more thoughtfully, a municipal anti-capitalist."[8]

What Howard was actually suggesting was the building of a vast network of social cities on low-cost land that was not too far from London and that was more or less abandoned by farmers. Each social city, with a population of about 250,000, would be quite self-sufficient in terms of food based on new agriculture in the greenbelts between the central city and the garden cities.[9] Each garden city, and there would typically be about six in each social city, would have housing, shopping, and workplaces, as in Howard's meticulously penned diagrams reproduced as Figure 2.2. The diagrams in the 1898 book show that the separate garden cities were only parts of a larger integrated society, but that diagrammatic representation of the whole integrated socioeconomic program was apparently too radical for him to include in the 1902 rewrite. The truly innovative aspect of Howard's idea was the economic analysis that underlay it. The modest financial burden he proposed to put on the residents of his social city was less than half of what the citizens of London were paying in rent and municipal charges. On that basis alone (to the putative despair of London landlords, but to Howard's delight that his new cities would bankrupt those landlords), citizens would be able and eager to migrate to a network of the new social cities. See the text of Howard's third diagram, which I have transcribed as Figure 2.3.

Howard was not against the ownership of private property nor particularly interested in Karl Marx's concept of public ownership of the means of production, but he was against the inequitable social system that was clearly emerging as cities grew larger.[10] He was anticapitalist only in the sense that land in social city was to be municipally owned, enabling the public to capture the unearned increments that come to a property owner when increased urban activities in the area make land more valuable than it was as raw or agricultural land. With social city itself receiving such unearned increment in value, there would be no need for a separate tax system—or for landlords for that matter—residents would simply make one payment covering what had been rent and local taxes. Howard put all those desirable attributes into one comprehensive package tying the environmental, industrial, social, governmental, and financial threads together as a challenge to mankind. Nothing before or since has matched his broad scope in providing a rationale for responsible "management of the territory," as the French would say. As Ray Thomas observes, in answer to his question of why Howard's ideas seemed so dangerous to people:

> A short answer to these questions is that Howard wrote about urban economics, but his book became popular because it was seen as being about planning. The Garden City became a symbol of his ideas. The supporting rationalities took second place and were forgotten—or never learned—by many supporters of the new towns movement. . . .
>
> Howardian theory indicates the normal urban growth process produces the opposite of what later came to be "self-contained and balanced communities." Unplanned urban growth in capitalist societies can be expected to result, in ever increasing scale, in social segregation. Howardian theory hypothesizes that the inner city problem is essentially the geographical manifestation of inequality in society.[11]

I think what happened then, and happens still, is that the builders and architects in the urban development community rarely saw the need to trouble themselves about the social and economic policies that cause inequitable distribution of economic benefits and eventually slums, nor about the finances of the municipal governments they rely upon for services to their development projects, and it was not until later in the century that they were forced to deal with both the environmental and fiscal

Figure 2.2 (a, b)   **Diagrams of Ebenezer Howard's "Social City"**

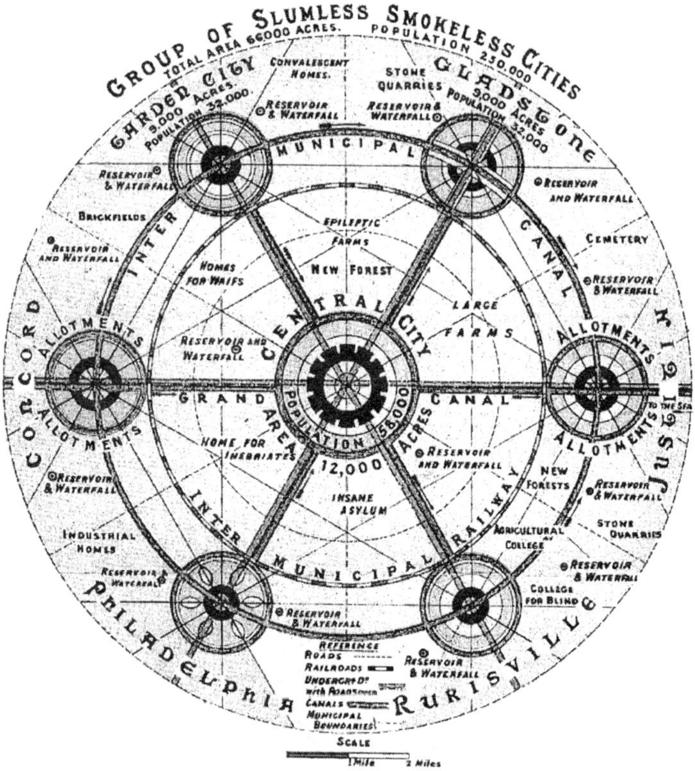

Source: Taken from the diagrams in Ebenezer Howard, *To-morrow: A Peaceful Path to Real Reform* (London: Swan Sonnenschein, 1898), p. 130.

impacts of their projects. Thus Henry George's single tax ideas never found wide support, and Ebenezer Howard's economic and social rationale for his concept of a network of communities surrounded by useful agricultural land was dropped. (According to Ray Thomas, little acknowledgment of his contributions was made in all the post–World War II negotiations in England over the building of new towns and over the compensation-and-betterment schemes.)

The Garden City (Instead of Social City) Becomes the Vision

Only the concept of a brand-new town more conveniently laid out and with more open space than in the existing cities fired the capitalistic

imagination of the architects and builders of the day (or since). The irony is that Howard apparently never even got to be considered a town planner in England; he is not included in *Pioneers in British Planning*.[12] The honored pioneers are eight in number: Thomas Adams, Patrick Geddes, Raymond Unwin, Patrick Abercrombie, George Papier, Thomas Sharp, Frederic Osborn, and Colin Buchanan, many of them exceptionally well known on both sides of the Atlantic in connection with the British New Town movement, which basically institutionalized Howard's physical concepts without the disturbing sociopolitical ones so integral to the self-sustaining garden cities of his social city.

In the preface to *Sociable Cities: The Legacy of Ebenezer Howard*, the book that Peter Hall and Colin Ward, stalwarts of England's Town and Country Planning Association, wrote to honor the centennial of *Tomorrow*'s publication, they write that its successor, *Garden Cities of Tomorrow*, became:

> the most influential and important book in the entire history of twentieth-century city planning. Over the following 70 years it effectively produced the pioneer garden cities at Letchworth and Welwyn, in which Howard took a personal role, and then—long after his death in 1928—some 30 new towns in the United Kingdom as well as countless imitations all over the world.[13]

Figure 2.3 **Howard's Analysis of Occupancy Costs in a Social City**

Rent and local rates of an average population are equal to about L 144,000 per annum being L 4.10 per head of population with a constant tendency to rise.

Available for landlord's rent . . . L 80,000

Available for municipal purposes . . . L 64,000

By migrating to Garden City rents and rates are at once reduced to L 2 per head, out of which a sinking fund is provided for the gradual extinction of landlord's rent. This being attained, all the funds hitherto devoted to that purpose may be applied municipally or to the provision of old age pensions.

On completion after 10 years/after 20 years/after 25 years/30th year/thence forward

Available for landlords rent L 2,600   2600   –0–   –0–   –0–   –0–

Sinking fund . . . . L 4,400   6,514   8,620   11,750   13,800   –0–

Available for municipal purposes . . . . . . L 44,000   44,000   44,000   44,000   44,000

Old age pensions. . . . . –0–   –0–   –0–   –0–   –0–   14,000

Source: Adapted from Figure 4 in Ebenezer Howard, *To-morrow: A Peaceful Path to Real Reform* (London: Swan Sonnenschein, 1898), p. 23.

Howard talked about the advantages that served as magnets to generate interest in social cities, here as Peter Hall described them:

> *The town* gave economic and social opportunities, but poor housing and a degraded environment. *The country* offered clean air and open country, but few opportunities for a decent livelihood and a narrow, exclusive social life. But a new combination—*"Town-Country,"* the town in the middle of the country—offered all the advantages of both, without any of the concomitant problems.[14]

Hall and Ward recast the three magnets into 1998 conditions, but, although much of what they write resonates with an American reader, their book is lacking in references to our experience with garden city projects in the United States. These began to appear on this side of the Atlantic early in the century and quite dramatically in the 1920s with the building of suburbs like Bronxville (New York), Shaker Heights (outside of Cleveland), and, notably, the creation of Radburn in New Jersey. The 1930s saw the construction of greenbelt towns by the federal government and the programs of the Federal Housing Administration (FHA) to encourage construction of projects featuring "garden apartments" (for residents with similar incomes) under FHA sections 207 and 608, programs that became the dominant mode for most of the postwar period.[15]

No one was more fervent about this type of development than Catherine Bauer, the preeminent "houser" of the midcentury whose statue graces the lobby of the headquarters of the U.S. Department of Housing and Urban Development in the nation's capital. A recent biography of her connects me to this topic in an unusual way: my mentor in city planning, Martin Meyerson, wrote the foreword, declaiming that "Catherine Bauer was a national treasure." Then in the text I read a story about Lloyd Rodwin, my dissertation adviser and mentor in the field of urban economics:

> One day her eye fell upon an article entitled "Garden Cities and the Metropolis" in the August 1945 issue of the *Journal of Land and Public Utility Economics* (later known as *Land Economics*). She noted with dismay that it criticized the Garden City concept espoused by the British urban theorist, Ebenezer Howard, in his 1898 book, *Garden Cities of Tomorrow*—a text she held dear. . . . A born and bred New Yorker who thought he understood the big city, Rodwin found Ebenezer Howard's ideas bizarre. . . . In Rodwin's view, Howard had paid insufficient attention to the regions in which Garden Cities were to play their strategic roles. He challenged Howard's assumptions on issues of rural migration, population growth, industrial location, journey to work, comparative urban costs, and municipal government administration. . . . Rodwin pronounced Howard's planning formulas simplistic.[16]

My further reading in H. Peter Oberlander and Eva Newbrun's book about this contretemps between Catherine Bauer and Lloyd Rodwin makes me think that this is a case of apples and oranges. Rodwin, quite properly, was asserting that an autonomous garden city built to Howard's scale, much less a whole Howardian social city complex, was impossible to contemplate in the existing metropolis that Rodwin, a city planner, had in mind. Bauer, using her architecturally trained imagination, was contemplating massive shifts of population to unpopulated regions served by recently constructed electricity-producing dams in places like the Columbia River watershed where, in theory, there would be space to build from scratch a social city that incorporated an array of garden cities. Both Bauer and Rodwin could be correct in their perceptions.

In any case, the garden city theme is a silent underpinning of any discussion of suburban living, residential building, and urban development in this country. While many books about garden cities in the United States and about the British New Town already grace the libraries of designers, architects, landscape architects, and social psychologists. Of greater importance to urban economists and planners, however, are the basic conflicts that throughout the twentieth century have raged about American cities' forms and functions, governance and glories, planning and processes, people and places. These conflicts erupted at the beginning of that century as Howard's ideas crossed the Atlantic. The suburban builders who have added the word "garden" to their projects have probably never known how Ebenezer Howard in 1898 had integrated the idea of garden city into his original dynamic proposal.

The nature of comprehensive planning in America is heavily influenced by the complex governmental structure that characterizes our far-flung federal system. In an England whose land area is as large as the state of Oregon, Parliament sets the rules, the appropriate ministries in London interpret them, and all local governments in the realm (are supposed to) comply in exactly the same way. In the United States, according to the 1997 Census of Governments, we had, in addition to one federal government and fifty "sovereign" state governments, 87,453 identifiable units of government, which was actually 29,303 fewer than in 1962, largely due to consolidations, especially of school and other special, single-purpose districts.[17] The total includes 3,043 counties, 19,372 municipalities or cities, 16,629 towns or townships, 13,726 independent school districts, and 34,683 other special districts.

Not all of the general, multipurpose governments exert the zoning and other form-giving powers they could exert under the various state enabling acts, which, of course, differ one from another, and not all the governmental units that might exercise some sort of planning function do so (and, in the 1920s and 1930s, only a very few local governments had employees trained in city planning).[18] However, all sorts of these governmental units (especially independent school districts, single-function special districts, and privately owned railroads, public utilities, and urban redevelopment companies given eminent-domain powers (and, by extension, many different agencies of state government, notably highway departments), have independent authority to site new facilities or to change existing facilities, thus influencing how development occurs in a particular part of a particular locality.

The stir about the garden city format began at the turn of the century. At the time, suburbs were beginning to sprout in the environs of existing urban hubs, the City Beautiful movement was in full flower (implemented by architects trained at the École des Beaux Arts in Paris), and city planning and regional planning as conscious activities were in their formative stages, as was the institution of zoning.[19] Engst and Hickerson observe:

> The English "garden city" of Letchworth, begun in 1903, was inspired by the ideas of Ebenezer Howard, whose book *Garden Cities of Tomorrow* (1902) started a worldwide garden city movement. Letchworth, thirty-five miles from London, was owned by a private corporation and originally designed to include residential, commercial, and industrial areas surrounded by an agricultural and recreational greenbelt. However, the area developed primarily as a commuter suburb of London.
>
> The influence of Howard's thinking in America can readily be seen in garden suburbs such as Forest Hills Gardens in New York City [1909]. While these American suburbs reflected the residential environment of Letchworth, they were, from the first, planned as suburbs rather than self-sufficient communities.[20]

Not until the 1920s did the English leadership in garden-citying become fully translated into American practice; the most visible manifestation of all was Radburn, a planned community in New Jersey, started in 1928. The social, economic, and architectural dimensions of town planning in the history of such new communities in relation to the development of cities and metropolises are important but beyond the scope of this book; most histories of housing and planning in the United States contain a number of references to them.[21] Over the years, however, the possibility of relatively autonomous garden cities in the United States on the scale of the British New Towns has dwindled away, becoming, in practice (possibly excepting such private-market ventures as Reston, Virginia, and Columbia, Maryland), the construction of suitably large real estate developments.

My hope is that readers by now will appreciate the dedication of the Ebenezers to the commonweal and their critical and complex view of the needs of urban society as compared to the simplistic approach of the Babbitts. In the early days, town and country planners were, by definition, Ebenezers. Late in the twentieth century, for reasons to be explored in later chapters, many planners were forced to focus on the kind of public-private partnerships dear to the hearts of those campaigning for even less regulation on real estate development. Possibly there are generational or even genetic differences between Ebenezers and Babbitts. We explore that possibility in the next section by considering some evidence about the characteristics of those in power at various times in the twentieth century.

II

Setting the Scene

3

Generations of Babbitts
and Ebenezers

Welcome to the theater of the twentieth century. Herewith a presenta-
tion of the cast of characters, with the *dramatis personae* composed of
the real generations and the fictional Babbitt. Obviously the whole century in America was pretty good theater; in addition to the dramas connected to real achievements in science and industry, literature and the
arts, and other good things, we can look to its beginning with the assassination of a president, its years full of news about the deaths of about
200 million people around the world from wars, starvation, atomic bombs,
other forms of pollution, lynchings, single and serial murders, and so
on, and its ending not exactly on the year 2000 but more properly some
months later with the total destruction of the twin towers of the World
Trade Center in New York City on September 11, 2001.

Ebenezers are in the cast, while the ghost in the plot is, of course,
Ebenezer Howard himself, whose voice offstage is barely heard above
the clamor of construction across the land. I still think our nation would
have been better off had we adopted as our own the dramatic proposals
advanced by Ebenezer Howard for England (see Chapter 2). Our
cityscapes, the fiscal structure of our federalist government, and our
ability to provide housing and open space for all our citizens would
have been significantly enhanced by adoption of his ideas for blending a
fair and efficient industrial economy with a sustainable agricultural sector to create a new form of livable metropolis. Whether they know of
him or not, his voice rings in the ears of the Ebenezers, my nickname for
citizens who work to create good housing and transportation for everyone, nonpolluting industry with lots of employment opportunities, sensible systems of taxation and public expenditures, and fairness and

nondiscriminatory behavior in our society, and, most important, for citizens who feel the system needs to reach out to lower-income, hard-working people who are functionally disadvantaged in some way.

And George Babbitt's voice rings in the ears of that other group I offer in contrast to the Ebenezers, the Babbitts (or what George Babbitt's creator Sinclair Lewis called "real" Americans). These are the folks who, throughout the bustling twentieth century, successfully avoided the Ebenezers' challenge to a Babbitt's right to develop land for the greatest personal profit and convenience. Accordingly, my purpose here as we begin to unfold the plot is to describe how the real-world Babbitts instrumented and structured cities and suburbs in the period from 1900 to 1930.

To contrast the worldviews and activities of the Ebenezers with the real world of the Babbitts, it is useful to envisage that period as a vast real estate ploy by the Babbitts to control every nook and cranny of every city and town across the nation. Sinclair Lewis, born in 1885 and thus a member of the Lost Generation, reflected the spirit of that age in all his writing. In *Main Street* (1912), the topical novel that established his place in American letters, his idealistic heroine Carol spends her life trying to turn Gopher Prairie, Minnesota, into one of the new garden suburbs with sidewalks. Such growth turns out to be possible only in the much larger cities, however, and at the end of the book Gopher Prairie is consigned to permanent status as a "dying small town." In *Babbitt* (1922), Lewis says that his eponymous protagonist is "nimble in the calling of selling houses for more than people could afford to pay" and shows him speaking at a real estate board dinner in 1920 in his hometown of Zenith, which is the kind of midsized midwestern city (said to be modeled on Cincinnati) that beat out the Gopher Prairies of the region:

> ... I wouldn't trade a high-class Zenith acreage development for the whole length and breadth of Broadway [New York] or State Street! [Chicago] ... it's evident to any one with a head for facts that Zenith is the finest example of American life and prosperity to be found anywhere. ...
>
> So! In my clumsy way I have tried to sketch the Real He-Man, the fellow with Zip and Bang. And it's because Zenith has so large a proportion of such men that it is the most stable, the greatest of our cities. New York has its thousands of Real Folks, but New York is cursed with unnumbered foreigners. So are Chicago and San Francisco. Oh, we have a golden roster of cities—Detroit and Cleveland with their renowned factories, Cincinnati with its great machine-tool and soap products, Pittsburgh and Birmingham with their steel, Kansas City and Minneapolis

and Omaha that open their bountiful gates on the bosom of the ocean-like wheat-lands, and countless other magnificent sister-cities, for, by the last census, there were no less than sixty-eight glorious American burgs with a population of over one hundred thousand! And all these cities stand together for power and purity, and against foreign ideas and communism— Atlanta with Hartford, Rochester with Denver, Milwaukee with Indianapolis, Los Angeles with Scranton, Portland, Maine, with Portland, Oregon. . . . Some time I hope folk will quit handing all the credit to a lot of moth-eaten, mildewed, out-of-date, old, European dumps, and give proper credit to the famous Zenith spirit, that clean fighting determination to win Success that has made the little old Zip City celebrated in every land and clime, wherever condensed milk and pasteboard cartons are known! . . .

I tell you, Zenith and her sister-cities are producing a new type of civilization. There are many resemblances between Zenith and these other burgs, and I'm darn glad of it! The extraordinary, growing, and sane standardization of stores, offices, streets, hotels, clothes, and newspapers throughout the United States shows how strong and enduring a type is ours.[1]

Each generation has its Babbitts and its Ebenezers, but each generation has its own characteristics that affect the whole process of urbanization while that generation is in power. Even those seminal decisions of the U.S. Supreme Court that helped determine the shape and feel of our urbanized nation can be usefully interpreted as the product of the generation dominant on the Court at the time.

One of the most exciting and intellectually rewarding challenges in the writing of this book was to identify the thought-patterns of the primary generation at certain critical junctures in the twentieth century. But it was not until I read *Generations: The History of America's Future, 1584 to 2069* by William Strauss and Neil Howe that I felt I had some useful tools to work with, and I promptly accepted the invitation in their book to use their formulations to create new insights into any subject matter not covered in their opus.[2] Although Strauss and Howe advance a refreshing concept of cyclical generational patterns for readers to digest, they rarely mention the kind of socioeconomic, legal, entrepreneurial, and land-development materials that I was sorting through. Thus I believe I am expanding their concept to new fields. Moreover, I was already partial to their notion of cycles in the operation of our political economy, for I had written earlier about cycles of inventiveness, greed, and stupidity in real estate investment from 1925 to 1980, all in tandem with cycles in the economy.[3] I found Strauss and Howe's approach to be dynamic and insightful, and so I have happily incorporated some of their ideas and terminology into my analysis of the development of the urban realm in the twentieth century.

Their book is an anatomy of eighteen "generations" from the Puritan whose 25,000 members were born between 1584 and 1614, to the most recent, the Millennial, those born between 1982 and, say, 2003, eventually to number perhaps 76 million persons. Strauss and Howe use a number of ways to categorize and name the generations, which were further classified by the major crises with which they struggled. The authors identify nine generations that have been or are active in the twentieth century, although only five or six held power in that period (as measured by majority control of the presidency, the Congress, and the Supreme Court, among other indicia).

The first two of these generations were dealing with the aftermath of the Civil War in what Strauss and Howe called the Civil War Cycle:

- Gilded Generation, those born 1822–42
- Progressive Generation, those born 1843–59

The next four generations, in what Strauss and Howe named the Great Power Cycle, worked to strengthen America's internal and international relationships:

- Missionary Generation, those born 1860–82
- Lost Generation, those born 1883–1900
- GI Generation, those born 1901–24
- Silent Generation, those born 1925–42

The most recent three make up the Millennial Cycle:

- Boom Generation, those born 1943–60
- Thirteenth Generation, those born 1961–81 and the thirteenth generation to know the American nation and flag
- Millennial Generation, those born 1982–2003(?)

Naturally, each generation's four basic periods of existence (youth, rising adulthood, midlife, and elderhood) pulsate in intimate relation to the experiences of the generations immediately preceding and immediately following it. For example, my own Silent Generation spent its youth

Figure 3.1 **Generations in Power, 1900–2000**

DECADE	PRESIDENTS	GENERATION	GENERATION THAT HAS MAJORITY IN: CONGRESS/GOVERNORS	SUPREME COURT
1900	McKinley	Progressive	Progressive	Gilded
	Roosevelt	Progressive	Progressive	Gilded
1910	Taft	Progressive	Progressive	Progressive
	Wilson	Progressive	Progressive	Progressive
1920	Harding	Missionary	Progressive	Progressive
	Coolidge	Missionary	Missionary	Missionary
1930	Hoover	Missionary	Missionary	Lost
	Roosevelt	Missionary	Missionary	Lost
1940	Roosevelt	Missionary	Lost	Lost
	Truman	Lost	GI	Lost
1950	Eisenhower	Lost	GI	Lost
1960	Kennedy	GI	GI	Lost
	Johnson	GI	GI	Lost
	Nixon	GI		Lost
1970	Nixon	GI	GI	Lost
	Ford	GI	GI	Lost
	Carter	GI	GI	GI
1980	Reagan	GI	Silent	GI
1990	Bush	GI	Silent	GI
	Clinton	Boom	n.a.	n.a.
2000	Bush	Boom	n.a.	n.a.

(Left margin, top to bottom: 1ST THIRD OF THE CENTURY · 2nd THIRD OF THE CENTURY · 3rd THIRD OF THE CENTURY)

Source: Data taken from William Strauss and Neil Howe, *Generations: The History of America's Future, 1584–2069* (New York: William Morrow, 1991).

while the GI Generation immediately before it was in its rising adulthood; my generation's midlife years were the Boomers' period of rising adulthood. For the purposes of analysis in this book, I am making the assumption that the most important societal decisions are made by whatever generations are in their midlife period. Strauss and Howe also characterized each of these generations by assigning one of four categories to it—Reactive, Adaptive, Idealist, or Civic—and I have interspersed definitions and comments about these designations in the various discussions below.

A generation's decision makers are undoubtedly a fairly elite group, better educated and more privileged than much of the population, especially those in the process of immigrating and being acculturated. Figure 3.1 shows the times when a given generation was in the majority in the decades of the twentieth century. And because the important events of the century seemed to fall quite naturally into three periods for analysis (1900–30, 1930–68, and 1968–2000), these periods are also indicated in the tabulation. I hope it is clear from this diagram that the Progressive and Missionary generations were most influential during the first third of the twentieth century, the Lost and GI generations during the middle third, and the GI, Silent, and Boom generations after 1968.

The plot of the drama that is the twentieth century unfolds in later chapters which serve as stages where the Ebenezers and the Babbitts battle it out decade after decade. Chapter 4 below describes what might have been in the minds and hearts of the generations that were active in 1900 concerning the past they inherited and the future that awaited them. When Charles Dickens's *The Mystery of Edwin Drood* was turned into a play, the director stopped the action in the middle of the last act and asked the audience to select one of two or three possible endings, at which point the actors continued with the ending thus chosen. Thus it is with this play, for we Americans, primarily those in the Boom, Thirteenth, and Millennial generations, will have some choices to make about the future of our metropolitan environments, and, with luck, there will be enough brave actors on the political stage to carry out our wishes for a better system.

4

Some Historical Themes and Sensibilities

The condition of the nation in 1900 constitutes our baseline for this study of a century of change. I want this chapter to connect us with the Americans who lived in 1900 and must have had a sense that the twentieth century would be very different from the nineteenth century. I want us to glimpse how citizens of the day might have felt about some of that past century's traumatic events. The Spanish-American War had just ended; the Civil War would have seemed no farther away in time than the Vietnam War seemed to us in the year 2000. The coming of electricity and telephones caused changes similar to those that the computer age is bringing to our lives. The great surge in immigration from Eastern Europe was well under way; in 1892 Ellis Island had been built to replace Castle Garden.[1] The separate-but-equal doctrine in *Plessy v. Ferguson* was only four years old, and unfortunately Jim Crow was becoming more and more the practice in the South. Resistance to and the need for control of unfettered corporate power was under way, and social Darwinism was being countered by the clergy and women's groups.[2] The muckrakers, led by Ida Tarbell against Rockefeller's Standard Oil, were operating in the interlude between passage of the Sherman Antitrust Act of 1890 and the Clayton Antitrust Act of 1914. As yet, the Federal Reserve System had not been invented, and there was no federal income tax. There was, I believe, a general fascination with the immense progress of industry and an increasing sense that we were changing from a fundamentally agrarian society to an industrialized, urbanized, more complex one, requiring many significant improvements to both the form and substance of our system. The Gay Nineties were definitely at an end.

As I got down to work on this book and began to deal with the ways in which successive generations had influenced the politics and economics of their day in power, I found that the stories I wanted to tell about the twentieth century reflected a fabulous evolutionary process in the nineteenth century that had generated an increasingly visible degree of urbanness. As young people moved from rural areas to the cities and families got smaller, the role of cities became even more important to the way in which the United States developed in the twentieth century. The process was fabulous because it generated fables about how we cast off European models of law, governance, and enterprise or recast them into modes appropriate for the American continent.[3] It was evolutionary because we did it experientially and experimentally in a thousand different places and circumstances throughout the century.

Evolution requires some dynamics, which I conceptualize here as continuous competition and interaction between public and private and macro and micro in all the various fields that make up our society. There is nothing like a 2 x 2 matrix, as shown below, to focus thought on such dynamic relationships; this one illustrates the basic relationships that I feel dominate discussions in studies, like this one, of political economy in the United States. We have big public projects, big private projects, little publicly supported projects, and little private projects, and all of them interact with one another because, in the typical case, each one needs some contact with or permission from the others, and one form of enterprise is constantly being compared to another. Our firm belief is that the general welfare is advanced by all this bubbling activity.

Public-Private Relationships

	Macro	Micro
	Macro	Micro
Public	Big government	Local, small government units
Private	Monopolies and big institutions	Individuals and small business

A good example of the evolution of our system by continuous competitions between large and small public and private forces was the U.S. Supreme Court's judgment in *Charles River Bridge v. Warren Bridge* in 1837, as recounted below by C.B. Swisher.[4] The effect of the ruling by Chief Justice Roger B. Taney (shortly after his appointment by President Andrew Jackson) was greater recognition of the power of government to limit property rights, both corporate and individual, in the public interest. This case is chock-full of the endemic conflicts in American life. It confronts important concepts about monopolies, about the relative rights of the state and corporations, about property ownership as a bundle of public and private rights (and obligations), and about broad and strict construction of constitutions and charters. The story began in 1650 when the Massachusetts legislature gave Harvard College the right to maintain a ferry across the Charles River:

> In 1785 the legislature incorporated the Proprietors of the Charles River Bridge and authorized the company to build a bridge across the river at the ferry location, with compensation to Harvard College for the ferry rights. Tolls collected for crossing the bridge brought returns beyond the cost of the bridge and the expectations of the legislature. The people grew tired of paying tribute, and in 1828 the legislature chartered another company to build the Warren Bridge a few rods distant from the first bridge. The Warren Bridge was to collect tolls until paid for and then become a free bridge. It quickly paid for itself and was opened to free transit, with the result that the public stopped paying tolls to cross the Charles River Bridge.
>
> The case arose from the attempt of the owners of the old bridge to get an injunction to prevent the construction of the Warren Bridge. . . . Daniel Webster and others who argued the case [but lost] contended that charters should be interpreted broadly to give all rights that might reasonably be conferred, much after the fashion of interpreting constitutions, which, it was agreed, as a matter of principle should be interpreted broadly. Opposing counsel [who won] naturally emphasized the power of the state to legislate to promote the public welfare, and contended that corporate charters should be limited to the rights clearly and specifically given. The case was decided in favor of the Warren Bridge at the first term over which Chief Justice Taney presided.

In effect, the Supreme Court in allowing the Warren Bridge to be built, determined that no private corporation could expect government to preserve its monopoly position as a matter of right, a concept that eventually led to the federal government's formal antitrust stance, beginning with the Sherman Antitrust Act of 1890. During the early part of the nineteenth century the common law of England that was the basis for American law was slowly being adapted to the needs of corporations and development generally, while later in the century, private corporations slipped into a new role as "fictitious persons" and began to claim the same rights under the Fourteenth Amendment as ordinary "natural persons." These changes and claims, in turn, have enabled large now globalized corporations to exercise extraordinary dominance of our economy. To preserve the rights of individuals, groups such as Program on Corporations, Law and Democracy (POCLAD) are leading a movement to take away such identity from the private corporation.[5] The movement is certainly being advanced as I write as a result of the disclosures of accounting frauds and other forms of criminal behavior at Enron and other major corporations.

Another example is the inevitable conflict between any two levels of government (or, for that matter, in any bureaucratic situation, between any headquarters and its divisional or regional sectors).[6] The relations between the federal government and the states are complicated by the fact that their basic relationship is neither hierarchial nor parent-child in character, for the original states created the federal central government rather than the other way around. On the other hand, the state governments, technically, created all their substate units of government, but, again, after the American Revolution, most counties and townships were older and more relevant than their state governments to which the new U.S. Constitution was addressed, so from the beginning a sense of grassroots power tended to offset any sense of automatic obeisance to higher levels of government, much less to neighboring governmental jurisdictions. Controversies about home rule as a basic right of local jurisdictions have characterized the relations between states and their subdivisions since the Republic got established; a famous debate in the late nineteenth century pitted Judge Thomas Cooley, who believed that localities have an inherent right to local self-government, against Judge John Dillon, whose more generally accepted dictum was that local governments are no more than creatures of their states, not sovereign in any sense.[7] The late twentieth century struggles between suburbs, central cities, and state legislatures regarding revenue-raising powers and mandates for spending attest to the persistence of these differing views.

One more example is the equally common competition between public corporations and private corporations for control of profitable markets. The concept of the publicly chartered, private-shareholder-owned, profit-seeking public utility corporation was a new feature in the late nineteenth century. The basic struggle in the nineteenth century was, and still is, between municipally owned corporations wanting to provide services at the lowest possible cost in such urban necessities as water supply, electricity, gas, and transit lines, and private firms that declared that such municipal activities constituted socialism and should not be allowed.[8] The arguments surrounding the New Deal's building of dams to generate

electricity and of federally assisted housing are two of many examples of
the dispute as it has continued in the twentieth century.

This evolutionary and competitive process reflects the wonderful but
daunting truth that cities, urbanity, the built environment, and the urban-
rural nexus involve just about everything in human society and governance, so the evolutionary, competitive process thereby becomes a factor
in any serious attempt to comprehend the urban situation. And urbanness
(or is it "urbanicity"?) is what we must deal with to understand what happened as America's urban areas absorbed the country's natural increase in
population, and almost all of the farming population, and a major share of
those who were able to immigrate into our country legally.

By about 1890, the frontier had closed, which meant it would not be
so easy for those who could not deal with civil society back home in the
East or the South simply to escape to the West, and the governments of
local areas and the states themselves were considered balefully inadequate if not corrupt. While the cities needed ever larger, more efficient,
and more attractive facilities and better organized and regulated utilities
and services, they would not be able to look to either the federal or their
state governments for much assistance. My doctoral dissertation dealt
extensively with the consequences of the record of defaults by states
and counties on their bonded debts at various periods in the nineteenth
century; as a result, only counties and cities were able to borrow funds
for capital projects, and then only under severe restrictions.[9] In 1806,
early in the history of the Republic, the states had turned down Secretary of the Treasury Albert Gallatin's plan for internal improvements
such as turnpikes to be financed and owned by the federal government.[10]
The federal government tried again under the New Deal to build new
towns and housing projects but was stopped by the courts, so its role in
local development has had to be indirect since then.

I think a bit more history will be useful here in order to interpret a
little more concretely the roles that the various levels of government
have come to play in our system of government, a system that defies
many of the precepts of academic theories of public finance. Our federalist government of fifty states, each with its own idiosyncratic system
for financing (or underfinancing) public activities, ensures that no simple
interpretations are forthcoming. In any case, the background story starts
with recognition that high on everyone's agenda at the beginning of the
nineteenth century were transportation projects to open up the lands
west of the Appalachian Mountains to commerce that otherwise would

be restricted to the St. Lawrence and Mississippi Rivers. Settlers, specu-
lators, and citizens of the Atlantic coasts busied themselves with plans
and looked to government for assistance, such as provided in the Ohio
Enabling Act of 1802, to build a National Road.

In 1806, Gallatin submitted to President Thomas Jefferson a selection of suitable projects in his "Report on Roads and Canals." Included
were the Cumberland (National) Road and connections between the
Hudson River and the Great Lakes. In fits and starts, the federal government did contribute some funds to these projects.

However, the War of 1812 destroyed the possibility of financing them
through customs receipts without new taxes or borrowing, for proceeds
of sale of the public lands were pledged to retirement of the wartime
debt. In 1822 President James Monroe vetoed a proposal for tolls to
continue building and maintaining the Cumberland Road, and the issue
of national preeminence in creating a transportation network, always a
threat to state, local, and private enterprise, died with President Andrew
Jackson's veto of the Maysville (Kentucky) Road in 1830.

Into the breach jumped the states, led by New York, which took control of the Erie Canal project after its construction had exhausted the
energies of the private entrepreneurs who had originated it. New York
borrowed money (largely from British banking firms) to finish it. The
smashing success of the Erie Canal, after it opened in 1825, induced
other states to borrow and spend on similar propositions, including development of railroads that would ultimately bring an end to the era of
canals and turnpikes.[11]

All went well until the economic storms of the late 1830s and early
1840s caused a number of the states to default on their debts. Several of
the southern and midwest states took refuge under the Eleventh Amendment of the U.S. Constitution, which says that no state can be sued on its
debt without its permission. The holders of these state debts had no re-
course, but, naturally, none of the world's banking houses (primarily in
the City of London) would lend any state any more money for more
internal improvements without its prior permission to sue it on the debt.
Since the states at that time would not give such permission, whatever
borrowing was done for such projects was done by counties and municipalities that could be sued. And, naturally, the counties and cities had
their own bouts of economic recessions, corruption, and bankruptcies in
the decades that followed, especially immediately after the Civil War.

How different our American society might have been if the federal government, from the outset, had been allowed by the states to be a full partner in the economic and social development of the nation's cities and towns.[12] These mid-nineteenth-century events, however, gave shape to federalism in America as we know it.

A number of important themes occupied much of the late nineteenth century. As the industrialization of the nation proceeded and new fortunes were made, women and clergymen fought vigorously against the doctrine of social Darwinism that rejected charity or concern for citizens who were poor and in distress. Lewis Mumford, among others, has described the process of "regularization" of cities, with the installation of paved roads, sewers, water supplies, electric and gas lines, and professional fire, police, and sanitation departments.[13] Lord Bryce and his researchers made a comprehensive study of the governmental and social systems and habits of Americans, while most of the economists and political scientists concerned themselves with problems of local governance and public utilities. Such domestic matters were presumably under the sole jurisdiction of the states, but the existence of slum dwellings that were health hazards and firetraps led to housing reforms in the 1870s in New York City. Comparable conditions in four of the largest cities in the 1890s convinced Congress to finance the very first federal government investigation into the social and economic conditions of American cities.

So by 1900 the basic themes of the great American social, political, and intellectual excursion were in place, and the nation became involved in what I have called the search for a better political economy. When the nineteenth century was just beginning, America's population, largely nonurban and engaged in agriculture, fishing, lumbering, and mining, occupied, however sparsely, just about the entire continent. The set of federal, state, and local institutions and private enterprises that emerged out of that nineteenth century nursery was reasonably appropriate in scale to the job in hand, although corruption and modes of unfair competition were clearly problems to be dealt with in the new century. The start of the twentieth century seemed to be a good time to begin improving and strengthening the various systems that had been created, but I think it is appropriate to look first at the lands and peoples that would be subject to development as the population grew.

5

Public Lands and the Native Population

"I Hear America Singing," from Walt Whitman's *Leaves of Grass*, was quite possibly as well known as any American poem in 1900, which leads me to wonder how Americans then felt about the vast extent of the continent. In the previous century, we had managed to get hold of all that land and, in the words of the 1964 Wilderness Act, "occupied and modified" much of it. How we continued to "occupy and modify" the rest of it—and to reoccupy and remodify much of it—during the twentieth century is one way of describing what this book is about.

All that land was certainly ours, bought and paid for, as the usual maps of our territorial acquisitions, such as Figure 5.1, tell us. We were protected from invasion by the Atlantic and Pacific oceans and were busy building the first of the great battleships that were ordained by Adm. Alfred Mahan's seminal analysis, *The Influence of Sea Power Upon History 1660–1783,* a book that stimulated the naval commands of the imperialist nations of the time: Great Britain, Germany, and the United States.[1]

All of the land we owned on the continent had been turned into states except some territories where the status of various Indian claims was still undetermined, but soon these ambiguities were cleared up and the states of Oklahoma (in 1907), New Mexico (in 1912), and Arizona (a few months later in 1912) were admitted to the union. Alaska had been a territory since 1867. We had invaded Hawaii two years before, and Queen Liliuokalani had lost her throne.[2] Cuba, Puerto Rico, and the Philippines had been touted as possible states after the 1898 war with Spain, but, for whatever reason (and could it possibly be what we now would call racism?), the idea of having a large number of Spanish-speak-

Figure 5.1   **U.S. Territorial Acquisitions**

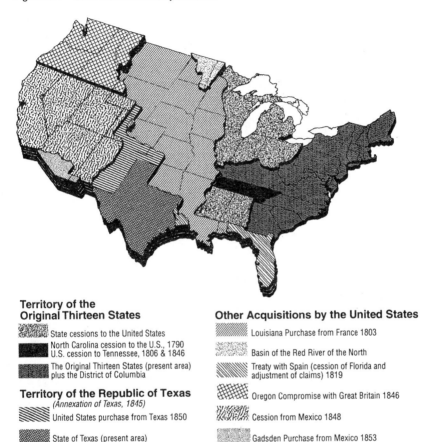

**Territory of the
Original Thirteen States**

State cessions to the United States

North Carolina cession to the U.S., 1790
U.S. cession to Tennessee, 1806 & 1846

The Original Thirteen States (present area)
plus the District of Columbia

Territory of the Republic of Texas
(Annexation of Texas, 1845)

United States purchase from Texas 1850

State of Texas (present area)

Other Acquisitions by the United States

Louisiana Purchase from France 1803

Basin of the Red River of the North

Treaty with Spain (cession of Florida and
adjustment of claims) 1819

Oregon Compromise with Great Britain 1846

Cession from Mexico 1848

Gadsden Purchase from Mexico 1853

Alaska
Purchased from Russia March 30, 1867

Source: U.S. Department of Interior, Bureau of Land Management, *Public Land
Statistics 1976* (Washington, DC: GPO, 1976), p. 5.

ing people becoming full-fledged U.S. citizens did not have enough appeal, although a number of those making predictions on the eve of 1900 guessed that Mexico and Nicaragua (after the canal was built there) would become states. Again they guessed wrong about statehood, and it turned out that the canal was built in Panama rather than Nicaragua.

The total area of the continental United States not including inland water areas, is about 3 million square miles or 1.9 billion acres, almost ten times the area of the original thirteen colonies. What became land in the public domain began when the new states that the original colonies had turned into ceded 233 million acres, mostly west of the Appalachian Mountains, to the new federal government. With the Louisiana Purchase (in 1803) and deals with Spain, Mexico, Texas, and Great Britain (in the 1840s), and not including Alaska's 375 million acres, the land in the public domain at its largest amounted to almost 1.5 billion acres.[3]

Then the federal government got rid of two-thirds of all that land, mostly before 1900. Twenty-four percent (277 million acres) of that public domain land was transferred to homesteaders, somewhat more (328 million acres) to the states for a variety of purposes, 94 million acres (or 8 percent of the total) to railroads, another 61 million acres to veterans, and the rest to many other types of recipients.

All of these acres, of course, were originally the homelands of Indian tribes, so we should think of those Indian lands as the canvas upon which the history of the United States was painted. While I wonder how many Americans in 1900 ever thought much about this historical fact, it is high time we wholeheartedly acknowledged it. Europeans began to occupy the Indian homelands in 1492. By 1800 we had claimed all the land east of the Mississippi River for the United States. By 1850, having settled matters with the British as to our border with Canada and with the Mexicans, the Spanish, and the Texans as to our southern border, the nation was getting serious about settling the West. The Oregon Trail dates from the mid-1840s and lasted until the railroads made traveling that much easier. The rush to dig gold in California began in 1849 with the discoveries at Sutter's Mill.

The grants to the railroads cut through the grasslands and hunting areas of the various tribes and decimated the buffalo herds upon which so many of the tribes depended.[4] Figure 5.2 gives a hint of how the railroads charged across the continent on land provided by the federal government, but it does not show the additional land donated to private railroad companies by the states themselves for the construction of hun-

Figure 5.2   **Land Given to Railroads**

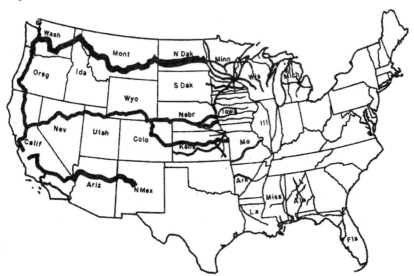

Source: U.S. Department of Interior, Bureau of Land Management, *Public Land Statistics 1976* (Washington, DC: GPO, 1976), p. 45.

dreds of short feeder rail lines out of the 328 million acres the states had received from the federal government.

Figure 5.3, which is intimately connected with the map of the railroads in Figure 5.2, shows the dates by which the Native Americans lost almost all of their western lands in the second half of the nineteenth century; the present small reservations are all that remain of these lost lands, and the United States still holds the title to all the lands in reservations ceded by treaties.

The Indian population was an estimated 1 million persons around 1500 when the Europeans first began to occupy parts of the area that would become the United States of America.[5] The number in 1900 (not including Alaska) was between 100,000 and 200,000 and increased dramatically to between 400,000 and 500,000 by the end of World War II. I have spent a great deal of time immersed in U.S. census data, I have visited and even worked in what is known now as "Indian Country," and I have a number of good friends who are Indians. However, I admit that, until I began to write this chapter, I had no clear idea when Indians began to be counted as part of the population or when they became citizens of the United States (since, as I learned to my surprise, adoption of

Figure 5.3 **Land Taken from Tribes**

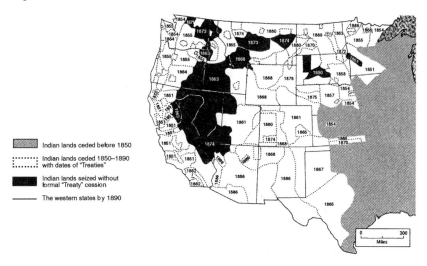

Indian lands ceded before 1850

Indian lands ceded 1850–1890
with dates of "Treaties"

Indian lands seized without
formal "Treaty" cession

The western states by 1890

Source: Adapted with permission from chart titled "Indian Lands Lost 1850–1890" in Martin Gilbert, *The Routledge Atlas of American History* (London and New York: Routledge, 1968 [1995]), p. 62.

the Fourteen Amendment to the U.S. Constitution did not bestow citizenship to Indians on the reservations as it did to African-Americans and, later, to business corporations). The story follows, beginning with the formal prose of the Bureau of the Census.

American Indians generally were not counted in censuses prior to 1890, unless they were considered to be part of the broader non-Indian society, as evidenced by their paying local taxes and living in settled communities, often alongside non-Indians. The censuses from 1850 through 1880 included estimates of American Indians "retaining their tribal character," sometimes by State or Territory.

In 1890, most Indians were enumerated, but were reported separately from the general population, usually by reservation rather than by county. A volume of the 1890 census reports dealt exclusively with Indians and included a historical review of earlier estimates:

The inclusion of most American Indians in the census beginning in 1890 naturally has some effect on comparisons for the relevant States and counties with censuses before that date. However, even if earlier censuses had enumerated all of the Indian population, much of it would not have been found at its 1890 location at the earlier dates, because of extensive forced removal, migration, and resettling as the settlement frontier advanced and Indian reservations were established.[6]

Imagine what stories underlie the bare words of that last sentence about removal and migration. According to the *Encyclopaedia Britannica*, Francisco de Vitoria, a Spaniard, and William Penn led the Europeans to consider the Indians "noble savages" who were to be not enslaved but brought up to civilized standards; in the meantime, they would be wards of the state and entitled to their own customs and laws (except where such customs and laws would interfere with the needs of their civilized guardians!). Lands would be acquired by the Europeans only by treaty or similar agreements, not by mere force, a concept enshrined in the Proclamation of 1763 and carried over into the new American Republic after the Revolution.[7] The first major departure from that policy was the Indian Removal Act of 1830, which moved large numbers of Indians from lands east of the Mississippi River to remote territories west of the river. But soon the remoteness disappeared, as noted in the encyclopaedia's quotation from Alexis de Tocqueville:

> Whilst the savages were endeavoring to civilize themselves, the Europeans continued to surround them on every side, and to confine them within narrower limits . . . and the Indians have been ruined by a competition which they had not the means of sustaining. They were isolated in their own country, and their race only constituted a little colony of troublesome strangers in the midst of a numerous and dominant people.[8]

The late nineteenth-century story, as sketched in the *Encyclopaedia Britannica,* is a continuation of those pressures. By 1871, Congress declared that thereafter no Indian nation or tribe would be recognized as an independent power with whom the United States would contract by treaty. The tensions continued to rise, culminating in such dramatic events as the massacre of Gen. George Custer's troops by the Sioux and Cheyenne in 1876, Nez Percé chief Joseph's battles in 1877, and Chiricahua chief Geronimo's dénouement in 1886. The very next year, Congress passed the infamous Dawes Severalty or General Allotment Act of 1887. Allotment meant that tribally owned reservation land could be divided into individual parcels to be given to individual members of the tribe, whether they wanted it or not. With the parcel would go all the rights and duties of citizenship. Such land could not be sold for twenty-five years. All land not so distributed would be declared surplus and available for settlement by non-Indians. Figure 5.3 above shows the extent to which vast amounts of such surplus land was made available. The Dawes Act and similar legislation assumed that Indians would not survive as tribes and would probably move to towns but that, in any case, they would all be assimilated. By the early 1920s, the government realized that the Indians were surviving despite Dawes and numerous epidemics, that the allotment policy had had few if any beneficial results, and that the United States had no effective policies concerning its Indian population. New legislation in 1924 followed this realization; it confirmed the citizenship of all Indians born in the United States. Further important changes in the relationship between the federal government and the tribes came with passage of the Indian Reorganization Act of 1934. The relations among tribal authorities, the Bureau of Indian Affairs (BIA), and the members of the tribes have never been smooth. By the late 1990s, the tribal councils got the authority to take over many of the BIA's administrative functions, ending the bureau's hegemony over the scores of activities on each reservation that were funded by the federal government, but the inability of the BIA to provide accurate accounting information about the thousands of trust funds for individuals and tribes remains a source of bitter dispute.[9]

As the Americans of 1900 looked ahead to the twentieth century, they were certainly aware that "the frontier had closed," as Frederick Jackson Turner suggested in outlining the immense influence that the concept of the frontier had had on American thought.[10] Nevertheless, even after the Indians emerged in the twentieth century as increasingly important components of our cultural mythology and our environmental ethic, as holders of large amounts of land newly wanted for non-Indian uses, and as trailblazers in adding gambling revenues and lotteries to our stable of public revenue, Indians are still hardly visible in contemporary histories and television specials.[11]

6

Visions of the Twenty-first Century

Nor did I find Indians present in the prognostications of 1900 that were exhumed by present-day journalists assigned by their editors to write background articles for us all to think about as we were crossing the bridge into the twenty-first century. Moreover, I could find almost no brave-new-urban-world guesses for the new millennium to compare to the multitude of those written in 1900; collectively we must have all been too busy dealing with current problems to speculate about what the cities and metropolises of the year 2100 might look like. Recall that in mid-1999 we were wondering whether hidden computer glitches known as the Y2K problem would plunge the world into darkness and chaos. A month earlier, at the teach-in in Seattle just before the World Trade Organization (WTO) meetings began, the question was whether the mafia in the former USSR and global corporations elsewhere were displacing nation-states as the governing authorities. And, of course, bioscientists were worried about all sorts of environmental degradations and global warming, while the political scientists were dealing with a score of civil wars and international quarrels on all the continents. The high-tech community, meanwhile, was basking in the glow of blazing stock markets (rarely thinking of possible downward adjustments in stock price levels which, indeed, came to pass in 2000–01 as this book was being written).

In comparison, as the Gay 1890s, also called the Mauve Decade, became fin de siècle, 1900 dawned with lots of positive ideas and not so many fears for the forthcoming twentieth century.[1] The *Ladies' Home Journal* guessed, wrongly, that the U.S. population would zoom to 500 million by the year 2000.[2] As for technological change, the German-language *Milwaukee Herold and Seebote*, abstracting predictions by others around the nation, wrote:

Photographs will be telegraphed from any distance. If there be a battle in China a hundred years hence, snapshots of its most striking events will be publicised in the newspapers an hour later. Photographs will reproduce all of Nature's colors. . . . Automobiles will be cheaper than horses today. . . . There will be Air-Ships, but they will not successfully compete with surface cars and water vessels for passengers and freight traffic. They will be maintained as deadly war-vessels by all military nations.[3]

The *Los Angeles Times Mirror*'s investigator unearthed a quotation that "Woman, having more leisure, will elevate her political and social status from subordination to equality with men," but he also reported a burning crisis, The Servant Problem, which had begun in the 1890s and lasted through the 1920s. The crisis was that middle-class women had always had servants such as cooks and maids, or a least a "housekeeper" who cooked and cleaned, but with rising prosperity, fewer and fewer Americans were willing to go into domestic service. And some observers felt that those who did go into service were less skilled, less contented in their work, and perhaps less honest.[4]

The *Times-Mirror* reporter found that people in 1900 were anticipating an explosive growth of cities. He quoted England's H.G. Wells who had forecast that the growth of vast suburbs and their shopping malls would be accompanied with "wayside teahouses, restaurants . . . dotted at every convenient position along the new roads, availing themselves no doubt wherever possible of the picturesque inns that the old coaching days have left us."

Back in the midwest America of 1900, however, the *Dodgeville Chronicle* (Wisconsin) reporter expected those large cities to be "marvels of cheapness and convenience" where municipal ownership of services would "reduce the cost of city life, which now appalls the economical visitor, to a merely nominal sum."[5] And the man at the *St. Louis Post-Dispatch* in 1900 compiled a wish list for his city: "Good clean streets and alleys. Filtered water. Adequate sewerage. A first-class lighting system. The equalization of taxation through the taxing of franchises and other property which has hitherto escaped taxation. An honest and efficient municipal government."[6]

The *Post-Dispatch* piece also included a prescient quotation from William Jennings Bryan, who was running for president in 1900: "The greatest political danger of the 20th century is that the increasing influence of wealth will lead to increasing disregard of the inalienable rights of man."

According to the narrator of the 1999 PBS special, "Across America, the [1900] presidential campaign was the great fall entertainment. Never before had candidates campaigned so hard, so far, or spent so much money." PBS's commentator David Nasaw then added: "Bryan is appealing to the plain people. Bryan is saying very clearly that the railroads, the manufacturers, the bankers, Wall Street were all fleecing the common folk, the farmers, the workers. Bryan was a demon, an absolutely frightening character for the upper classes, for the wealthy. And there were moments in 1900 where fear ripples through the upper classes."[7] But, in the event, the Republican Party's William McKinley won the election (McKinley was killed on September 6, 1901, and was succeeded by Theodore Roosevelt). What PBS called "ugly labor disputes" in the construction trades and many different industries, all demanding better working conditions and higher pay, were endemic that year. J.P. Morgan's troops won a major battle with the United Mine Workers just before the election. In 1900, all across the South, black men were kept from the polls by new laws, intimidation, and violence, and, in the words of Margaret Washington, a participant on that PBS show:

> Yes, it is a period of demoralization, 1900. . . . African Americans, they've had a bad time. Jim Crow is there. But they're not slaves, the world is open to them . . . and they want things to get better and they're working to make it better. It's amazing that this song "Lift Every Voice and Sing" was composed in 1900. It has become the African American national anthem. And what is there to sing about. Sing about the past. And sing about how far we have come. In spite of oppression, lift your voices and sing. It's a new century. This is 1900. This is a new day.

Cities were obviously going to get larger decade by decade. Thirteen million people had been added to the population of the nation in the 1890–1900 decade and it did not take much imagination to predict an even greater number for the 1900–10 decade. The actual census of 1900 found 76,212,168 persons in the country. To have the population reach 500 million in 2000, as the *Ladies' Home Journal* had predicted, would have required the population to grow at a compound rate of 20 percent in each decade of the twentieth century, a not altogether unreasonable, albeit simplistic, guess given our actual history, as spread out in Table 6.1.

From 1790 through 1860, our population increased more than a third in each decade, the rate of increase declining slowly and unevenly there-

Table 6.1

Increase in U.S. Population by Decade

Decade	Population increase in decade (in millions)	Percent increase in decade
1790–1800	1.4	35
1800–1810	1.9	36
1810–1820	2.4	33
1820–1830	3.3	33
1830–1840	4.2	33
1840–1850	6.1	36
1850–1860	8.2	36
1860–1870	7.2	23
1870–1880	11.6	30
1880–1890	12.8	25
1890–1900	13.2	21
1900–1910	16.0	21
1910–1920	13.8	11
1920–1930	17.2	16
1930–1940	9.0	7
1940–1950	19.1	15
1950–1960	28.0	19
1960–1970	23.9	13
1970–1980	23.3	11
1980–1990	22.2	10
1990–2000	32.7	13

Source: Population of States and Counties of the United States 1790–1990, pp. 2–4, and for the 2000 Census, calculated from the U.S. Census Bureau Summary Files on the Internet.

after, except for the 1930–40 decade, running from the Great Depression until the beginning of World War II, which is notable for "slow growth" in just about every socioeconomic indicator.

About 281.4 million Americans were accounted for in the U.S. Census in 2000, up about 205 million from the 76 million in 1900. Much about America in the twentieth century is explained by the absorption of 205 million people, or almost three people for every one alive in 1900. America's cities, rural areas, and ways of life had to change in fundamental ways to accommodate that growth. One way of gaining perspective on the process by which the physical, visible landscape (or urbanscape) changed in America in the twentieth century is to suggest that at least 100,000 square miles of undeveloped land would have had to be converted into more urbanized densities for those 205 million people who were added to the rolls in those 100 years.[8] The size of the estimate depends upon one's assumptions about density of population, amount of land required for each housing unit, average size of a household, and so on. The amount of land involved, however calculated, is minor compared to the totality of land in the United States, but the importance of these land conversions depends upon the locational, economic, ecological, and aesthetic characteristics of the parcels of land involved, upon the kinds of private and public developments and infrastructure placed thereon, and upon the capacities and attitudes of the governmental entities that might come to have responsibilities for them. It is thus at this point that our story of life after 1900 begins.

III

Notes on Suburbanization

7

The Suburbs According to Richard T. Ely in 1902

Urbanization

The ideas of Richard T. Ely (born 1854), in his professorial and advocate roles, were particularly influential in the debates early in the century about the future of the American economic system and of the infrastructure of its municipalities. Ely, one of the founders of the American Economic Association, and his fellow academic, John R. Commons (born 1862), are perfect examples of the Progressive Generation at work.[1] The preeminent institutional economists, they are also my intellectual guides to the institutional, sociopolitical context of much of the work in finance, real estate investment, economic development, housing, city and regional planning, and community organizing that I have done as a professional urban economist and city and regional planner.

Their fellow members in that progressive generation were dominant as the twentieth century opened, fully conscious of America's emergence as a Great Power; the Spanish-American War and the Great White Fleet that President Theodore Roosevelt sent around the world made sure of that. It was not until after World War II that America was further defined as *the* Great Power by the returning GIs of that generation, a stance that Boomer George W. Bush has adopted for his presidency.

Ely's *The Coming City*, published in 1902, is a pithy lecture with some useful appendices, and in it he encapsulates a whole range of ideas that were percolating as the twentieth century began.[2] That year 1902 is near the end of the forty-year period, 1870–1910, of the municipal reform or "good government" movement. Municipal reform was a hallmark of several generations (in the preceding Civil War cycle) that had been forced to recognize the national need to improve cities so that corruption and inefficiency did not interfere with business activities that were described by Commons as manufacturing capitalism. Ely's little book, which provides an introduction to the thinking about cities at that time, touches upon many vital concerns: the nature of corruption, control by the business elite, the search for an economic base and for culture, with, of course, his suggestions for improved methods for governing the cities.

The stage is thus set for the first thirty years of development in the twentieth century, with some of the Progressive Generation working to get new levels of municipal reform passed by their legislatures and with others, led by such Wall Street tycoons as J.P. Morgan, working to replace manufacturers with investment bankers in what Commons designated as the era of finance capitalism.

Ely then was professor of political economy at the University of Wisconsin. The term "political economy" is not as fashionable now as it was, but it connotes much more than the two words considered separately. It recognizes not only that politics is based on the economy (as in President Clinton's 1992 reelection campaign slogan, "It's the economy, stupid") and that the economy is instinct with politics, but more importantly that the relationships between economic interest groups determine politics and the structure of society, so that the term nowadays has a somewhat Marxian or at least European tang to it.

Ely himself, even though he was a ranking member of the established order, was interested and knowledgeable about topics that the establishment was chary about: social trends, socialist thought, and the political economy of cities. He began his lecture with remarks about the vast changes in the 1890–1900 decade and continued:

> The twentieth-century city is destined to embrace more than half of our population, and this makes its government of vital significance to every man, woman and child in the United States, and, indeed, in the entire civilized world. The frontiersman in the far West, the woodsman in the pine forests of Michigan and Wisconsin, the miner delving in the bowels of the earth in Pennsylvania, Colorado, and far-away Alaska, all are feeling, and will feel still more forcefully, the influences proceeding from the character of our great cities as truly as the dweller in London, Paris, Berlin, or New York. . . .

THE PROBLEM OF THE CITY, THE PROBLEM OF A REVOLUTION BROUGHT ABOUT BY EVOLUTION, BUT IT IMPLIES IN SOME RESPECTS A RETURN TO EARLIER CONDITIONS

The problem of the city is the problem of a revolution—a revolution brought about by industrial evolution, if you will. Strangely enough, too, it involves in some particulars a return to the conditions of classical antiquity. When we speak of the nation as a whole, we use words which are rural in their primary significance. We say this country of ours, this land of ours, whereas the Athenians said, this city of ours—their state being essentially a city-state, with rural districts, land added as a subordinate part of the state, ruled from the city as a centre. . . .

Rural votes have controlled our destinies, and men from the country have given shape to our national life. But we are entering a period in which men from the city are certain to have an increasing influence in the councils of the nation, and are very likely to become dominant.[3]

We will spend much of the remainder of this book examining what happened to this set of 1902 projections. In short, urban and industrial problems did come to dominate the nation's political economy through the World War II period, but the economic and financial power of cities by then had been truncated by the rise of autonomous suburbs. With the coming of "one person, one vote" in the 1960s, the political power of suburbanites became superior to that of city people. And a case has been made that metropolitan areas, with cities and suburbs recognizing their mutual interdependence, are inherently stronger in economic terms than nations in the era of globalization that characterized life in 2000.[4]

But now we need to pick up the thread of Ely's thought. He had interested himself in the growing urbanization of the nation, the only tabulation in his book being the percentage of the U.S. population that had been counted as "urban" from the time of the first census in 1790; he wrote, "This increase in urban population is not something brought about by sentimental considerations. Men have not, as a rule, left the country and gone to the city as an outcome of changes in their feelings and desires."[5]

For the latter years of the twentieth century, new definitions and various statistical strategies needed to be employed to deal with vastly larger populations. Population counts were technically more accurate in the eighteenth and nineteenth centuries because each person had to be ex-

Table 7.1

Percent "Urban" in U.S. Population, 1790–2000

	Share of population defined as "urban"		
Year	In Ely's book	Previous U.S. census	Current U.S. census
1790	3.35	5.10	
1800	3.97	6.10	
1810	4.93	7.30	
1820	4.98	7.20	
1830	6.72	8.80	
1840	8.52	10.80	
1850	12.49	15.40	
1860	16.13	19.80	
1870	10.93	25.70	
1880	22.57	28.20	
1890	29.20	35.10	
1900	—	39.70	
1910	—	45.70	
1920	—	51.20	
1930	—	56.10	
1940	—	59.00	
1950	—	56.50	64.00
1960	—	59.60	69.90
1970	—	63.10	73.60
1980	—		73.70
1990	—		75.20
2000	—	n.a.	n.a.

Source: Ely's data, actually for places with more than 8,000 people (very large for the time), are found on his page 20. Urban definitions for Census 2000 are presumably the same as published by Census for 1995. Census data for the 1790–1990 periods shown as "previous" and "current" in Table 7.1 and can be found at www.census.gov/population/census data/table-4.pdf.

plicitly included in the enumerations; recent censuses have resorted to estimates based on statistical measurements of groups that were most likely to be undercounted. Urbanization, however measured, has been the dominant mode since the days after World War I when nothing managed to "keep them down on the farms after they've seen Paree." The steady decline over the decades in the percentage of total population that is nonurban or rural is easy to calculate from Table 7.1.

Ely was certainly not the first to observe that a large number of simple but interrelated happenings cumulate to create the movement from country to city. Perhaps the first major writer on the subject was Adam Smith, whose *Wealth of Nations* in 1776 analyzed how the need of the city for agricultural products not only elevates the farmer from growing for his own needs to supplying the city but ultimately makes the countryside dependent upon the city's markets and the city's ability to derive income from its exports of commodities, manufactures, or services.[6] In fact, the whole set of modern ideas concerning land value and local economic development differ from Smith's more in technique than in substance.

Among the simple changes to a rural existence are the introduction of farm machinery that frees the farmer's children to migrate cityward, and the improvements in transportation and post offices that make the trips to and from the urban centers easier and cheaper, often allowing one member of a farm household to earn a good cash income in town, while the expansion of commerce in the city tends to limit the nonfarm development of rural market towns. The results of these changes were summarized a century later by the editors of *The Economist* magazine:

> In truth, the defining issues of the next 100 years cannot yet be defined, any more than for the 20th century they could securely have been outlined in 1900. But demography, at least, is the most forecastable of trends, because it takes so long for the statistics of births and deaths to have an impact on the population structure of the living.
>
> And it is worth recalling that even in 1900 one thing was, or should have been, clear: that industrial and social change in the developed countries was shifting millions of people into the cities and the factories. The political and economic consequences of that were unpredictable but the rise of urban working classes did indeed prove one of the century's defining issues.[7]

Suburbanization

Ely was among the first to observe that something called a suburb was beginning to redefine the nature of urbanism in America:

THE SUBURBS AND THEIR CHARACTER

We are witnessing some changes which are making it easier for men to live in suburbs, but the suburbs are urban in character, and the dwellers in the suburbs are urbanites in their mental attitudes, feelings, and sympathies. Rapid transit of the local kind operates chiefly to widen out the city and extend it farther into the country. There is some scattering of manufacturing plants from large to small cities, and occasionally even to the country; but, as yet, we have no reason to anticipate a cessation in the growth in numbers of those who live under essentially urban conditions.[8]

The changes that made it "easier" to live in the suburbs were only partly related to the creation of rapid transit systems, primarily the trolley lines that were built at the turn of the century and that met an untimely death in the 1930s (a story to be explored later in this book). The main reason was legislation by the states that allowed suburbs to become independent, autonomous, municipal corporations with no responsibilities to the cities that generated them. The suburbanites could work and get their income from the city, avoid the city's property taxes that paid for things like public schools and public baths for immigrants and other poor people, and devote the suburbs' property taxes exclusively to benefits for the relatively affluent and primarily white suburbanites. Once this disconnection between city and suburb became the norm in America, the nation was fated to a century of increasing disparities in wealth and power between suburbs and central cities (and I have little doubt that most educated people of the period knew and accepted the inevitability of that fate).

Meanwhile, city governments were noted for corruption, and the cities themselves needed vast amounts of physical improvements, from public buildings and streets to improvements in housing and living conditions in slummy neighborhoods. Ely noted the demands for municipal reform that began right after the Civil War and continued with the cry that cities should be run like well-ordered households, or rather as businesses by businessmen. The reformers, according to Ely, said, in effect, let us get rid of professional politicians and political bosses, and create a civil service, and lower taxes, and get home rule with absolute separation from the politics of state and nation, and, please, let good men come forward and be the saviors of their city.[9]

Ely did not like the idea that an idealized businessman would be killing off the politicians. In fact, he did not think that most businessmen would be qualified to run a city. He preferred the idea of making municipal service an honorable profession. On that score, he wrote:

> I jotted down a list of the kinds of experts required for municipal administration. My list is as follows: The sociologist, the economist, the bacteriologist, the chemist, the engineer, the physician, the educator, the administrator (that is, the man skilled in public administration), the lawyer, the sanitarian . . . and, of course, we need efficiency, honesty, and common sense.[10]

and further,

But there is an esthetic side to this, and it is receiving rapid development in these first years of the twentieth-century city. It is coming to be felt more and more that the city should be a work of art.[11]

And, of even greater significance, he went on to discuss the role of women in promoting either the governmental reforms or the municipal aesthetics, or both:

Wherever you see any peculiarly excellent work going forward in the development of the twentieth-century city you may be sure that the women have something to do with it. They are cold and unmoved when we talk about municipal government as business, but when we bring forward the household ideal they think of the children, and their powers are enlisted, and when they are once aroused you may be sure that something is going to happen![12]

Two types of municipal reform were emerging at the time of Ely's work. The first was to enable the citizenry (outside the South, which continued to restrict voting to whites and to restrict initiatives to the legislature) to create and vote on legislative initiatives and various kinds of recall petitions and referenda. All these were seen as useful additions for reformers, who could hardly have imaged how use of these governmental tools expanded at the end of the twentieth century to the detriment of reasonable governmental processes.

The other type of reform was establishment of autonomous commissions and municipal corporations that provided a wide range of engineering and other technical services to improve the economic and social aspects of urban life, in such fields as health, sewage systems, and sometimes utilities such as electricity, water supply, and gas. It was clear, said Ely, that a city had to exercise a significant measure of control over any private corporations that received monopoly franchises to furnish public utilities, and it was equally clear—in fact, "absolutely inevitable"—that those private corporations would be involved in politics.[13]

But then Ely had to come up with some reason for the apathy and indifference of the men (who, I suppose, were from the Gilded Generation) who were not getting as involved with municipal reforms as their wives might have been, and the main reason he found is that "those best citizens . . . are gaining more than they lose by precisely the kind of [unreformed, read corrupt] municipal government that exists at the present time." He told this story:

A distinguished divine, in an address before the Marquette Club of Chicago, expressed himself as follows: "If we were to awake to-morrow morning and find that all the aldermen in the city hall were honest men, a lot of our most respectable citizens would be found running around town like chickens with their heads cut off, seeking to protect the franchises their attorneys have plotted and schemed and bribed to get for them. You say our intelligent men, our wealthy men, our brainy men, should be aided in this reform. It is our intelligent men who are looting the community. They don't want municipal reform. Present conditions are too profitable."[14]

and Ely added a quote from Mayor Swift of Chicago:

Who is it that comes into the common council and asks for [special] privileges? Who is it who are accused of offering bribes for such franchises? It is the same ones—the prominent citizens.

I tell you, these questions come home. Talk about anarchy; talk about breeding the spirit of communism! What does it more than the representative citizens of Chicago? Your high-toned business men, your patriotic men, your prominent citizens of Chicago are the men who knock at the door of the council and ask for illegal franchises. It is not the common people.[15]

Ely was not alone but part of an educated, reasonably idealistic, rather elitist, and nevertheless relatively politically astute group of citizens widely distributed around the country who felt the time had come to reestablish confidence in government and to create whole new realms of citizen activity. The reformers' demands for "municipal reform" meant rejection of political machines and corrupt officials and adoption of such techniques as a civil service based on merit rather than political connection, voting reforms such as the referenda and initiative, and use of autonomous "authorities and special districts" to be operated by professionally trained people and removed from intrusion by elected officials after the professionals were elected or appointed. His economist friends meanwhile were debating the question of whether any government expenditures or investments could be ranked with those of manufacturing, mining, and agriculture businesses and whether governments' investments were "real" investments (such as privately owned brick-and-mortar projects and heavy equipment were). Ely had little doubt that governments were necessary and economically productive.

Much of this activity was concentrated in the major cities. Reform leadership was tied into the great social reform movements of the day, with such extraordinary women as Jane Addams in Chicago and Lillian D. Wald in New York at the head of the parade.[16] On any given day, these women and their allies would be tending to their settlement houses, testifying to state legislatures (in company with groups like the then-influential Women's City Club of New York and League of Women Voters) about dismal conditions for laboring families and small children and urging factory laws limiting hours and improving working conditions, and attending some function for international peace. Such groups as the Women's International League for Peace and Freedom and the Visiting Nurse Association stand as monuments to their organizing skills.

Ely's mental picture of a future city was probably a powerful center with a few suburbs and a few metropolitan districts, such as Boston had invented in the 1880s, for parks and sewers. He thought of suburbanites as displaced urbanites; he would be unhappy to see them describable at the end of the twentieth century as uninterested and unknowledgeable about the central city and not dependent on the central city for either jobs, commerce, or culture, enjoying the power of their doughnut-shaped ring of suburbs to govern the hole-in-the-doughnut that the central city has become, meanwhile making sure there was no metropolitan-wide power to replace it. And almost none of all these reformers really considered how our social and economic systems create the physical conditions that made cities so difficult to live in, particularly for poor people. It is that challenge and what happened to it that concerns us most.

8

Patterns of Transportation and Metropolitanization, 1900–2000

Importance of Land Use

Professor Ely's predictions about suburbia came true with a vengeance, as suburbs and smaller cities in the West and South absorbed most of the population added in the twentieth century. Much of the so-called urban development that ensued was tinged with a "garden suburb" label. This chapter deals with this changing environment created by revolutions in transportation and in governance, while the focus shifts from "the city" to "the metropolis." However, in the process of recognizing change, a writer on these subjects must always remember that each hamlet, village, town, and city across the nation becomes a unique environment for whatever urbanizing pressures exist in its region, because each state in the United States creates its own set of building codes and development regulations and gives its local governments a range of choices as to how such laws can be adopted and applied.

We also must acknowledge that neither government nor the private sector can do much to alter permanently the reality of the geological formations of these local environments. Indeed, much of American history is encompassed in the stories of how humans have coped with and tried to change the facts of their geology and the plant ecology that reflects the soil composition and climate at a given site, especially when such change improved possibilities for profitable agriculture. Any drive or flight across the United States reminds the traveler of the innumerable stony, dry, unforgiving landscapes that are the size of oceans, while all the towns, cities, and suburbs look like little islands and networks of activity encased in greenery. In fact, Jean Gottmann, a famous French

geographer, observed in 1949 that much of the United States is uninhab-
itable without modern technology to bring water and utilities from far
away. It was the pre-contact Indians of New England who made the first
changes in the American landscape, according to William Cronan, by
instituting annual burns of forest lands to open them up for grazing ani-
mals and even planting of crops.[1]

Europeans began their occupation on the shores of the Atlantic Ocean
and the Caribbean. Apparently, many of the indigenous peoples on the
mainland succumbed soon after from disease. After the Revolution, settlers moved west of the Appalachians, eventually meeting up with Europeans moving up and down the Mississippi from Canada and New
Orleans and, half a century later, with those moving up to the Southwest
and California from Mexico.

Many of the increasing number of immigrants from Europe in the
early nineteenth century headed for the mid-central states. Gold in California drew folks to the far West, a westward movement enhanced after
the Civil War as southerners moved to Texas, the Southwest, and the
Northwest.

Clearing, selective cutting, timbering, and mining were the major ways
of changing the face of the land. Many of the settlers in the New England states left the difficult land on the slopes of the Green and White
Mountains as soon as the Erie Canal made the trip to the lands west of
the Appalachians easier and cheaper after 1825; some towns in Vermont
and Connecticut are said to have less population today than they did
before the exodus to the West. The railroad builders created little towns
along the way to generate commerce for their railroads. The South, including Texas, developed large areas for sugar and cotton. Vast tracts in
the western states were fenced off; the last great cattle drives over un-
fenced land were in the 1880s. The millions of buffalo on the Great
Plains were pretty much gone by that time, replaced by wheat and corn.
Our national literature features great tales about trappers, cowboys, cattle
drives, the competition between sheep and cattle that Zane Grey wrote
about, the tough times for the immigrants to Montana in the 1890s that
Ivan Doig writes about, but in 1900, there was not yet much to write
about the towns and cities of the developing West. The deserts in Texas
were just on the brink of sprouting oil wells after oil rushed to the sky at
Spindletop on that fateful day in 1900. The Rocky Mountains were still
spotted with little mining towns, some of which would become ski re-
sorts after World War II, frequented by Texas oil barons and their fami-

lies. The Dust Bowl was still in the future in 1900. Ancient forests were being felled at a great rate in the Pacific Northwest.

In 1900 there was still a great deal of land that was barely or not at all occupied by the humans marching through the last paragraph. Most land uses were relatively gentle on the environment; we had not yet gotten into such twentieth-century habits as (1) building megadams for irrigation and electric power generation, (2) clear-cutting vast areas for timber, (3) strip mining, (4) plowing up the plains, (5) polluting vast areas with nuclear or industrial waste, or (6) farming by use of incredible quantities of agricultural chemicals, to name a few of our national habits that have come under intense criticism in recent years. That first year of the twentieth century merely marked the continuation of a process that began by converting arable coastal land—and land accessible to sea-lanes—away from occupancy by indigenous people to occupancy by people of mostly European stock, who went on to open up new areas for settlement on the plains and rocky steppes of the West.[2] Chapter 5 laid out the broad strokes by which the federal government came to have jurisdiction over the land; much of the acreage had been passed on to states and private hands by 1900, and much of the land that had been reserved earlier in the nineteenth century for Indian tribes was privatized out of tribal hands as people poured west and later southwest. The pioneers and settlers certainly made great strides at taking over, occupying, and modifying the North American continent; the process, as it continued, changed the face and fate of our rivers, significantly drained our aquifers (as in Colorado and Nebraska), and created all sorts of environmental and species-protection problems for the twenty-first century.

For the purposes of this book, however, we must skip the environmental side of development and consider where the millions more people anticipated in 1900 actually settled by 2000. Table 8.1 begins the story by looking at major regions in the United States, using the standard regional boundaries established by the Census Bureau early in the twentieth century. The table shows how each region absorbed the population increase and illustrates the shift of population from east to west over the last 150 years. In the 1850–1900 period (with its 53 million increase), the Midwest fills up rapidly, with only a little population going to the West. In the 1900–50 period (with its 75 million increase), the percentages are fairly evenly distributed among regions. In the post–World War II period and the rest of the century (with its 130 million increase), the trends to warmer western and southern areas stand out clearly. And in-

Table 8.1

Percentage of Nation's Population Growth by Region, Half Centuries, 1850–2000

Census region	1850–1900	1900–1950	1950–2000
Northeast	23.4	24.6	10.8
South	29.2	30.1	40.8
Midwest	39.4	24.2	15.3
West	8.0	21.1	33.1

Note: U.S. Census distributes states into regions and subregions as follows: Northeast = New England + Mid-Atlantic, South = East South Central + South Atlantic + West South Central, Midwest = East North Central + West North Central, West = Mountain + Pacific.

creasingly over time, the growth has channeled itself into metropolises, and I was amused to learn from my dictionary that the root of *metro* is "mother," *polis*, of course, meaning "city." The dictionary suggests that the metropolis is the mothership, but there are certainly some who would still maintain that it is the city that is the mother of the metropolis.

Metropolitanization

Granting that some mountainous or otherwise barren areas would never attract much population, we can turn our attention to the question of why some areas emerged as the locus for great agglomerations of urbanites while other areas, equally livable or with arable land, remained relatively rural. This book about the process of urbanizing, suburbanizing, developing, and redeveloping thousands of square miles a year should, after all, be based upon some reasonably sound theory to explain the phenomena of settlement patterns.

A certain amount of theory does provide the foundation of land economics and regional science. The most common form is central place theory, in which distance from the center is the critical factor in establishing economic value.[3] Even Adam Smith in his *Wealth of Nations* recognized these principles, observing that cities, by generating effective demand for agricultural products, were the ultimate justification and sustainers for farmers producing beyond their own needs for subsistence.

The mathematical models used in central place studies usually concentrate on a single central city surrounded by concentric circles of less dense populations and lower economic activity levels. These models become a little fuzzy, in my opinion, even though more complicated, when dealing with urbanized areas with multiple activity nodes or emerging centers scattered about the various suburbs. In truth, the logical way to contemplate or evaluate an urban area is to consider the metropolis as an organic whole rather than as a central city with spokes of development radiating outward or as a congeries of suburbs.

In many countries, the span of the local governing entity is the metropolis, while the typical U.S. practice is to give governmental autonomy to each suburb as well as to the central city and, even more confusing, to grant autonomy to independent school districts and the multiplicity of overlapping county and single-purpose special districts that provide fire, water, library, port-development, and many other urban services.

I was always fascinated by the contribution to central place theory made by a German geographer named Walter Christaller.[4] He explored the use of geometrical relationships in illustrating the regular hierarchies of market towns in Germany. My favorite visualization of central place theory has always been the cascade of hexagons he employed in some of his work. One day while flying from coast to coast, I attempted to analyze the metropolises beneath me in the same way Christaller did for market towns in Germany. The result was a sketch now adapted for publication as Figure 8.1. I selected Chicago, New York, Los Angeles, and Washington, D.C., as the major foci for they were already the leading urban agglomerations, presumably exerting irresistibly magnetic attractions to all the other metropolises and economic areas on the map. The task then became to fit scores of these other metropolises into the prescribed nodes and centers of smaller hexagons that reflect the areas of influence of larger centers.

My diagram reflects the fact that real relationships between cities do not depend entirely upon the distance factors that are critical to true central place studies of subregional areas. For example, a given city in the United States may have a good deal of centrifugal power, able to span mountains in a single bound, because of administrative as well as market power, as in the array of Federal Reserve districts: Kansas City is the home of the central bank facility for Denver, and San Francisco serves as the central bank for Seattle. My intuitive distribution at this interregional scale of major urban agglomerations to appropriate nodes on the diagram suggests (as may be the fact) that all sorts of market forces are combining to make the four major foci (New York, Los Ange-

Figure 8.1   **My Christaller-type View of the United States**

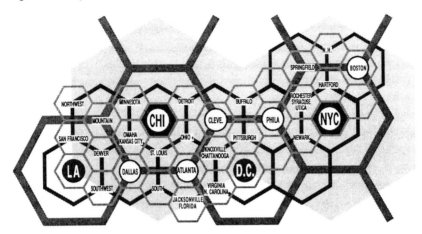

les, Chicago, and Washington, D.C.) larger and larger decade after decade, retaining thereby their present dominance.

Physical distance can be measured in miles and kilometers but, even more relevantly, in travel time and convenience, all of which means that modes of transportation created the economic framework for the existence of metropolises. The ways that changes in modes of transportation deeply affected America's nineteenth-century cities are nicely portrayed by Kenneth Jackson in his magisterial *Crabgrass Frontier:*

> Between 1815 and 1875, America's largest cities underwent a dramatic spatial change. The introduction of the steam ferry, the omnibus, the commuter railroad, the horsecar, the elevated railroad, and the cable car gave additional impetus to an exodus that would turn cities "inside out" and inaugurate a new pattern of suburban affluence and center despair. The result was hailed as the inevitable outcome of the desirable segregation of commercial from residential area and of the disadvantaged from the more comfortable.[5]

The greatest influence in the twentieth century on the shape and function of metropolises in America is surely the change in transportation praxis that made the automobile so indispensable. Changes in transportation methods and facilities have happened in a variety of ways, some pernicious or resulting from such factors, others merely cumulative adaptations to economic or social conditions prevailing at various points

Figure 8.2   **Diagram of Change in Transportation Factors**

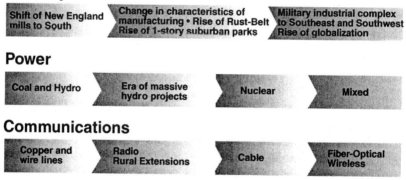

| 1900 | 1920 | 1940 | 1960 | 1980 | 2000 |

Trains

Intercity Trucking

Interurban Trolleys

Automobiles

Ocean Liners

Interstate Highways

Air Traffic

Numbers of branch banks, small retail stores, scattered warehouses, small gas stations

Industry

Shift of New England mills to South

Change in characteristics of manufacturing • Rise of Rust-Belt Rise of 1-story suburban parks

Military industrial complex to Southeast and Southwest Rise of globalization

Power

Coal and Hydro

Era of massive hydro projects

Nuclear

Mixed

Communications

Copper and wire lines

Radio Rural Extensions

Cable

Fiber-Optical Wireless

during the hundred years. Figure 8.2 is my attempt to illustrate these changes over time by charting the relative importance of each mode of transportation, with the apex of each triangle at the point in time it began its rise in importance or its descent into less importance. The comments that follow regarding each mode are meant to recognize the importance of the subject and to be suggestive, for it is clearly beyond the scope of this book to provide a proper set of references to the hundreds of books on the theories and techniques for each mode, on the impact of new types of transportation on the shape and facility requirements of particular metropolises, and on the economic aspects of national networks of roads, railroads, and airlines.

Trains

Trains were understood to be the basic intercity mode of transportation as the twentieth century opened. The great railroad days petered out during the Depression. The various bankrupt lines kept merging, keeping as much freight handling as they could and giving up as much passenger service as they were allowed by the Interstate Commerce Commission. Some hidebound financiers and trustees kept believing in railroad stocks and bonds as the safest of investments, since no one could imagine a nation that was not wholly dependent upon rails, and railroads never lacked for partisans during the transportation debates late in the nineteenth century. Posters of streamlined trains, on electrified lines that kept coal-burning locomotives out of the cities, decorated our walls since the first of the streamliners, such as the Burlington Road's "Zephyr," about the time of the Century of Progress World's Fair in Chicago in 1933–34. The railroads were essential during World War II, but the decline in traffic was steady thereafter until Amtrak was established by Congress in the 1950s to salvage at least a minimal amount of passenger service. Lots of people, including me, think that the nation's continuing cold-shouldering of high-speed, well-appointed trains with frequent intercity trips is a form of collective insanity.

Buses and Trucking

As the price of passenger travel and freight handling dropped as a result of increasing competition among the highway transport companies after World War II, and as more and more customers moved away from fixed-rail lines, the final kibosh was given to the railroads, and inter-metropolitan surface transportation became the almost exclusive domain of rubber-tired vehicles.

Interurban Trolleys

Complementing the major railroads were numerous interurban trolleys.[6] These streetcar lines were of great importance from the 1890s through

World War II, by which time virtually all of them had gone bankrupt; their rails were ripped up and sold as scrap iron, mostly to Japan, which converted it into munitions for the war in the Pacific. Their demise was caused, it is said, by the loose financial practices and greediness of their promoters and was hastened, it is clear, by automobile companies that connived and conspired to advance the use of automobiles. In any case, they had served their urban customers well while they lasted, for they provided convenient means for people commuting daily from "streetcar suburbs" to the city and for city folks making weekend expeditions to the country.

What happened to them? Here is a cogent summary by Louis Guilbault of the acknowledged conspiracy as it emerged from testimony before Congress and from Department of Justice lawsuits:

> General Motors hated competing with streetcars, and the company became very successful at ditching them. . . . From 1932 until the early 1980s, many auto, oil and rubber firms—but especially General Motors—engaged in all manner of questionable activities, usually under a pervasive blanket of secrecy, to achieve a rubber-tired, internal-combustion transportation monopoly. . . .
>
> Let's start in 1932. It was the Depression, and Yellow Truck and Coach—which GM bought control of in 1925—was a dog, a chronic money-loser. Even before the Depression, Yellow lost money. . . . Red ink gushed for seven of the ten years after GM got into making heavy trucks, buses and taxicabs, a business vastly different from automaking.
>
> So how *do* you sell buses, say, if competitive bids don't do the job? Well, the best way is to ditch the competition, which GM proceeded to do. In 1932, competitor #1 was the electric railway. GM later pointed out that many of the railway transit companies were in dire financial straits. This is true, but of course in 1932 the giant automaker's bus division was no goldmine itself. Yellow Truck and Coach, however, had what the little railway companies didn't—a rich uncle. GM provided money to replace streetcars with Yellow buses in a few small cities in the Midwest. . . . Omnibus Corporation of America, which had a web of interlocking directors and managers with GM, tore up 92 miles of Manhattan (NY) streetcar lines and started putting in hundreds of Yellow buses. . . .
>
> [And there were] unexpected destructive effects of the Public Utilities Holding Act of 1935. The big electric utilities, manufacturers like Brill, Pullman and St. Louis Car, and suppliers such as General Electric, Ohio Brass and Westinghouse could have served as effective competition to the likes of General Motors. However, electrical interests were prevented

from any ownership of transportation companies, while auto, oil and rubber companies ran amok.[7]

General Motors, in partnership with the Fitzgerald brothers of Minnesota, then set up National City Lines (NCL). Guilbault continues:

NCL didn't mess with niceties like public hearings or democratic process. . . . NCL's tactics were simpler; they bought streetcar companies, tore up the rails, torched or sold off the streetcars, and put in buses. GM almost always made the new vehicles. . . .

World War Two forced a change in tactics, since bus conversions were largely put on hold. But this certainly didn't hurt NCL. Transit was booming, with gas, auto and tires rationed. Cash-rich, National could buy into really big operations: the railway from Chicago to Milwaukee, transit systems in Baltimore, St. Louis and Los Angeles, as well as smaller operations in California, Florida, Iowa, Texas and Washington state. NCL, GM, Firestone, Standard Oil, Mack Truck, Phillips Petroleum and executives from each firm were indicted on anti-trust charges in 1947. They were acquitted on some charges and convicted on others in Chicago in 1949. . . .

As manufacturer after manufacturer dropped out of bus manufacturing, GM found itself in overwhelming dominance of the transit vehicle market. This again attracted the attention of the antitrust people. After years of litigation, the company signed a consent decree with the Justice Dept. in 1965. . . . Market forces were working against GM's buses by the 1970s. Transit authorities were demanding more innovative buses than the standardized product built at the firm's huge plant in Pontiac, Michigan, and European and American competitors were offering them. In 1979, GM made its last intercity bus and in 1987 it shut down transit bus production as well.

A substantial literature[8] (and a PBS film[9]) deal imaginatively with this rarely understood conspiracy, but the main complaint found in much of the literature on transportation in the metropolis is that, whatever the cause, our urban system is utterly beholden to petroleum and asphalt and that we have not yet found a way to put less polluting, more cost-efficient electricity (and ultimately fuel cells to produce hydrogen as fuel) to work.

Automobiles

What more can be said? But actually there are a few thoughts to be recorded. First, in the last decade or so, a number of museums dedicated to the impact of the automobile on our national culture and on the form of a particular locality (for instance, the great museum in and of Los Angeles, located across from the LaBrea dinosaur pits!) have appeared. Second, the size, functioning, and gas-guzzling character of the automobile itself continue to amaze. Third, automobiles and trucks create unacceptably high levels of noise, and one form of amelioration, the screening fences erected as an afterthought along major and even minor highways, constitute one of the more remarkable alterations to the urban landscape in recent years.

Interstate Highways

Conceptualized by New Deal agencies in the 1930s, glorified in the General Motors exhibit at the New York World's Fair in 1939–40, justified in 1956 as necessary for the defense of the nation, visualized in bits and pieces by everyone everywhere during the endless process of actually building them during the 1960s and 1970s, stimulating the creation of innumerable grassroots organizations defending their neighborhoods from total demolition by authoritarian state highway departments (although the urban renewal programs got more of the opprobrium than did the highway programs), and responsible for as yet unmeasured shifts of population all across the United States from towns remote from the interstates to emergent urbanizing centers adjacent to highway interchanges: interstate highways were undoubtedly the single greatest influence on our automobile-dominated urban growth patterns in the 1950–80 period.

Ocean Liners and Fishing Fleets

Gone from America's harbors are the trans-Atlantic and trans-Pacific fleets. No longer can you drive to the dock, see your automobile hoisted aboard, take your morning constitutional around the decks where, later in the day, you would sit in deck chairs for reading, socializing, and afternoon tea before the nightly dancing and "horse-racing" programs, and, after landing, drive to your business and tourist destinations in Europe (trans-Pacific tourism being much less common). But my generation and many earlier ones knew the ocean liners as a wonderful way to travel. Gone also, as a result of declining stocks of fish, are most of the fishing fleets. Increasingly in the United States and elsewhere, dockside areas are being redeveloped for non-maritime uses, still another example of how changes in transportation affect the uses of space in cities.

Air Traffic

Transocean flights were scarce before World War II, still characterized by short hops and one or more fueling stops in the first few postwar decades, and the norm by the end of the century. Domestic air traffic increased year by year without as much governmental subsidy as in the developmental period before World War II. Year by year the airports serving the major (and even minor) metropolises have become larger, busier, and more expansive in the services available to travelers and to the business-office parks nearby and lining the highways into the central city. More and more high-value, light-weight freight is carried by air (together with private mail services that are slowly making the U.S. Postal Service's monopoly obsolete), creating in the process footloose industries no longer rooted to particular locations.

The fallout from the deregulation legislation of the Reagan years is not complete yet. As airlines consolidated, a few cities became major "hubs," many smaller metropolises became accessible only by monopolistic feeder lines, prices for flights became skewed between high ones for top-class passengers and quite low ones for the economy class. All in all, the organization and finances of the airline industry remain in turmoil.

These transportation phenomena are important contributors to manifold other changes in technology that collectively constitute the real shapers of urban form. For example and only barely suggested in Figure 8.2, better communications enable financial firms to merge and become globalized, at the same time diminishing the need for branch offices (partly because of increased use of ATMs), which changes the demand for space in downtowns or shopping malls. Shopping areas are also impacted by the rise of retailing by catalog and the Internet, with orders mostly sent by telecommunications, and, by the same token, modern communications systems decrease the need for inventories held by business firms, in consequence of which a variety of scattered warehouses become surplus. These changes in retailing and wholesaling are reflected in the creation of new megastores and megawarehouses and in the conversion of some major malls into suburban centers for upscale globalized franchise operations to compete with the new outlet malls being built along the interstate highways in what used to be called "exurbia."[10]

Table 8.2

Population of Top Twenty Metropolitan Areas, 1860–2000
(in thousands)

Rank	1860 Census (1950 definition)		1900 Census (1950 definition)		1950 Census (1950 definition)		2000 Census (complex areas)
1	New York	1,400	New York	4,850	New York	13,100	New York
2	Philadelphia	600	Chicago	1,850	Chicago	5,260	Los Angeles
3	Boston	340	Philadelphia	1,575	Los Angeles	4,100	Chicago
4	Baltimore	225	Boston	1,165	Philadelphia	3,300	Washington, DC
5	Cincinnati	205	Pittsburgh	675	Detroit	3,025	San Francisco
6	New Orleans	185	St. Louis	650	Boston	2,475	Philadelphia
7	St. Louis	175	Baltimore	580	San Francisco	2,050	Boston
8	Chicago	120	Cincinnati	490	St. Louis	1,540	Detroit
9	Pittsburgh	115	San Francisco	470	Cleveland	1,475	Dallas
10	Louisville	90	Cleveland	420	Washington, DC	1,470	Houston
11	Buffalo	90	Buffalo	390	Pittsburgh	1,460	Atlanta
12	Washington, DC	72	Minn-St. Paul	375	Baltimore	1,325	Miami
13	Troy, NY	65	Milwaukee	325	Minn-St. Paul	1,100	Seattle
14	Albany, NY	65	Detroit	310	Buffalo	1,000	Phoenix
15	Providence	63	Washington, DC	310	Cincinnati	955	Minn-St. Paul
16	San Francisco	60	New Orleans	300	Milwaukee	925	Cleveland
17	Detroit	50	Providence	280	Houston	795	San Diego
18	Rochester	50	Louisville	265	Kansas City	770	St. Louis
19	Milwaukee	48	Kansas City	235	Seattle	705	Denver
20	Cleveland	48	Rochester	180	Atlanta	690	Baltimore

Source: Adapted from table titled "Population and Rank of Twenty Large St. Metro. Areas, 1860–1969," one of the miscellaneous tables on population trends in the United States from Rand McNally Commercial Atlas submitted as part of the testimony of Richard L. Forstall, senior research editor, cartographic division, Rand McNally & Co., to *U.S. House of Representatives, Ad Hoc Subcommittee on Urban Growth of the Committee on Banking and Currency, Ninety-First Congress,* "Population Trends," Part 1, June–July, 1969, Washington, DC: GPO, plus my estimates from U.S. Census 2000.

Meanwhile, after World War II, high-tech industries drifted to the Southeast and Southwest. Nuclear reactors, which took years to get located and regulated, generated tons of waste that made many localities unlivable. Massive dams produced most of the electricity while coal-fired plants lost popularity, and so coal mines shut down. Cable and fiber-optic wires created new networks in and around the webs of telephone and power wires that formerly defined urban space. As the century ended, nationwide and metropolitanwide debates about electric and nuclear power, and communications merely increased in intensity.

And as all of this was going on, places were found for the 200 million people added to the population in the twentieth century. Increasingly over the years, metropolitan areas absorbed many of those people. The top twenty metropolitan areas housed 12 percent of total population in 1860, 22 percent in 1900, 30 percent in 1950, and 48 percent in 2000. Table 8.2 ranks these metropolises by size of population.

The population data shown in Table 8.2 are for groups of counties as defined in 1950 by the federal government's Bureau of the Budget as "standard metropolitan statistical areas" or SMSAs. Each SMSA included at least one central city with more than 50,000 residents plus the adjacent counties whose economies were primarily related to those central places. No data are given for the areas listed for 2000 because, in the last half of the twentieth century, so many people moved to suburbs and exurbs of the old central cities and the areas between the old SMSAs that the Census Bureau was forced to include many more counties and combinations of the old SMSAs for the larger metropolises. The new definitions and the more comprehensive polycentric areas are currently known as metropolitan statistical areas (MSAs), primary MSAs (PMSAs), consolidated MSAs, and New England consolidated metropolitan areas (NECMAs), which combine scores of townships rather than counties. The rankings shown for 2000 are for the largest definition used for each metropolis, so that the column represents a mixture of CMSAs, PMSAs, and some MSAs, thus making it very difficult to make direct comparisons between the area populations in 2000 with the data for the collections of counties providing the 1860–1950 data.

In the 1900 ranking, Minneapolis-St. Paul and Kansas City joined the top-twenty list, while Troy and Albany in the Northeast dropped off. In 1950 rankings, New Orleans, Providence, Louisville, and Rochester had been replaced by Los Angeles, Houston, Seattle, and Atlanta, all reflecting population shifts to the South and the West. For 2000, that trend

Table 8.3

Top Twenty Metropolitan Areas, 1990–2000

Rank	Area	CMSA 2000	CMSA 1990	PMSA 2000	PMSA 1990
1	NY-NJ-CT	21,200	19,550	9,314	8,547
2	Los Angeles-Riverside-Orange	16,374	14,532	9,519	8,863
3	Chicago-Gary-Kenosha	9,157	8,248	8,273	7,410
4	Washington, DC-Balt-MD-VA-WV	7,608	6,727	4,923	4,223
5	San Francisco-Oakland-San Jose	7,039	6,353	1,731	1,603
6	Phila-Wilmington-Atlantic City	6,188	5,892	5,101	4,922
7	Boston-Worcester-Lawrence	5,819	5,455	3,407	3,228
8	Detroit-Ann Arbor-Flint	5,456	5,187	4,441	4,266
9	Dallas-Fort Worth	5,222	4,037	3,519	2,676
10	Houston-Galveston-Brazoria	4,669	3,731	4,178	3,333
11	Atlanta MSA	xx	xx	4,112	2,960
12	Miami-Fort Lauderdale	3,876	3,193	2,253	1,937
13	Seattle-Tacoma-Bremerton	3,555	2,970	2,415	2,033
14	Phoenix-Mesa MSA	xx	xx	3,252	2,238
15	Minnesota-St. Paul MSA	xx	xx	2,969	2,539
16	Cleveland-Akron	2,946	2,860	2,551	2,202
17	San Diego MSA	xx	xx	2,814	2,498
18	St. Louis MSA	xx	xx	2,604	2,493
19	Denver-Boulder-Greeley	2,582	1,980	2,109	1,623
20	Baltimore	xx	xx	2,552	2,382

Source: Calculated from U.S. Census tapes.

continues, with Dallas, Phoenix, Miami, and Denver moving to the top-twenty list and Buffalo, Cincinnati, Milwaukee, and Kansas City, all in the northeastern or north central states, dropping off. Table 8.3 shows how the populations of the top twenty agglomerations for 2000 shifted between 1990 and 2000 and what the difference is between the different definitions.

Table 8.4, showing the density of population in the central city and its environs, is a most unusual tabulation made for SMSAs as of 1960. I selected nine of them as reasonably representative of new and old metropolises around the country and calculated that they had average density of 1,609 persons per square mile. The figure for population per square mile in the place I grew up, Manhattan, is higher than for New York as a central city because lower density areas in Queens, Staten Island, and the other boroughs are included, and similarly the figure for Cambridge in the Boston SMSA is higher than for the Boston area as a whole. Obviously Seattle, to which we moved in 1971, felt less popu-

Table 8.4

Land Area and Population Per Square Mile in Selected Standard Metropolitan Areas, 1960

Standard metropolitan area	Land area (square miles)	Population per square mile (thousands)		
		Total SMA	Central area	Outside SMA
Average of the 9 SMSAs	n.a.	1,609	10,797	821
New York	2,149	4,977	24,697	1,588
Chicago	3,714	1,675	15,836	765
Los Angeles/Long Beach	4,842	1,393	5,638	903
Boston	969	2,672	14,586	2,054
San Francisco-Oakland	3,313	840	11,013	522
Washington, DC-MD-VA	1,485	1,348	12,442	869
Houston	1,711	727	2,860	220
Seattle	4,234	262	6,295	133
Atlanta	1,723	590	3,802	332
Average persons per acre (1 square mile = 640 acres)		2.5	16.9	1.2

Source: Calculated from U.S. Census data.

lated than the places on the East Coast we had left, and Seattle's environs seemed almost undeveloped. The table illustrates more particularly the manner in which the suburbs of the rapid-growth areas of the early postwar period, such as Houston, Atlanta, and Seattle, were developing at quite low densities, while relatively older areas with significant growth in the postwar period, such as Los Angeles, San Francisco, Washington, D.C., and Chicago, were developing at measurably higher densities. Presumably a comparable analysis of the Census 2000 data would show the extent to which densities in such suburban areas might even begin to match the 1960 data for the smaller central cities.

Planners enjoy talking about the economic and even social advantages of increased residential density. While many property owners like the idea of making money by increasing the number of residential units that can be built on their parcels, politicians usually find that the neighbors do not want the "up-zoning" required to obtain higher-density construction (even if effective mass transportation services might then be considered more feasible). The game of the profit-seeking real estate developer is to obtain control of a lower-density parcel and to get permission to redevelop it at an appreciably higher density. The game of the planner is often to figure out which areas in a community can be up-

Table 8.5

Acreage by Category of Land Use, Augusta, Georgia

Land use category	Acreage	Percentage
Residential (more or less "net")	4,269	37
Business (retail, wholesale, industrial)	1,556	14
Transportation (streets, raillines, and utilities)	3,339	30
Institutional and other public uses	2,167	19
Total developed acres	11,331	100
Total vacant, nonurban, wet acreage	33,474	—
Total acreage in study area	44,805	—

Source: Adapted from F. Stuart, Chapin, *Urban Land Use Planning*, 2nd ed. (Urbana: University of Illinois Press, 1965), p. 296, Table 24 "Summary of Land Uses, Augusta, Georgia, Planning Area, 1952."

zoned with the least amount of political opposition.[11] Data that suggest how much land is available for up-zoning or "infill" in any particular community are notoriously hard to come by, usually because every piece of land in that community has all sorts of emotions and personal predilections embedded in it.

If the 200 million people added to the population in the twentieth century were settled at the average density of 1,609 people per square mile as shown in Table 8.4, some 124,300 square miles of raw land would have had to be converted (but because all metropolises encompass much land that is completely undevelopable, I rounded this figure down to 100,000 square miles for the last paragraph of Chapter 6). The expectation for the next 100 million people added to the U.S. population is that most of them will reside in metropolitan areas that will expand their boundaries and "infill" existing areas to accommodate them. How much actual acreage will be required for houses and housing, and how much for all the other needs of an urban community, such as roads, commerce, industry, utilities, mass transportation, and institutions, is hard to estimate closely. My diligent search for data good enough to generalize this aspect of development policy was not successful, but one study by competent analysts done in 1952 for the Augusta, Georgia, Planning Area (presumably more or less equivalent to its SMSA) does provide some useful data to use in our exploration of the question.

The data in Table 8.5 show that the Augusta study area encompassed 44,805 acres, of which 33,474 or three-quarters of the total, was listed as vacant, nonurban, or under water (just the kinds of lands that generate controversies and lawsuits between environmentalists, neighbors, and developers). Land uses in the developed segments of the planning area are shown as a total of 11,331 acres, one acre for every three undevelopable ones.

The implications of the Augusta study, with regard to the 11,331 developed acres are that, for every one of the 4,269 acres dedicated strictly to residential use, the community needed approximately two more acres (or 7,062 acres in all) in 1952 for business, transportation and utilities, and public and private institutions. By the end of the century there might be even larger amounts that might be needed for nonresidential development, not to mention that there well may be, in addition, three other undeveloped and possibly undevelopable acres set aside for every one acre that might be developed.

If the data in Tables 8.4 and 8.5 are at all applicable now, the gross area required to take care of the next 100 million American citizens at 1,609 persons per square mile (as calculated for the metropolitan areas in Table 8.4) will amount to about 62,000 square miles or about 40 million acres. Because so much more of the development in the twenty-first century will be infill rather than expansion into raw land, we might expect the portion of land that is considered undevelopable to be a smaller proportion than in the Augusta study, say 10 million acres instead of 20 million. This leaves 30 million acres for actual development, perhaps 60 percent or 18 million acres of which would be consigned for industrial, commercial, transportation, utilities, and public and private institutional use, and the remaining 12 million acres for "net residential" or housing use. The anticipated 100 million people on those 12 million acres would thereupon be living at an average density of 8 persons per acre, a figure quite representative of current practice and more or less halfway between the 16.9 average density in the central areas and the 1.2 average in the areas outside, as reported in Table 8.4.

In any case, providing land for the comprehensive needs of the next 100 million people coming into our present metropolises is obviously a critical issue for the twenty-first century. The actual amount of acreage converted to these urban uses will reflect decisions that are made, metropolis by metropolis, concerning densities higher than in our example but required for the typical "smart growth" proposal that is discussed in Chapter 12.

IV

The Record: 1900–2000

9
Structuring the Political Economy of America, 1900–30

Almost every part of the economic and political machinery that was the America of 1900 was upgraded in the first third of the twentieth century, with especially visible changes in the cities themselves. Some 47 million people were added to the population as 1900's count of 76 million persons grew into 1930's 123 million, and all of them needed roofs over their heads. No one knows how much building occurred in the decade and a half before World War I because the federal government, unfortunately, did not collect or publish estimates of total construction of residential and nonresidential buildings for the years prior to 1915.

While the cities were building the kind of physical infrastructure needed to handle not only the increases in population from births over death and the steady immigration from Europe but also the rising migration of rural career seekers to the urban scene, America was overhauling all the other systems that were necessary to manage its changing society. Expenditures by local, state, and national government were low by any standard at the end of the nineteenth century but obviously had to rise to deal with such changes. The increasing use of automobiles brought demands for better streets in the cities, for better highways paralleling the streetcar lines that had opened up the suburban environs for settlement, for rural roads to help the farmers get their produce to the spreading cities, and even for the creation of a national park system to protect those special places that automobilists could now reach. For the first time, the federal government found itself making outright grants to the states to fund the building of rural roads and facilities. Whatever the actual rate of construction might have been before World War I, an impressive amount of building came after it, despite the postwar recession, until dropping dramatically after 1929.

The amount of such activity in the prewar decades, however, must have been vastly larger than at any time in the nineteenth century, for a short tour around any central area of any of the cities, large and small, that existed in those pre–World War I years usually reveals that most of the fanciest eight- to ten-story apartment houses (using Mr. Otis's new elevators) in the community, the grandest of the public buildings, and the most ornate of the private clubs date from that period. In my home town of New York, I offer as examples the New York Public Library, Grand Central Station, the Metropolitan Museum, the elegant department stores (such as Russeks on Fifth Avenue by McKim Mead and White, and the Siegel-Cooper colossus on 18th Street and Sixth Avenue), and scores of distinguished apartment houses. Union Station in Washington, D.C., is another example of the genre. The best of the urban parks and boulevards, generally following the City Beautiful/Beaux Arts fashions that caught the nation's interest after the 1893 Chicago World's Fair and that often had been laid out by Frederick Law Olmsted's civic design firm, also came in this prewar time.

Governments obviously needed a better revenue system, and so the U.S. Constitution was amended in 1913 to permit the taxing of income from property and earnings. A more stable banking system was necessary as "finance capitalism," John R. Commons's description of the mechanisms by which Wall Street firms operated the great industrial corporations, with their multitudinous stockholders, that were coming to dominate the economy, replaced nineteenth century's "manufacturing capitalism," characterized by smaller, independent, privately owned companies that were the mainstay of hundreds of the cities and towns across the nation.[1] And so the Federal Reserve System was invented a year later.[2] At the same time, the field of economics was becoming professionalized (the American Economics Association was founded in the early 1890s) as the use of quantitative analysis was growing, and in 1908 Harvard led the way with the nation's first graduate school of business administration.[3] By the late 1920s, Wesley Clair Mitchell and his colleagues at the National Bureau of Economic Research had operationalized a set of national income and product accounts in order to comprehend the totality of the U.S. economy.

And, for the first time, in these same years the real estate industry was able to obtain money from Wall Street's capital markets and thus able to build larger-scale developments than had been possible before. Some of the major urban projects (such as Shaker Heights, Ohio), were built by railroad companies to create markets for their lines but, increasingly, entrepreneurs were able to float issues of stocks and mortgage bonds for their projects. In earlier times, the scale of a project was limited by the financial resources of a small group of partners and their local banks and mortgage lenders.

But the mortgage lenders and the other members of the banking and investment fraternity wanted protection for their investments in real estate, and the favored form of protection was land-use zoning. Zoning would keep uses separated so that a factory could not be built next to a department store, or a shopping area too near a new single-family housing estate. The owners of the real estate on lower Fifth Avenue are often given credit for instituting the use of zoning shortly before World War I, and the practice spread steadily during the 1920s. The basic idea of land-use zoning as a preemptive strike against nuisance suits between property owners was approved in 1926 by the U.S. Supreme Court.[4] A series of reports by advisory committees in the U.S. Department of Commerce developed the legal framework for state enabling acts for zoning (1922–1924) and city planning (1928). Secretary of Commerce Herbert Hoover, serving under President Calvin Coolidge, actively promoted their adoption.

Zoning codes actually came on the scene somewhat after public health codes, building codes, and town planning had become familiar in urban areas. Public health was the subject of municipal ordinances at least as early as the early Roman Empire, certainly in medieval towns, and, in America, in New Amsterdam (before it became New York in 1664) with respect to pigs running loose in the streets. Building codes, covering structure and utilities, became more and more common, with increasing concern about occupancy in the mid-nineteenth century. New York City took the lead with regard to occupancy standards by requiring light and air in bedrooms and commissioned architectural studies that led to the promotion of model tenements.

The modern practice of comprehensive city planning gets discussed in various ways later in this book. Here we need only to mention that its formulation owes as much to the leadership of the American Public Health Association (APHA) early in the twentieth century as to any other of the many forces that converged to create comprehensive planning as an intrinsic element of competent municipal governance. APHA's concern began with observations that bad housing was generating epidemics of tuberculosis and other diseases in the slums that had come to characterize so many of America's major cities (primarily on the East Coast). In former ages, towns burned down from time to time for any number of natural or political or accidental causes, but one of the features of municipal progress in the late nineteenth century was creation of full-time professional fire departments, with a resulting increase in old, rotten, densely occupied buildings that had not had the good sense to burn down at an appropriately earlier stage of decay.

APHA began to convene all the actors on the municipal stage who could help prevent the creation of more slums and who might help eliminate the existing ones. The actors included lawyers interested in codifying municipal regulations, the municipal engineers trying to be more efficient in building streets, public utility systems, and rapid transit facilities, representatives of the neighborhood houses and the municipal arts community (including members of the City Beautiful movement), architects, and sociologists. From the beginning, city planning has had to be completely interdisciplinary (just as Professor Ely described), always attempting to provide a basis for decisions by city councils that would merge the drive for efficiency with the need for equity and beauty.

All these fundamental changes to the law and look of America continued until the onset of the Great Depression of the 1930s. The passing of the presidency from Herbert Hoover to Franklin D. Roosevelt seems to me to mark the end of a third of the twentieth century that willy-nilly had been devoted to fashioning a political economy far more complex than had been required for life in the nineteenth century, and it marks the beginning of the next third of a century when most of the systems that had first appeared in the preceding decades got restructured.

As described in Strauss and Howe's *Generations*, the Gilded Generation was fading from the scene as the century began. [5] Gildeds were Reactives who as youngsters had fought and endured the Civil War, reacting to the mess it left by becoming determined and pragmatic, building the great business trusts, exploiting the South, moving to the West, patenting numerous inventions, and enduring the first major depression in 1893 at the same time as they braved criticism in order to enjoy the opulence of the Chicago World's Fair that same year.[6] The Gildeds, embedded in the Civil War Cycle, were pretty much off center stage as the twentieth century began.

The first third of the century was dominated by Strauss and Howe's Progressive and Missionary generations, while their Great Power Cycle begins. The people in these two generations over these first three decades transformed America with important "good government" reforms of state and local administrations, with factory-safety and child-labor legislation, with land-use zoning introduced and popularized, and with impressive City Beautiful public buildings, parks, and boulevards and a variety of multistory, multifamily apartment houses built in virtually every city across the nation.

The Progressive Generation was deemed Adaptive because its members, said Strauss and Howe, began as conformists, developed their own ethos, and finally partnered with their juniors. They rejected the Gildeds and campaigned for the Spanish-American War. They figured that "calibration and communication would eventually make America a nicer country," so theirs was the first generation to obtain advanced academic degrees, to define "professional," and then to establish a wide variety of professional associations, all in order "to apply their credentialed expertise toward improving" what the previous generation had pioneered, in the process attempting to "blend the rugged West with the effete East."[7]

The Missionary Generation was termed Idealist. To Strauss and Howe's way of thinking, such a generation struggles with its elders' institutions until it is able to become self-absorbed with its own patterns, ending, however, as uncompromising moralists. Their elders had created idyllic childhoods, scouting, and manly college heroes for the youthful years of this generation, but the Missionary Generation turned against constraints on women and against the trusts that had grown up in the elders' time, writing books like Upton Sinclair's *The Jungle* and Jacob Riis's *How the Other Half Lives*. The Missionaries saw that America had the potential to be a Great Power, crusading against the Huns of the world, but, where the Progressives had the ideal of Temperance, the Missionaries advanced both the ideal and the laws about Prohibition. The genius of Franklin D. Roosevelt, a member of the Missionary Generation, was that he surrounded himself with younger Lost Generation men and women, but most Missionaries retreated from both his New Deal and from the generations that followed their own.

The Babbitts, in contrast to the Ebenezers, are generally satisfied with existing class and racial disparities and not afraid to embrace programs that might even widen the gaps. At the end of the eighteenth century, Alexander Hamilton would have been their hero. They transformed Ebenezer Howard's radical ideas into the kind of garden city that would be palatable to the real estate developers and municipal boosters who populate not only Sinclair Lewis's novels but also what Robert Goodman, in 1971, termed the "urban industrial complex," composed of all those with a pecuniary or political interest in building roads, pouring concrete, putting housing developments on suburban land, running mortgage loan institutions, and collecting property taxes.[8]

In the 1920s we can associate the Babbitts with the creation of real estate boards and the introduction of land-use zoning. During this period Calvin Coolidge triumphantly declared that the business of America is business (the same kind of triumphalist attitude associated with the claim at the end of the century that capitalism had won over all other economic systems and that the full globalization of the economy was inevitable). Thereafter, as suburbanites, we can associate the Babbitts with all the shifts of the urban scene toward conformity and sameness. They were increasingly unhappy with what they considered the socialistic tendencies of the New Deal; in the early postwar period they were fervently in favor of the Taft-Hartley Act, which began to limit the growth of labor unions; and they were generally conservative politically during the Cold War and the Vietnam War and dubious about regulations to protect the environment.

While our next chapter has to report that Coolidge's capitalism had to be rescued by the early New Deal measures, here we look at the structuring of the urban scene during the first third of the twentieth century, seen as the blossoming of modern-day community building in which private real estate ventures go hand in hand with public works to create a solider urban structure than had been necessary in the nineteenth century, and in which innovations in both the public and private sectors drive the search for "highest and best use of land" steadily onward to larger and larger projects. This concept of "highest and best use," the watchword of the Babbitt-style landowning capitalist, is intended to trump all other planning or environmental considerations; the origins of the term are somewhat obscure, but its use is ubiquitous.[9]

All of this is consistent with Strauss and Howe's view of how the Missionary and Lost generations operated at the beginning of the Great Power Cycle. In particular, the garden city folks worked to link their new suburbs to the central cities by intercity rail and telephone and telegraph lines, with paved roads for automobiles and delivery trucks to be installed as soon as possible. They were happy to see slums eliminated by building new towns and new suburbs, but my impression is that they also assumed that these new suburbs would have to be stratified by income and race "in order to preserve property values." Indeed, such institutionalized racism is a major theme throughout the twentieth century, a theme that appears in various guises throughout this book.

Planning and Construction in the First Third of the Century

Planning

In the two decades before World War I, some form of city planning, with leadership from the local power elite, began in literally every city of any size in the nation. One of the major impetuses to the new practice was the desire to avoid some of the inconvenience of constantly tearing up the same street for construction of public works and public utilities. Finally a number of groups in the community, representing a wide range of interests and professional skills, began to see the mutuality of their interests and would start meeting regularly to see what could be achieved by cooperation and collaboration among municipal departments and other interested parties. At a typical conference would be "good government" lawyers and civic leaders; public health officials, usually members of APHA, who were especially concerned about health conditions in the slums and even more especially about the control of diseases, such as tuberculosis, associated with slums; the first generation of "housers" hoping to replace slums with standard housing and to get adequate occupancy standards for residential units; real estate owners and downtown merchants exploring notions of land-use zoning and other regulations; Beaux Arts architects wanting to create a City Beautiful; economists seeking ways to improve the efficiency of municipal operations and investments; and assorted business leaders, including executives of transportation companies, public utilities, and banking and financial institutions. Probably absent were women and any reference to racism.

Defining what planning is or is not in the kind of mixed economy we have in the United States,[10] and then articulating how it should be done, occupies much of a planner's working, and even social life, because every citizen living in an urban area seems to have a clear notion of why urban snafus are the fault of the local planning agency and what planners should be doing about the situation. When asked for my personal view, I usually respond that, if planning did not exist, it would have to be invented in order for the body politic to make sensible decisions. In the event, the most limited definition of planning, its role in providing a basis for local land-use zoning (and attached map of the community), soon became known as planning's major technique for preserving "good" districts by keeping jarring uses separated and by minimizing the number of nuisance suits that might ensue if supposedly incompatible uses were allowed to exist side by side. Planners themselves have been engaged through the years in all sorts of much needed studies essential to making reasoned judgments about population growth and migration, land for industry, housing, transportation, public works of all kinds, open space and parks, historic preservation, cultural institutions, and, more diffidently, proposals regarding income distribution, racism, pollution controls and remedies, and measures to limit growth. But, in the public mind, the power of the local government to limit property development through zoning continues to stand out as the primary purpose and tool of planners.

Obviously zoning, which limits private property rights in the name of a larger public interest, had to confront the inevitable legal challenges. In 1926 the U.S. Supreme Court in *Village of Euclid v. Ambler Realty*, 272 U.S. 365, approved the creation of zoning districts and triggered broad acceptance of the basic concepts of zoning. Shortly thereafter, Herbert Hoover, President Calvin Coolidge's secretary of commerce, promulgated model zoning legislation and campaigned vigorously, cheered on by mortgage bankers and real estate interests, for adoption of the codes by state and local legislatures.

Fast forward to the latter years of the twentieth century to discover how disputatious the subject of zoning as either policy or practice can be. As policy, it often appears that zoning has limited influence or power to direct developmental pressures within a given governmental jurisdiction or to preserve a given piece of property (such as beach access) for public enjoyment. In practice, the codes can become extremely varied, inherently complex, and inordinately competitive and poorly matched both with plain and fancy types of city/regional and town/country planning and with all manner of environmental protection laws. A considerable literature exists for anyone interested in the battles about land-use regulations and about the litigation that determines the outcomes.[11]

Yes, zoning codes have helped shape the urban scene, but, the shapes of most cities were pretty well determined by decades of private and public decisions before a zoning map and zoning regulations were adopted in a particular locality, and ordinarily the zoning map merely translated the three-dimensional reality on the ground to a two-dimensional presence in the building-permit office. And even as I write at the beginning of the third millennium, critically important areas in and around the cities of America have never yet been brought under the zoning yoke.

Regional planning in America has had a less contentious but similarly amorphous history compared to city planning. The lower level of combat is a result of its being somewhat removed from the local politics about zoning and subsequent building permits that together determine a person's power, right, or privilege to develop a given property. The form and nature of different varieties of regional planning, however, generate enthusiastic support far more than local plans. At the broadest level, hearts are stirred by visions of entire watersheds carefully developed for combinations of environmental uplift, industrial power, broadly enjoyed economic development, efficient transportation, and outdoor recreation. Examples of this level of planning begin with the works of Benton Mackaye, who conceptualized the Tennessee Valley Authority in the 1920s. Equally famous is the multivolume *Regional Plan of New York and Its Environs*, funded in 1923 by the Russell Sage Foundation as the basis for planning a score of bridges and tunnels to make transportation among the cities and suburbs of the region efficient and capable of handling expected future growth.[12] One of the icons of "landscape architecture" in the late twentieth century is Ian McHarg, whose seminal work, *Design With Nature* (published by the American Museum of Natural History in 1969) was inspired in many ways by Benton Mackaye.

A second form of regional planning is primarily concerned with intrametropolitan distributions of population, land uses, housing, industry, commerce, open space, employment, and transportation. Such concerns are politically easier to accept and use when some form of regional planning is a prerequisite for various forms of federal grants, as was common when the federal government was making large grants for transportation and health facilities in the 1960s and 1970s. However, with rare exceptions (such as the Regional Plan Association of New York), regional planning is performed by a public agency, typically a confederation of local governments, although a number of metropolises sport nongovernmental organizations to advocate ecologically sound policies. Unfortunately, these confederations tend to either disband or become mute when issues such as a fair distribution of publicly assisted housing among rich and poor suburbs are proposed or mandated. Regardless of the actual power of planners to influence events, however, some degree of regional (or even metropolitan-wide) planning is manifestly required to complement local planning and to create an adequate basis for responsible government and intelligent private decisions.

Construction

Amazingly enough, I know of no statistics, even rough estimates, about the total volume of construction, otherwise known as the creation of "real" wealth, for the intensely productive period between 1900 and World War I. The first official estimates begin to appear about 1915 and grow increasingly accurate and provide greater detail as more and more communities adopted some sort of building permit control over both residential and nonresidential construction and were able to begin providing consistent regular reports on numbers, types, dollar values, and timing of construction starts and completions to the U.S. Department of Commerce.[13] An added impetus to the development of estimates was the development of national income and product accounts in the 1920s, naturally by members of the Missionary and Lost generations.

An accurate record of construction in that first decade and a half before World War I might astonish us by its range and magnitude. Every city of any size began to build a variety of apartment houses for upper-income families, buildings with about ten stories, elegant exteriors of cut stone or terra-cotta, well-decorated foyers, and either hydraulic or lift elevators.[14]

As immigration continued and urban populations grew across the nation, uncounted masses of solid, freestanding, one-family houses in the central areas, built for the large families of the day, began to appear; many of these remain standing, fully rebuilt in the latter half of the century for upmarket families or offices. After World War I such ample structures were built in the upper-income suburbs more than in the central areas. Nearby, in the outer edges of the central areas and in nearby towns, were equally large numbers of two-family and three-decker flats for working families. After the real estate lobbies of the 1920s began to define private ownership of a single-family house on its own lot as the only proper way for true-blue Americans to live, fewer two-family homes were built although, in truth, this type of construction was perfectly attuned to a working family's life cycle. At times the other half of the house could be rented out to strangers to supplement income; at other times, it could shelter just-married children or elderly parents. The minimal single-family house that World War II veterans could get with the GI Bill benefits did not provide such intergenerational or economic cycle capabilities.

The great art museums, public libraries, and City Beautiful boulevards got built in this early period, together with monumental railroad stations, such as Grand Central in New York and Union Station in Washington, D.C.; New York City's Park Avenue was transformed when the New York Central's tracks were put underground to accommodate the construction of fashionable apartment buildings, many with expansive interior courtyards. Most of the railroad lines had been laid down by the time the twentieth century opened, but privately financed intercity and interurban trolley lines were being built at a great rate, and the subway and elevated lines in some of the major cities were built then. One by one these private lines went bankrupt. In New York City they were handed over to the city and became the patchwork of lines that for years retained their original corporate designations until succumbing to renaming in the last part of the century. The trolleys (see story in Chapter 8) had a different fate.

Industrial activity in the first part of the twentieth century, equally poorly documented, seems to have been pretty much centered in the cities, occupying vast areas and served by railroad trackage. Many factories had multiple stories with complex systems for moving goods and messages between floors. One of the consequences of the San Francisco earthquake of 1906 was the financial burden on the casualty insurance companies that were then forced to jack up premiums on nonfireproof buildings, making the occupancy of these buildings economically impossible for small firms.[15] This was of special importance to my father, Aaron Rabinowitz, who had established his own real estate management and brokerage firm in Manhattan in 1903, when he was only nineteen. His firm, Spear & Company, became one of the earliest members of the New York Real Estate Board. Between that fateful date in 1906 and the mid-1920s, much of Spear & Company's work was devoted to moving small manufacturing firms from little four- or five-story structures with rickety hand-operated elevators to new fifteen- to twenty-story fireproof buildings in a new "garment center" between 14th Street and 42nd Street on the West Side.

These central-city fireproof loft buildings mirrored the national change in industrial processes that favored horizontal workspaces and disfavored multistory operations. This change made the suburbanization of industry that much more feasible and the ultimate abandonment of central city buildings that much more advantageous. Such changes in industrial processes accelerated in the new facilities built during World War II and continued thereafter, making obsolete the Depression-era challenge for the New Dealers of getting existing factories to puff smoke out of their smokestacks once again as visible evidence that the national recovery was under way.

The heightened activity in all forms of real estate during these early twentieth-century decades led inevitably, given the organizational pro- clivities of the Missionary Generation, to the formation of a variety of professional associations in the field: the National Association of Real Estate Boards (NAREB), the American Institute of Real Estate Apprais- ers, the Building and Owners Management Association, and so on.[16] States began to license brokers, so the professional groups developed certification programs. Locally, the new real estate boards exercised a good deal of power concerning planning, zoning, and building permits; at the national level, NAREB became a major pressure group, espe- cially against any government subsidy of housing for lower-income fami- lies. And so we come to the subject of "housing," a term dear to the Ebenezers of our world but disdained by the Babbitts of the real estate world who deal with "homes and home-building." For them, "housing" implies the intrusion of a socialistic government into private markets; in reality, much of the private market for homes in this country is sup- ported by government mortgage insurance programs and related agen- cies authorized by Congress.

"Housers" Make Their Appearance

Housing is the result of work by Ebenezers in society to help less fortu- nate people have "decent, safe and sanitary" abodes. The term also be- came useful to the Census Bureau when it began to inventory the residential stock of the nation, the first full-count census becoming part of the 1940 decennial census. Concern for housing became the province of the various good government leagues early in the twentieth century and of city and regional planning (or town and country planning groups), such as New York's Citizen Planning and Housing Council, one of the earliest and most effective of the big-city, city-wide, community-action groups that played such important roles in the later eras of urban rede- velopment and renewal. By contrast, the real estate industry thought of itself as involved with "home-building" and "residential construc- tion" rather than with "housing," the proponents of which became known as "housers."

Much has been written on the history of America's housing policies and programs (and on the English and European programs that served as models). Many writings focus on New York City's attempts in the nineteenth century to find designs for "tenements" that would provide light and air for occupants, on the role of philanthropists as pioneers in the housing movement, and on attempts at creating the perfect garden city. These garden city writings, largely for the Babbitt trade, abandoned Ebenezer Howard's fiscal and regional underpinnings but often held on as idealistically as possible to his concepts for joining living, working, shopping, and usable open spaces and parks with safe pathways for pedestrians and unobtrusive parking for automobiles and trucks. Creating projects for model tenements and model neighborhoods in garden-type planned communities has actually been the province of architects and landscape architects rather than of planners, for the lot of planners is to struggle with improving and maintaining life in existing places rather than having the luxury of new construction on open land.

The general problem of housing, for all classifications of the people who live or will come to reside in an existing community has, however, traditionally been a part of both the planners' world and the philanthropists' world. As such housing became of major significance in mid-century, the Ford Foundation instituted many related programs. These are the subject of retrospective monographs written by Louis Winnick as he retired from the Ford Foundation. Louis Winnick has had a distinguished career as an urban economist and planner. He took his doctoral degree at Columbia University's Institute for Land Use and Housing Studies (where I was a fellow student in 1951 before I was recalled by the Navy); for many years he was director of research for New York City's Department of Planning, then head of the Ford Foundation's Division of National Affairs and instrumental in guiding the foundation's work in the urban realm. As he moved toward retirement in the late 1980s, he was asked to write a set of histories of the foundation's urban interests. These were primarily for internal consumption and have not been published, but the foundation's archivist, Alan Divack, provided me with the full set of papers Winnick had written. I consider them of such originality, scope, value, and authoritativeness that I have incorporated particularly illuminating chunks of them in the chapters that follow.

The earlier contexts of housing as a praiseworthy activity are wonderfully considered in the paragraphs below, the first of the material I have been privileged to use from Louis Winnick's writings at the Ford Foundation:[17]

Housing's appeal to the philanthropic impulses of past and present rests in part on its status as a merit good—as instrumental to a larger vision of social reform—and in part because, more so than other sectors, it can be a crucible of innovation. Earlier generations of philanthropists viewed a decent dwelling to be not just an end in itself but the sine qua non of a healthy society. The eradication of contagious disease, a salubrious environment, and the extension of life expectancy were not to be achieved without attending to housing's sanitary facilities, fire protection, light and ventilation, and overcrowded dwellings and building sites. Sound housing was likewise a means for perfecting a moral and democratic republic. There could be no stable social order unless everyone possessed a satisfactory stake in the system. . . .[18]

Associated with the philanthropic investors, and often inspiring them, was a vanguard of social reformers. These advocates sought more than a scatter of investment models that might or might not be replicated by the marketplace, but comprehensive laws and regulations to be imposed on all tenements, old as well as new. The most renowned was Jacob Riis, whose journalistic exposés and powerful books stirred the influential and, through them, the state legislature. New York's Governor Theodore Roosevelt poured his boundless energy into Riis's cause and became Riis's lifelong friend and confidant.

Riis's genius was to create a public climate conducive to housing reform rather than to formulate concrete proposals or draft statutes and regulations. Those technical skills belonged to other housing reformers, notably Elgin Gould, Robert DeForest, and, most of all, Lawrence Veiller. Veiller was the perfect embodiment of the philanthropic duality, one face technocrat, the other advocate. Self-taught and indefatigable, he acquired a mastery of the technology of constructing and operating tenement buildings as well as an unparalleled legal expertise in translating the physical principles into comprehensive and enforceable laws. A peerless organizer of committees and commissions, Veiller was the acknowledged leader of the reformist campaign that culminated in New York State's Tenement Housing Law of 1901, the triumph of 50 years of model-building and advocacy and a landmark in the march of the Progressive movement. Most but (to Veiller's bitter disappointment) by no means all the innovations derived from the models and architectural competitions found their way into that law. The real estate lobby, then as now, was not without countervailing power.[19]

The housers' campaign in America for governmental attention to programs for slum clearance and replacements was led off by activists such as Edith Elmer Wood, author of a seminal book, *Recent Trends in Ameri-*

can Housing.[20] A few years earlier, one of the first public steps to get governments to shoulder some responsibility had been New York State's passage of the Urban Redevelopment Law. This law was instigated by the reformers operating under the aegis of Gov. Alfred E. Smith, a democrat and a Democrat.

The purpose of the 1926 legislation was to induce private investors to put their money into slum clearance, providing housing for low-income families inside cities, obviously a program requiring use of eminent domain to acquire sites so that land assembly would not be hijacked by an individual owner holding out.[21] State government granted power of eminent domain to a private limited-dividend housing company if the company had at least 50 percent of a site approved by the local government for such construction (a provision that seems to assume that such a city already had a full panoply of appropriate zoning and building codes, etc.). Local government also could confer a property tax exemption on the improvement for twenty-five years. The developer-sponsor had to agree to limit dividends from the project to 6 percent on the investment.

The state housing commission was established to implement the new law. At the insistance of Lillian D. Wald of the Henry Street Settlement, Aaron Rabinowitz was appointed to the commission. He and Lieutenant Governor Herbert Lehman helped finance one of the most famous of the projects built under that pioneering statute, Grand Street Housing; it was built by the Amalgamated Clothing Workers Union's housing corporation on the heels of its first project, erected in the Bronx before governmental assistance of any sort was available.[22]

The private developers of limited-dividend housing projects had to arrange for their own mortgages, since these were the days before any form of mortgage insurance or guarantee existed. Obviously "housing" began to attract more attention as the New Dealers saw it as a Keynesian-economics tool to counter the failing economy during the Depression, and there ensued many long chapters on the subject for the rest of the century. In those days before the system was overhauled by the New Deal, home mortgages came from savings banks, commercial banks, pension funds, and individuals and typically did not run for more than five years, with no amortization by regular partial monthly or annual repayments of the mortgage loan, which meant that the mortgage came due with a bang, represented in classic melodramas by bankers demanding payment and the hapless homeowner pleading for help.

Not until the 1920s, however, were the large banks and insurance companies able or willing to offer large mortgages with twenty- to thirty-year terms to builders. When large mortgages became available, builders could begin to plan large-scale projects, while Wall Street investment bankers figured out ways to package or syndicate these large mortgages or groups of mortgages to small investors. Such financial developments combined to change the landscape by enabling real estate promoters for the very first time to create building corporations with hundreds or thousands of small investors as holders of stocks or certificates of participation in large mortgages. Before these institutional changes in the 1920s, larger building projects were only able to be financed by large corporations for their own use (with perhaps some spaces for rent to others), by charitable trusts (such as Sailor's Snug Harbor in downtown Manhattan), by churches (such as Trinity Church, also in New York), or by small groups of wealthy investors forming partnerships for the purpose.

The emergence of large mortgage bond issues and real estate corporations, each with thousands of investors in the corporation's stocks and bonds, is one of the most important features of the decade and a half following World War I, and the chapters about these phenomena in my book, *The Real Estate Gamble*, are, I think, among the first written from the perspective of institutional change and adaptation.[23] In the middle of the Depression, the U.S. Congress felt the need for new banking and securities laws and held hearings about the devious ways bankrupt mortgage bond issues had been reorganized by bondholder committee and court-appointed trustees.[24] These hearings are reviewed in the book, together with a report on original research about the rise and fall of the securities issued by some 300 of the new real estate corporations whose finances were reported to *Moody's Financial Institutions and Real Estate Manuals* from the 1920s through the Depression until World War II. In general, a minority of these corporations avoided bankrupcy, and these survivors lost a minimum of 50 percent, but sometimes up to 90 percent, of their pre–1929 market values before recovering somewhat as the economy improved during World War II.

Several of these new real estate corporations became cases to be studied at Harvard Business School during the 1920s. Among them was the pyramid of corporations created by Frederick Fillmore French in New York and Connecticut. French managed to raise several hundred millions of dollars from some 10,000 investors, each one receiving some preferred stock in a corporation erecting a specific building or providing a managerial or financial service to the family of corporations he created in the 1920s. The preferred stock paid for one-half of the cost of the building, the other half being financed by a conventional first mortgage from a single institution. With each share of preferred stock, French gave the investor a share of common stock, taking another share for his investment firm (whose shares could also be bought). The intention of this quite famous "French Plan" was to retire these preferred stocks from profits over the ensuing ten-year period, after which the common stock would begin to have real value and pay dividends.[25] Under the plan, French built a significant number of what were then considered large apartment and office buildings, including the twelve buildings and parks known as Tudor City on East 42nd Street in Manhattan. "Live in Tudor City and walk to work" was the slogan, cartooned in *The New Yorker* magazine and shown here as Figure 9.1.

Stories of Frederick Fillmore French and his extraordinary real estate ventures have been told elsewhere, but my major reason for recounting some of those experiences here is that they are a superb example of 1920s-type activity in the then-emerging markets for real estate securities and for dense high-rise construction; also, as noted below, I have personal reasons for dwelling on this case. French's pyramid of holding companies fell upon the usual hard times as the Depression developed, with rents received by the separate corporations falling to no more than one-half of 1920s peaks and with stock prices down to one-tenth of the price at which they had been issued. At the same time, the French companies attracted lawsuits by disaffected stockholders, beginning in 1930; the last of these suits was not settled until 1968. French's Knickerbocker Village project provides an almost unique example of how the federal government was moved, out of desperation, to invest directly in a real estate project that promised to provide employment as the Depression continued. French, using scores of dummy corporations in the late 1920s, had secretly acquired some nineteen square blocks just north of City Hall in Manhattan to "build another Tudor City." Most of these properties were ultimately lost to foreclosure, but a number of them became the site of Knickerbocker Village, financed by the only big-city loan made by the Reconstruction Finance Corporation, established by President Herbert Hoover but headed, by the time Knickerbocker Village opened, by Jesse Jones, a Roosevelt appointee.

Knickerbocker Village, built before the era of high-rise public housing projects, was almost as high as some of the projects that were blown up and left as rubble later in the century, and it served as a demonstra-

Figure 9.1   **Gluyas Williams's Cartoon About Tudor City**

Source: Used by permission of Joyce Williams and family. Originally published in the *New Yorker* magazine in 1927, as part of Gluyas Williams's "Industrial Crises" series with the caption "A Resident of Tudor City Is Discovered Not Walking to Work."

tion of how many people could be housed in a redevelopment project. However, arguments were raging on both sides of the Atlantic at the time concerning the economic feasibility of high-rise construction for both residential and office buildings. Baron Haussemann, working on Napoleon III's Paris, and the French architect Le Corbusier, who advo-

Figure 9.2   **Knickerbocker Village**

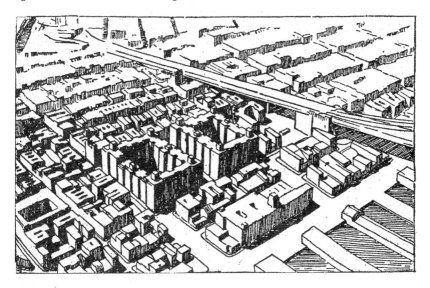

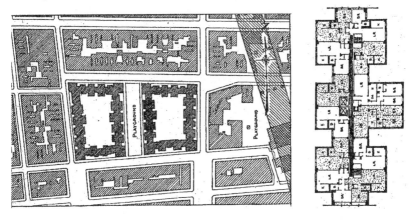

Source: Reproduced with permission from Werner Hegemann, *City Planning Housing*, vol. two, *Political Economy and Civic Art* (New York: Architectural Book Publishing Company, 1937), p. 275.

cated enormous new skyscrapers, could also be cited on the many issues presented by new levels of height and density, as illustrated by the quotation (which includes Figure 9.2) below by Werner Hegemann, a learned city planner writing in 1937 about French's project:

But it is not Le Corbusier alone who thus returned to the obsolete policy of Napoleon and Haussemann who thought it good finance to rebuild congested cities by increasing land values and building heights. This same policy is continuously being revived in the congested sections of New York. The outstanding example is the so-called Knickerbocker Village. It is called village probably because it is no village at all but one of the most congested and tallest conglomerations of dwellings in the world. This unpleasant fact is supposed to be veiled by giving it a name suggesting quaintly pleasant and country-like conditions. The Knickerbocker "Village" replaces congested six-storied "tenements" by twelve story "apartments," tripling (with 1047 persons per acre) the former population congestion per acre of this area, and even quadrupling the average population density of Manhattan Island.

Immediately after the opening of these Knickerbocker Apartments the tenants, dissatisfied by the inefficiency with which the buildings were operated, organized. They staged their first strike and refused to pay rent. This strike could be pacified by strategic concessions to the new tenants and by equally strategic evictions or threats of eviction. The strike, however, carried a foreboding of the greater things which may develop if this policy of increasing congestion should be carried further.

The attempt to abolish slums by building higher, instead of lower, is false economy. . . . It is again true that the late Mr. F.F. French, promoter of Knickerbocker Village, claims: "The high cost of land in lower Manhattan does not render slum clearance impracticable . . . the cost of land is rendered less expensive per room by building twelve or sixteen stories on it rather than six."

The weakness of this argument, however, is emphasized by the 1933 report of the New York State Board of Housing: "on land as expensive as $6 a square foot commercial practice cannot produce a cheaper room in a twelve-story building than in a six-story building. In both, only a room rent as high as $18 a month would be remunerative. But under the regulation of the State Housing Law, a room on one-dollar land costs $10.21 in a twelve-story building and only $9.51 in a six-story building." These figures again prove the accuracy of the late Eberstadt's often quoted contentions. This German master in the science of housing has established the fact that the higher a dwelling is the more is it apt to be burdened with unproductive expenses. *He has also proved, as has been said before, that the individual two-story row house is the most economical unit for housing the masses* and for distributing the heavy financial burden connected with a large-scale project. [Hegemann's footnote:] A similar conclusion [was reached by famous architects:] Aronovici, Churchill, Lescaze, Mayer and the late Henry Wright in their illuminating analyses of housing economics in New York.[26] [Emphasis added]

The large developments of garden apartments after World War II were, in many respects, no more than clusters of two-story two-unit modules. Two-family houses had been the mainstay of working-class families in the Northeast earlier in the century but were generally snubbed by the generations that gravitated to the post–World War II suburbs. In any case, height and density won not only the day but the century (and I believe all of the architects cited by Hegemann sooner or later produced high-rise buildings for their clients). The larger cities in the United States built high-rise towers under the public housing programs (many of which were demolished as failed experiments later in the century) and, using federal urban-redevelopment capital grants under the Housing Act of 1949, sold downtown land at $1 or $2 a square foot to developers of both residential and commercial facilities in order to get rents down. By the end of the twentieth century, virtually every town and city of any size sported a crop of high-rise buildings. The World Trade Center towers in New York City were classic examples of the triumph of the economics of prestige over the economics of cost and conservation, and the debates over the optimal size of buildings still go on.

Knickerbocker Village had been built under the 1926 limited-dividend housing laws, and, at the dedication, the speech on behalf of the New York State Housing Commission was given by one Aaron Rabinowitz, my father, who met Mrs. Fred F. French for the first time at the ceremony. At that time, Aaron Rabinowitz was also one of Gov. Alfred E. Smith's appointees on the New York State Insurance Commission, the supervisory authority for all the insurance companies licensed to do business in the state. Several years later, Mr. French died unexpectedly of a massive heart attack, and Mrs. French, inheritor of the controlling stock in the Fred F. French Investing Company, Inc., which stood at the pinnacle of the holding company pyramid, hired Mr. Rabinowitz to be head of the firm, with an option on her stock if ever she sold it. His knowledge of both real estate and insurance companies stabilized the firm, one of the relatively few "public" firms that survived the Depression without reorganization by bankruptcy proceedings. Ultimately buying Mrs. French's stock, he devoted the rest of his life (he died at age eighty-nine in 1973) to dealing with the lawsuits, amortizing the mortgages to extinction, and learning to live under the various sets of federal, state, and local rent control laws that began in the middle of World War II.

Urban Studies and the History of the Real Estate Industry

Another adequate history that has yet to be written would cover the early stages of development of the real estate industry in the twentieth century as it intersected with comparable developments in city and regional planning, in zoning practice, and in the economic analysis of construction starts. Our nation is too big, state laws too varied, and local situations too unique or idiosyncratic to allow for the collection of accurate data for the whole. Instead of a comprehensive treatment of these sets of interactions, mostly what we have are biographies of individual builders and descriptions of the growth (but rarely the decline) of their projects and ventures, together with business histories of thrift-mortgage institutions or particular governmental programs (involving mortgages, rent control, etc.), either for particular places or the nation as a whole.

Marc Weiss is perhaps the best analyst we have on twentieth-century real estate history, but his best-known book, *The Rise of the Community Builders: The American Real Estate Industry and Urban Land Planning*, can begin only in the mid-1920s for lack of reliable information, with little grounding in changes generated in the earlier part of the century. One of the reasons for such lack of data, as documented by Leo Grebler while compiling data for his study of long-term investments in investment-grade real property, is that most of the financial data are secrets closely guarded by the various owners, lenders, and tenants of a major building project, and such data tend to be discarded as one set of owners passes the structure on to another set over the long life of a building.[27]

Weiss's extensive essay, "Real Estate History: An Overview and Research Agenda," is the best introduction I know of to the raft of subjects that must be included in any comprehensive survey of the real estate industry and is cited frequently in the passages that follow.[28] In this essay, he makes a number of references to my own writings and puts them into a context that makes sense of the rather heterogeneous set of topics that have occupied my time over the years. My main objective here, however, is not expressing my satisfaction with his treatment of my work but expressing my appreciation of the way he has broken the field into manageable topics for discussion. I have followed his categorizations and the essence of his thought in the summary that follows:

Category 1. Predecessors

Weiss acknowledges his predecessors by beginning with reference to economists such as Adna Ferrin Weber, who wrote that already-cited seminal book in 1899, *The Growth of Cities in the Nineteenth Century*, and Richard M. Hurd, who pioneered the microeconomic approach with his *Principles of City Land Values* in 1904.[29] Then, he writes,

> The formal launching of the field of urban land economics during the 1920s led to further advances both in data gathering and in methods of scholarship. World famous Richard T. Ely, then in his seventies, provided leadership to a new generation of political economists and social scientists who worked directly with industry and government to produce pathbreaking research monographs on many aspects of the real estate business and urbanization.

As examples, Weiss cites Homer Hoyt and Helen Monchow in the pre–World War II years, and, for the 1940s, a stable of economists, writing under the aegis of the National Bureau of Economic Research (NBER), that included Miles Colean, Wesley Clair Mitchell, Arthur Burns, Ernest M. Fisher, Leo Grebler, Raymond Goldsmith, Saul B. Klaman, Raymond J. Saulnier, and a number of other well-known researchers. He also cites "some academics trained as 'institutional' economists, such as Arthur M. Weimer, Leland S. Burns, Fred E. Case, Alan Rabinowitz, and Maury Seldin [who] have continued into the 1980s the Richard Ely–NBER philosophy of understanding real estate economics in historical perspective," plus those who have written credible histories of the various trade associations and what he calls "sagas of personal success."

Category 2. Real Estate Development, Construction, Land Subdividing, Sales, Leasing, and Property Management

These topics cover the small-scale, ordinary processes of real estate and government, in the contrasting contexts of incremental suburbanization, the building of "new communities," and central-area urban redevelopment.[30]

Category 3. Financial Institutions, Mortgages, Lenders, Investors, Insurers, and Tax Collectors

Weiss comments that

The business of real estate revolves around money, yet surprisingly few historians are directly engaged in tracing the flow of funds through the financial system. [Many books] document the tremendous changes that have taken place during the past century in the financing of housing production and consumption, . . . and the securitization of mortgages. . . . Mortgage lending for multifamily dwellings or apartments has received less attention from researchers. Financing for commercial and industrial properties, for land acquisition and development, and for equity investment have all been relatively neglected topics of historical analysis. One broadranging exception is Alan Rabinowitz's *The Real Estate Gamble* (1980), which explores the history of real estate investment since 1920 . . . and also discusses the history of boom and bust cycles in real estate investment.[31]

Pages later,

Few scholars have followed Alan Rabinowitz's lead in examining the evolution of investment mechanisms and financial instruments such as mortgage-backed securities, syndications, real estate investment trusts, and other devices involved in structuring often complex deals. We also need to know more about the changing historical role of institutions in the financing of commercial and industrial development, including life insurance companies, pension funds, commercial banks, syndicators, and securities firms.[32]

And further, there has been "almost no significant historical research on the crucial role of taxation in real estate finance." There was notable growth during the 1970s in both the quantity and quality of academic and intergovernmental studies on the economics and politics of the property tax, but those efforts at theory-making seem to have tapered off somewhat in recent years; however, ever since passage of Proposition 13 in California about 1978, politicians and citizens in almost every state have been forced to deal with both angry challenges and practical limits to their existing property tax systems.[33]

Category 4. Large Property Owners and Users

This category covers analyses of investment in large-scale real estate developments. The genre was pioneered by Leo Grebler at Columbia University. Also here are reports of the many investments by major life insurance companies in such housing projects as Stuyvesant Town in New York, LaBrea in Los Angeles, and Lake Meadows in Chicago, and by the California community builders of the 1950s and 1960s.[34]

Category 5. Property Relations

Here the Ebenezers blossom, beginning with Henry George's *Progress and Poverty* (1879), Richard Ely's *Property and Contract in Their Relations to the Distribution of Wealth* (1914), and John R. Commons's *Legal Foundation of Capitalism* (1924), through the trailblazing work of the sociologists at the University of Chicago and the many books on urban race relations in housing, to the neo-Marxian examinations of socioeconomic stratifications in capitalist cities.[35]

Category 6. The Public Sector

This last of Weiss's basic categories recognizes the role of government and the realms of laws, taxes, municipal finance (including a welcome reference to my book on the subject[36]) and fiscal policy, planning, development, and redevelopment.

However, in this essay Weiss does not include the contributions that universities have made to the compiling of real estate history and to many other aspects of urban economics, urban policy making, and state and local finance. Their role in the early decades of the twentieth century, is represented by Harvard's Bureau of Municipal Research where work on the economics of public utilities attracted the elite of the economics profession. The New Deal agencies employed many otherwise unemployed economists and academicians, and two of them, Ernest Fisher and Leo Grebler, both of whom had worked at the Federal Housing Administration (FHA) for many years, received a most innovative research grant authorized in the Housing Act of 1949. The grant enabled them to establish the first of a new breed of university-connected operations, the Institute for Urban Land Use and Housing Studies at Columbia University's Graduate School of Business. Here Fisher and Grebler began training a new generation of land economists (including Louis Winnick and me) capable of bridging the gap between economics, political science, public administration, and the practice of urban planning and real estate development.[37] Columbia's Institute was shorn of its federal support when Dwight Eisenhower, a former president of Columbia, became president of the United States; his Republican cohorts went to work to strip the federal government of a variety of New Deal agencies involved with "planning" or "research" that had been created to enhance the nation's urban and regional resources. The research component of the Housing Acts did not survive the cuts. Fisher and Grebler carried on their work, however, at new centers at such institutions as the University of Southern California, the University of California at Berkeley, the University of Pennsylvania, and the University of Wisconsin. Decades later, a similar center was established at Massachusetts Institute of Technology.

In the 1950s, the Ford Foundation attempted to "urbanize higher learning" and proceeded to fund centers at "many of America's first-rank private universities, among them Harvard, Princeton, Columbia, Chicago, Johns Hopkins and Northwestern," as further described by Winnick acting as historian for the foundation:[38]

> The notable actions of the early phase included the establishment of a Joint Center for Urban Studies shared by Harvard and MIT. The expectation was that if two world-class institutions could be induced to turn their gaze on the cities around them, it would set a challenge to others. Moreover, Cambridge boasted outstanding scholars of urban studies, among them Edward Banfield, Charles Haar, Martin Meyerson, Daniel Patrick Moynihan, Raymond Vernon, James Q. Wilson and Robert Wood. The total outlay for the Center was $2.5 million. It survives in a truncated version, supported mainly by contributions from the private housing industry.
>
> During that early phase there was also an attempt to raise the aspirations and standards of urban scholarship by creating a Committee on Urban Economics (CUE). The economics discipline (at least then) stood at the apex of the social sciences, the nearest approximation to the physical sciences. Much would be gained, it was held, to bring the analytic capacities of that prestigious discipline to the study of cities and their problems, a field hitherto left in the main to the ministrations of historians, sociologists and schools of social work. A total of $1.25 million was allotted over eight years to CUE, predominantly in support of doctoral dissertations for young economists plus the conferences and research monographs of the more established for whom urban studies was typically a new interest. Some products of that program can be seen even now in textbooks, learned journals and the rosters of academic departments and policy institutes.[39]

The emergence of research and well-documented histories as a basis for generalizations and prescriptions for the American city and metropolis is, in part, a product of people inspired earlier by Richard T. Ely, but much of the implementation of his vision was postponed until after World War II. My speculative thoughts about why there was not much earlier a higher degree of consciousness about land economics and real estate (as categorized into areas of interest by Weiss and then incorporated into the work of the institutions about which Winnick writes) include the following:

1. The national mood of the first third of the twentieth century was epitomized in the wistful title of the Chicago World's Fair of 1933–34, "A Century of Progress," at a moment in the middle of the Depression when progress seemed to have halted. I imagine that, during these early decades, everyone was too busy building to worry about historical analysis of the urbanization process. Not until the Lost and Silent generations had taken over from the Gilded and Missionary generations was there either need or opportunity to wonder what had happened in the previous decades.

2. The tools for such research and analysis were lacking. I have mentioned the slow buildup in essential data series by various units of the federal government and cooperating private sources. Concepts such as national income accounts, users of such data, were just being developed. And adding machines and card sorters were the only machines useful for analytic work to be had; mechanical calculators, electronic calculators, and creaky first-generation computers were hardly dreamed of before World War II!

3. The relatively new professional and trade associations, and the new real estate corporations and the large projects they built, had not been around long enough for evaluative histories, although Grebler was fairly successful at assembling data for investment-grade buildings that had been under one ownership for a number of decades in New York City. The people Weiss writes about, however, were ready when the time came to gain perspective on the New Deal initiatives and on the prospects for the economy and the society of the postwar decades, especially as legislation such as the Full Employment Act of 1946 mandated attempts by the federal government to modulate and control economic cycles by influencing the levels of residential construction and business investment.

4. Few of the pre–World War II changes in the urban realm occurred without controversy, but the raucous level of dissent between Republicans and Democrats, as well as more generally between Babbitts and Ebenezers, mounted steadily thereafter, at least with respect to race, socialism, and especially, as reviewed below, the "taking issue."

5. After the war, controversy about race and the political economy bred more propaganda as well as more scholarly detachment. In the

following paragraphs, I sketch out a few of these areas of continuing dispute:

a. Race makes a difference. Clauses in housing contracts that discriminated on the basis of race, religion, or national origin were outlawed in the late 1940s, as the civil rights campaigns moved into high gear. But those who object to fair housing programs have never ceased overt and often covert opposition nor completely prohibited activities such as blockbusting, or unwillingness to show houses to persons of differing income, class or race.

b. Since the concepts of socialism were articulated in the nineteenth century, a charge of socialism arises whenever any governmental initiative does more than offer straight subsidies to private interests and, instead, does something that complements, supplements, regulates, or appears to compete with private interests. Charges of socialism were common when cities were building essential public utility systems late in the nineteenth century and even housing for war workers in World War I. The post–World War I years were scarred by the depredations on civil liberties by the socialist-hunting Mitchell Palmer, U.S. attorney general. The federal government was eventually forced to discontinue New Deal initiatives such as low-rent housing in greenbelt communities and in old cities because of such opposition. Every bit of housing and urban redevelopment legislation in the post–World War II period, a period that coincided with the Cold War and militantly anticommunist activities, was criticized as socialistic by the rightist factions of the real estate community, even when their businesses were ultimately helped or underwritten by the federal programs.

c. Over the years, increasingly so in the 1970s and 1980s, programs to control urban growth, in addition to local zoning, building, environmental, and occupancy regulations, increased in number and complexity. Any number of situations ended up in the courts, and the Supreme Court accepted many of them for review. Many of the cases revolved around the "taking issue," the claims by property owners that particular governmental acts have so limited their ability to enjoy the benefits of private ownership that their property has been "taken" and they should receive compensation in the same manner as people whose property has been taken by the government by eminent domain receive just compensation as specified in the Fifth Amendment of the Bill of Rights.

The history and the future of the taking issue itself have occupied the minds of almost everyone connected with real estate and land development in recent decades in a way that high-level analysis of the real estate industry itself never has and probably never will. The famous decision in 1926 in *Village of Euclid v. Ambler Realty*, 272 U.S. 365, was followed for the next forty years or so by various cases having to do with state and local powers and procedures concerning zoning and other controls on construction, but it was not until the environmentalists became active around the time of the first Earth Day in 1970 that a whole new set of cases began to drift into the courts and a whole new branch of the literature for city planners and municipal officials appeared to provide them with some background on the subject. The names of Richard Babcock, Fred Bosselman, David Callies, and Daniel Mandelker come to mind, lawyers writing the early books and articles. In my opinion, the single most useful introduction to the challenge of the taking issue was a slim volume titled *The Quiet Revolution in Land Use Control* prepared by Bosselman and Callies and issued in 1972 by the new Council on Environmental Quality.[40]

What had happened was the attempt in many jurisdictions and in many different ways to use land-use regulations on privately held property as an inexpensive way to obtain open spaces, to protect particular places or buildings, to limit the volume or timing of construction, and, often, to create new facilities or new public access to scarce resources such as beaches. Different courts making decisions at variance from one another all through the last third of the century paved the way to the U.S. Supreme Court.[41] Some of the wisest of the participants in this chapter of the great land-use game in the United States came to the conclusion that if a local community really wanted to own or have full control of a piece of property for the benefit of the public, that property would have to be bought and paid for up front; it could not be gotten by regulations or side agreements at the risk of having to buy it anyhow as a judgment for having effectively "taken" it not directly by condemnation but by what was said to be "inverse condemnation."

The 1990s were not a good decade for the regulators as one case after another went against them—for example, in such as the 1992 *Lucas* case, the Supreme Court "found a *per se* taking where a South Carolina coastal protection law permanently barred a landowner from developing the property and reduced the market value of the property to zero"; not until April 2002, with a reasonable decision coming down from the Rehnquist court in a case involving a moratorium on development around Lake Tahoe, California, was there any joy in the regulator's world; according to the Community Rights Counsel group, "The ruling is a major victory that preserves the ability of local governments to protect fragile resources from environmental harm."[42]

The accomplishments on many fronts in the first three decades of the twentieth century were instrumental in creating the basic frameworks of American cities as we know them. The accumulating forces of economic depression brought a clearly defined end to that era and opened up opportunities for the New Deal to restructure the institutions that had emerged during those years.

10

Restructuring America
1930 Through World War II

The 1930s

Much of the restructuring of the systems created in the century's first decades took place in the single decade of the 1930s during the New Deal, and the new systems kept being expanded in range and intensity during World War II and the postwar periods until the sharp break with the past wrought by the Nixon administration after 1968. More details will be found in the chapters that follow; here it is enough merely to suggest the nature of the restructuring I believe actually happened:

1. Activist New Deal programs across the whole spectrum of federal activities effectively changed the banking and securities industries, the housing and mortgage industries, and the whole process of evaluating and developing the nation's natural and human resources.

2. Mobilization of the nation's economy to fight in World War II led to novel attempts to stabilize the postwar economy and prevent the kind of depression experienced in the 1920s after the accumulated savings of war workers and veterans had been used up.

3. The outpouring of support for the 12 million GIs being demobilized provided unprecedented opportunity for them to get college educations or vocational training and to buy small houses in newly created suburbs.

4. The decision in 1949 to provide capital to municipalities for urban redevelopment and renewal programs enabled old cities to compete (somewhat) in economic terms with the emergent suburbs.

5. The invention of the atomic bomb and other methods of mass destruction reinforced a desire to decentralize industry; as E.B. White ob-

served about New York City in 1949, "The city, for the first time in its long history, is destructible."[1]

6. At the same time, industry itself was making a transition from heavy machinery and railroads to lighter-weight "footloose" industry, using vast networks of new roads and airways, all in conjunction with construction of the National Defense Interstate Highway System.

7. Massive migrations continued throughout the period. African-Americans moved steadily from the South to northern industrial cities from the 1920s; later the general population moved out of the cities to the suburbs and from east to west. These migrations were manifestations of the post-Depression suburbanization and automobilization of our culture; the postwar urban redevelopment and renewal programs were invented as counterbalancing forces to salvage the central cities.

8. The struggles for civil and voting rights, the restoration of Native American tribal rights, and the restructuring of state legislatures after one-person-one-vote decisions changed many of the nation's programs and procedures affecting the urban sector of the nation.

9. The increased consciousness of environmental threats to our world led to establishment of numerous new forms of federal and statewide regulation concerning development and pollution control.

My second third of the twentieth century begins as the New Deal battles the depressed economy and reconstitutes most of the private and public institutions that had been developed in the earlier part of the century, including the banking and securities industries, the housing and transportation sectors, and the agricultural, hydrographic, forest-based, and other natural resource complexes of the nation. World War II had the effect domestically of producing a postwar period with those tidal waves of babies, suburban buildings, redevelopment projects in the cities that were being left behind interstate highways, and an industrial base redesigned and reconstituted. All of these collectively represent a kind of flowering of New Deal programs mixed with the need to clear away much of the past and to explore an America newly based on broad education under the GI Bill and on the civil rights battles that began in the postwar period.

Strauss and Howe's Lost Generation, which took charge before World War II and continued through the Eisenhower years, had fought in World War I and was outraged to return from France in 1919 to an America encumbered with Prohibition and crusades against communism. Labeled

Reactive by Strauss and Howe, the Lost Generation fought those new ideologically based movements with their own notions "of pleasure, fought Babbittry with binges, and fought moral crusades with bathtub gin and opulent sex."[2] The authors cite Malcolm Cowley, who called 1930 a year of "doubt and even defeat" for his generation, a year of broken friendships, sudden poverty, and suicide . . . the start of a collective midlife hangover that lasted through the Great Depression.

The GI Generation that followed the Lost Generation earned the moniker of Civic from Strauss and Howe, who write:

> Throughout their lives, these G.I.s have been America's confident and rational problem-solvers: victorious soldiers and Rosie the Riveters; Nobel laureates; makers of Minuteman missiles, interstate highways, Apollo rockets, battleships, and miracle vaccines; the creators of Disney's Tomorrowland; "men's men" who have known how to get things done. Whatever they accomplished—whether organizing "big bands," swarming ashore in Normandy, or making "Bible Epic" movies, they always seemed to do it *big*, to do it *together*. Among G.I.s, says the inscription on their Iwo Jima shrines, "uncommon valor was a common virtue."[3]

The size and scope of the federal government expanded immeasurably during the earlier part of their lifetime, with most of the new programs focused on their needs, first as children and then as the aged. Between Eisenhower and Clinton, all of our presidents were from this warrior group, all but Reagan having been in the navy.

Enter my generation, the Silents, deemed Adaptive by Strauss and Howe, because we had to adapt to our GI predecessors and then to our Boomer successors, with no president from our own generation and not even a memorial to our war, the Korean one.[4] "Outer directed," we were considered juniors to battle-tested GI vets:

> The Silents widely realize they are the generational stuffing of a sandwich between the get-it-done G.I. and the self-absorbed Boom. Well into their rising adulthood they looked to the G.I.s for role models—and pursued what then looked to be a lifetime mission of refining and humanizing the G.I.-built world. Come the mid-1960s, the Silents found themselves "grown up just as the world's gone teen-age" (as Howard Junker put it at the time) and fell under the trance of (their) free-spirited next-juniors, the Boomers.

According to Strauss and Howe, we Silents stressed expertise over simplicity, participation over authority, process over result. As a rule, we were very suburbanized and wanted to use our real estate gains to get rich and safe; we also assumed, however, that the taxes that went up to finance World War II would never come down, meaning that our Silent Generation could not expect the kind of financial accumulations that the Lost and GI generations were enjoying.

Changes During the Depression and the New Deal

Leading up to the Depression were the Roaring Twenties. By all accounts, the general public at the time seems to have thought that the America that had been built in the first third of the century was just swell, with a few rough edges that would disappear with a little work, especially since the endless flow of immigrants had been checked. The nation was disarming, since there were to be no more wars. The mobsters created by Prohibition were sort of glamorous, as were the Hollywood stars, and nothing seemed to keep Americans from the speakeasies and jazz clubs. Socialism was nothing to worry about, and Attorney General Mitchell Palmer was taking care of the radicals (although in a way that stimulated Roger Baldwin to establish the American Civil Liberties Union to protect what was left of the Bill of Rights). Practically everyone, it seemed, was making extra money in the stock market. Then came the Depression as an unwelcome surprise, and the time had come for the Lost Generation to assume responsibility for straightening the mess that their forebears had left.

The biggest surprise may have been how each of the institutional pillars of that America melted down so quickly after the stock market's crash in October 1929. I was fascinated to learn, as I did research about residential and nonresidential real estate markets in the late 1920s and early 1930s, how eagerly business leaders (and President Herbert Hoover) tried to reassure everyone that "better times were just around the corner." A popular ballad suggested that the way to get the economy restarted was to have another cup of coffee and another piece of pie. The fact was that, soon after the 1929 crash, the markets for new and existing houses slowed and kept on slowing; in retrospect, these markets had been soft for several years before the crash, as we discovered later, were agriculture and other sectors of the economy.

President Hoover's administration was concerned enough to convene the first President's Conference on Housing and Home Ownership, which acknowledged that the existing array of savings institutions was not able to serve the needs of middle-income families even in good times, not to mention times of economic turmoil and widening unemployment. At such times, mortgage foreclosures skyrocketed because workers could not pay their loans back when due. In the 1920s mortgages were not amortized systematically month by month; borrowers paid only interest and were faced with the full amount when due.

Hoover had long been a proponent of zoning, but he was not familiar with the financial and real estate worlds that were falling apart month by month. In addition to troubles for individual homeowners, income for the multitude of large-scale projects and apartment houses was falling fast, the mortgage-bond houses were collapsing, and banks were going bankrupt. There was almost no investment in new construction of any sort. Playing the game of real estate during the Depression was often restricted to playing the brand-new game of Monopoly, whose inventor was said to have made lots of money for his contribution to the happiness of all his distraught (and possibly unemployed) customers while unemployment was said to be peaking at about 25 percent of the labor force.

Hoover, a member of the Missionary Generation, as was his successor Franklin D. Roosevelt, finally got energized before the 1932 election that brought Roosevelt into office. Hoover had few precedents for federal action, especially with regard to urban areas, where some housing had been built in 1918 for war workers, but he did get Congress to establish the Reconstruction Finance Corporation (RFC), which helped major corporations and banks borrow otherwise scarce funds.[5] Congress also created the Federal Home Loan Bank (FHLB) to operate across the nation. A wide variety of thrift institutions could become members of FHLB and thus be in line to borrow money "upon the security of home mortgages which met the requirements of the Act."[6]

What did the country look like at that time? There were lots of cold smokestacks, mostly in multistoried brick factories in the downtown industrial areas, with a few located in rural communities. There were only a handful of office buildings or apartments higher than ten or fifteen stories. There were lines at soup kitchens for the unemployed and Hoovervilles full of shanties (often in the middle of towns; while I was growing up in a Manhattan brownstone house, they were located in Central Park and between Riverside Drive and the railroad tracks). For me, the scene included the trolley line on Eighth Avenue, the Sixth Avenue and Third Avenue elevated lines, sturdy apartment houses (mostly built in the previous two decades), and, in the outer boroughs like Queens and the Bronx, rows of small attached houses and smaller apartment houses. Suburbia meant either towns like Bronxville or Cedarhurst, with family houses and small apartment houses within walking distance of the commuter raillines, or, further up the socioeconomic scale, the Scarsdales and East Oranges, with larger houses but still within easy reach of the commuter raillines. So far as I could see when I got to travel around the country during and after World War II, whatever the cities and towns of America looked like in the early years of the Depression is more or less what they looked like, except fifteen or twenty years older, in the 1940s and 1950s. Many of those existing cities and towns obtained one or more new facilities built by the New Deal's Public Works Administration, perhaps a high school or post office, but most new construction took place only during the war and then in areas that would become the new suburbs of the postwar period.

Roosevelt, entering the White House in March 1933, found one-third of the nation poorly fed and one-third of the nation poorly housed. Very quickly, "housing," a term then relatively unfamiliar to the American public but meaning homes for poor people and a stable banking and mortgage system for those able to keep up with much lower mortgage payments than ever before, became a key element of the New Deal. Writing in the 1980s and looking back over the century, Louis Winnick described four basic trends and challenges that made it difficult to get "adequate, safe and sanitary housing" for the "working poor." I have paraphrased his view:

His first point is that the demand for funds changed from providing temporary assistance to needy families to assistance for permanently disadvantaged persons, the latter a group much less attractive to legislators. At the same time, the costs of construction rose inexorably. As a result of these two trends, the need for funds rose faster than public and private groups could handle, and, as a result, the effort to provide costly new construction diminished, only partly replaced by smaller programs to rehabilitate old structures.[7]

At this point a summary of what the objectives of the New Deal for getting housing for the working poor seem to have been will be useful:

1. To get the banking system reorganized, with a new system of long-term amortizing mortgages offered by the reorganized banks and a group of new savings-type institutions with, for the first time, charters from the federal government instead of from the states.

2. To get foreclosed houses back into the former owners' hands, financed by new mortgages arranged by the new (federal) Home Owners Loan Corporation (HOLC).[8]

3. To get some construction going: the Public Works Administration built schools, post offices, dams, and reclamation projects; the Civilian Conservation Corps improved national parks and similar facilities; and the Works Progress Administration put planners and architects to work mapping cities and delineating their economic bases and historical properties, planning circumferential highways and other traffic facilities, and, with some economists, "discovering" that local economies were an intrinsic part of the national economy.[9]

4. To get small homeowners investing by obtaining rehabilitation loans insured by the new Federal Housing Administration (FHA), which later began to insure rental garden apartment projects and single-home developments under Sections 203 and 207, but all, of course, in racially and economically homogeneous locations.

5. To get some housing built directly by the federal government; after three of these new greenbelt garden cities were built, further such building was proscribed, but, as a consequence, a mechanism to support local public housing projects was invented and the ideas implemented by the housing act in 1937. It was not until the mid-1960s that the federal government returned to the idea of supporting "new communities."

For the record, here is a slightly more detailed view of relevant legislation in the early New Deal years:

1. 1933, June: Home Owners Loan Act
   a. Creates Home Owners Loan Corporation (HOLC) that over the ensuing decade enabled 1 million homes to be refinanced with long-term mortgages at interest rates of less than 5 percent.
   b. Establishes a system for having the federal government charter savings and loan associations.

2. 1933, June: National Industrial Recovery Act. Over time it helped employment by building fifty low-rent public housing projects with 21,600 units in thirty-seven cities, plus 15,000 units in resettlement and greenbelt towns.

3. 1934, National Housing Act (as amended over the following five years) creates Federal Housing Administration (FHA)

a. Title I authorizes FHA to provide insurance to banks for housing renovation and modernization loans.

b. Title II authorizes FHA to establish mortgage insurance programs on one- to four-family structures, including Section 203 for unsubsidized construction and Section 207 for construction for low-income families under federal and state programs.

c. Title III authorized FHA to establish the Federal National Mortgage Association (FNMA, later known as "Fannie Mae") to provide a secondary market for first mortgages.

d. Title IV created the Federal Savings and Loan Insurance Corporation (FSLIC) to insure the accounts of depositors in a wide variety of thrift institutions, including the federally chartered savings and loan associations.

e. A number of sections in these housing acts related to farm properties to the work of Reconstruction Finance Corporation and the Interstate Commerce Commission, and to a variety of other federal programs and agencies.

4. 1937 U.S. Housing Act, Public Housing Program. United States Housing Administration is put into Harold Ickes's Department of the Interior.[10]

The New Deal is well known for beginning the public housing program, but even at the 1934 meeting of the National Association of Housing Officials, full of strong supporters of such housing work, some cautions were being expressed:

> The question of public assistance cut right to the bone of the American philosophy—private ownership of home and land. Public assistance was viewed as a revolutionary and socialistic concept and found few adherents. [As stated in the final report of President Hoover's Conference on Home Building and Home Ownership,] "if business, financial, and industrial groups fail to take the task in hand and apply the large sums of capital required and the utmost of planning genius and engineering skill to the problem, it seems likely that American cities will be forced to turn to the European methods of solution to this problem, through subsidization by the state and municipal treasuries and probably through actual ownership of housing projects by municipal authority. It can hardly be doubted that the next 10 years will determine which choice will be made between these two alternatives." It didn't take 10 years.[11]

What had happened was a turn to Europe's models with Roosevelt's authorization of a construction program by a new Public Works Administration under the National Industrial Recovery Act of 1933. Over the next few years, the housing pioneers formed the National Association of Housing Officials (adding the word Redevelopment to the title after the 1949 Housing Act) and worked successfully to get the Housing Act of 1937 passed. An authoritative interpretation of what happened to public housing over the ensuing five decades or so was penned by Elaine T. Ostrowski, former director of the Division of Housing Management of the Department of Housing and Urban Development:

> Public housing in the United States was introduced in 1937, largely in response to the Great Depression. It was designed to address a number of problems created by the Depression. While providing decent housing for families that needed it was one of its objectives, others included creating employment opportunities, stimulating the construction industry, providing investment opportunities, and eliminating slums. As a concept, public housing was conceived as a temporary platform for families who had been made poor by the Depression. It was assumed that once these families were back on their economic feet, they would move back into private sector housing.
>
> Administration of public housing was vested at the local level where cities or counties, at their discretion, created public housing authorities as operationally self-sufficient agencies. (Housing has never been a mandated program of government at any level.) To construct the housing, PHAs then, as now, contracted with the federal government through the Department of Housing and Urban Development to issue 40-year bonds. HUD guarantees the bonds and assists in paying the principal and interest due on the bonds annually. In the early years of the program, PHAs could offer relatively low rents for their units because they only had to charge enough to cover operating expenses and to establish and maintain an operating reserve.[12]

This is as good a place as any to describe how public housing projects that looked and felt quite middle-class when they were introduced into the cityscape in the early years of the program changed character in the second half of the twentieth century.[13] Public housing was originally intended to deal with what were then considered deserving working poor families, often politically connected because slots in the prewar housing projects (providentially located in racially segregated or ethnic areas, where "ethnic" in those days primarily referred to the Irish, Italian, and

Polish populations) were few and the need widespread, so it made sense for the politicians involved in creating the projects to help people who had helped them. By war's end, the kind of families who had managed to get into such prewar housing were able to buy FHA–insured houses in the suburbs using either veterans' benefits or accumulated savings from well-paid jobs in war plants, and this cadre of conventional families was thus lost to the public housing market.

Their places in the old projects were taken by families with fewer mainstream attributes. This change in the character of families to be housed increased the difficulty, in the latter years, of finding sites for the construction of additional multiracial projects. One consequence of that difficulty was the development of low-rent housing for the elderly, because the elderly were considered less troubling as potential neighbors, in preference to projects for large families. And one consequence of that set of preferences was that many very large families were crammed into older apartments designed for smaller families, thus accelerating the depreciation of the properties as acceptable living areas. Elaine Ostrowski writes,

> In the 1950s, . . . the [housing] program underwent a number of modifications in response to changing economic, political, and social conditions. These modifications had the net effect of transforming its basic concept.
>
> The evolution of public housing into a program directed at the very poor began in 1949 when federally financed slum clearance efforts put the burden on PHAs to house the families that were being displaced by the efforts. These were not temporarily poor families, these were families that had been poor for generations, and, as such, they could not afford the subsidized rents of public housing. So the federal government took a number of steps to make the housing more available to these families. Income limits were introduced as a qualification for occupancy, and while this gave the poor first priority for housing, it also made it difficult for PHAs to raise rents when operating expenses went up.
>
> In the 1960s, subsidies were introduced for special segments within the population, such as the very poor, large families, and the elderly. As a result, the resident composition began to shift slowly as PHAs gave preference to more of these families because they could supply badly needed revenue through the special subsidies they brought with them. Then, in 1969, a formal, comprehensive, subsidy program was imposed on PHAs that limited the rents all families paid to no more than 25 percent of their adjusted income.
>
> The federal government makes up the PHAs' shortfall in revenues by providing operating subsidies . . . [which], however, have almost without

exception been inadequate to enable PHAs to provide fiscally sound, socially responsible housing. It is important to note that local government makes no contribution to the public housing program beyond some relief on local taxes (rates).[14]

And so we go to the end of the decade of the 1930s. Many people knew that war was coming. The climax of the decade was the New York World's Fair of 1939, so successful that it was extended for a second year (but, sadly, without the wonderful Czechoslovakian Pavilion, for that country had succumbed to Hitler after the Munich Agreement). The 1939 fair was looking to the future, in sharp contrast to the Chicago World's Fair of 1933–34, which only celebrated the past century's progress. The visit of England's King George VI and Queen Elizabeth was important, partly because after visiting the fair they went to Hyde Park where Roosevelt served them hot dogs, thus indicating his belief that England was worth saving from Hitler despite what the America First isolationists were saying. The World's Fair was offering a vision of a future after the coming war, and the biggest hit of all was the General Motors Corporation's pavilion with its incredible scale model of an urban area with superhighways, moving automobiles and trucks, and tall buildings in the center of the city.

The basic infrastructure of America was changed in important ways during the New Deal years. By the end of the 1930s, much helped by defense orders starting a few years earlier, smokestacks had begun to emit their heavenly smoke, but the Age of Iron, characterized by large pieces of heavy machinery, powered by coal, requiring large factories within walking distance of workers' housing, was drawing to a close. It was being replaced by the Age of Electrical Motors, making one-story factories more feasible and liberating the factory from reliance on deliveries of coal and raw materials by railroads. The airlines, subsidized by lucrative contracts to haul mail, were able to service many more localities than before. Workers could now come to the plants by their own automobiles. Eventually, as the century wore on, plants would be "footloose," and future wars would be fought largely with products emerging from factories in the West and the Southeast, while factories in the older industrial sectors of the country were in danger of rusting away. Among the other happenings were the following:

1. Some farms were saved from blowing away by various types of reclamation projects, and the Rural Electrification Administration did its job.

2. The nation discovered its regions, its great watersheds and rivers, and began to build multipurpose dams providing flood control, erosion control, irrigation, electricity, and recreation.[15]

3. Urban highways got planned as a precurser to metropolitan-scale road systems (just in time for implementation when siting war plants and wartime housing projects), cities were mapped street by street, their historic buildings were identified and measured as a precurser to preservation, and the blighted slum areas of the cities were identified and mapped as a precurser to what would become the urban redevelopment and renewal programs. Taken all together, these improvements became the standards and formats for postwar America's urban places.

4. Average family size was getting smaller, affecting the kind and location of housing that would get built in the new suburbs.

And then came Pearl Harbor and our entry officially into World War II.

Changes During World War II

During the war we spent billions of dollars for new war plants, new highways to reach them, and new suburban housing for war workers. Beginning in 1943, both government and business leadership groups such as the Committee for Economic Development did a lot of thinking about America and the world after the war. By late 1942, a year or so after Hitler decided to invade the Soviet Union instead of invading an England that was reeling after the Battle of Britain in the summer of 1940, after the British had routed Rommel out of North Africa, the feeling was strong that the Allies would eventually win the war, although at what cost and when were puzzlements. The war economy had made the Depression a thing of the past, and in both England and the United States there was a growing sense that prosperity for all should be permanent and stable, an idea that in America led to passage of the Full Employment Act of 1946 and later to President Lyndon Johnson's Great Society antipoverty programs. What was good for society would also be good for the returning GIs, good for cities, good for labor unions as well as the corporations. And the rest of the world was not to be forgotten, for plans were made to stabilize the international scene, beginning with the establishment of the United Nations and the Bretton Woods agreements, which led to the creation of the World Bank, the International Monetary Fund, and the General Agreement on Tariffs and Trade (later to transmogrify into the World Trade Organization).

Wartime production had required new facilities. The government had decided that all of them should be outside of the old cities, partly as a defense measure against attack by enemy bombers. Only after the atomic bomb was developed did the war planners draw those concentric circles around the centers of cities.[16] The new highways to these suburban plants had, coincidentally, been mapped in the 1930s by the Works Progress Administration (WPA) planners. The plants required new housing nearby, provided by the Defense Housing Act of 1940, the Lanham Military Family Housing Act of 1940, and the FHA Section 608 program for warworker and later veterans' housing which started in 1942, the same year that federal rent controls were initiated. Add a few military airfields converted to civilian use after the war, and voilà, we had the infrastructure for postwar suburbia, including a new transportation system.

Many problems lay in wait for the postwar period. One portent was continuing racism, manifested earlier in riots originating in disputes about wartime employment practices; the further concern was that postwar economic adjustments would send female and black workers back to the ranks of the unemployed. Whether there would be sufficient raw materials from foreign sources to serve America's needs as a superpower was a concern that generated a number of study commissions and initiatives.[17]

Building materials were rationed during the war, and rationing and some price controls would continue through most of the 1940s. The fear that there would not be enough materials for all the housing that needed to be built to please the 12 million GIs returning to their communities also fed the fear of inflation, especially as the wartime accord between the U.S. Treasury and the Federal Reserve Board to keep interest rates very low was expiring as of 1950. In addition to whatever new construction was being put into the new suburbs, the economists were aware that the old infrastructure of roads, bridges, public buildings, and older houses had been quietly deteriorating since the beginnings of the Great Depression some fifteen years earlier; the bill was coming due and would fan the inflationary fires, for money in the form of vast wartime savings, larger than in any previous epoch, was available for higher than ever outlays on consumption and business equipment. At the same time, no one knew whether the United States would have a serious postwar recession like the one that had followed World War I instead of the promised bout of prosperity; many old-timers who had weathered the Depression spent the better part of the 1950s waiting for that recession to occur. Among a long list of changes for the nation's leaders to think about as the war began to turn into the postwar period were the implications for urban areas generally, and those outside the old South particularly, of the stream of individuals and families that moved from rural areas to urban areas, a migration that began in earnest in the 1930s (well-documented in paintings by the redoubtable Jacob Lawrence) and that increased in volume year by year during and after the war.

Migration

That America's population was redistributing itself internally had become a set of facts that was never far from people's consciousness after Gunnar Myrdal's epic study from 1938 to 1942 of race relations in the nation, *An American Dilemma: The Negro Problem and Modern Democracy*.[18] Here is how Winnick related these movements to the "plight of the cities," as the migrations continued in the middle third of the century, roughly 1930 to 1968.

> The nature of America's urban crisis has been depicted by many writers in many ways. A useful way is to resolve the phenomenon into three of its principal origins: [1] tidal waves of metropolitan and interregional migration; [2] a legacy of poverty and racial discrimination; and [3] a belated discovery, the emergence of a seemingly self-perpetuating underclass.
>
> The sources of the urban predicament are analytically distinguishable, though fused by history and registered on the mind's eye as an amalgam. Thus "inner city," a common idiom of urban-crisis parlance, connotes simultaneously geography, race and pathology. The devastation visited upon older neighborhoods and older cities was a consequence of sweeping changes in the size and social composition of their populations and of profound changes in the behavioral values of many of their residents. These causal factors may be usefully surveyed one at a time.
>
> . . . . The first, metropolitan and regional migration, concerns massive and concurrent movements of people, industry and markets. One heavy stream swept past the legal boundaries of established cities, transporting millions of people from tightly-packed neighborhoods to new, open environments. A second stream carried additional millions from older, colder regions of the country to its younger, warmer ones. These outmovements imposed severe stresses in most mature cities, leaving them with derelict neighborhoods, boarded-up stores, decaying housing, abandoned factories, vanishing public transit and weakened tax revenues. The neighborhoods of exodus were incompletely refilled by a third migratory stream, as millions of poor people tracked northward from the Cottonbelt South

and the Caribbean; to them, even cities of diminished vitality promised jobs, wages and housing far superior to the hopeless unemployment and decrepit hovels left behind. There is now a fourth stream, to be only lightly covered in this study, of millions of immigrants predominantly of Latin and Asian origin.[19]

Winnick, writing in the late 1980s, saw that this fourth stream was a result not only of upheavals precipitated by the Cold War and the Vietnam War but of overwhelming pressures in the less developed and underdeveloped nations of the Third World.

Back at home, Strauss and Howe's Great Power Cycle was in full swing. The Lost Generation that had been in charge during the war was giving way to the GI Generation. The idealistic Lost Generation wanted to do whatever it could for the returning warriors, which meant helping them in their university, business, and political careers and supporting their desires to move to the new suburbs, away from the old cities of the east and central parts of the country and certainly away from the farms. Naturally, not every one was on the move, and many veterans did return happily and permanently to their old haunts. Meanwhile, the Silent Generation learned to adapt to the preeminence of the GI Generation. Here's a bit more of Winnick's wisdom on the subject:

> Large-scale geographical redistribution was inevitable even had America been a racially-homogeneous nation. The exploding metropolis was a universal phenomenon, occurring in legions of urban areas whose racial and ethnic composition bore no resemblance to America's; it was as much evident in Tokyo and Stockholm as in New York and Philadelphia.
>
> Mass dispersion was a response to fundamental improvements in the technology of transportation and communication and to pervasive increases in living standards. Throughout the modern world, the automobile and the superhighway, the jet plane, and sophisticated electronics drastically reduced the time and cost of physical movement, information retrieval and market exchange. Everywhere, households and firms had conferred upon them a new abundance of locational choice. And everywhere the social and economic benefits of central agglomeration were devalued, starkly so in cities with obsolescent industry and housing, and whose street patterns were inhospitable to auto and truck. The unfolding locational options were promptly exercised by millions of postwar families who were by now possessed of cars, low-interest mortgages and an irrepressible yearning for a home in a leafy suburb.[20]

Social Pressures

The GIs coming out of World War II felt individually empowered to take advantage of opportunities to refashion the country they returned to, as much as any other generation in American history. And one of the first effects, I believe, was to see their own generation refashioned, at long last, into two mutually incompatible groups whose incompatibility had been suppressed in earlier decades.

To epitomize the different ways of thinking about those opportunities to refashion American life into a proper post–World War II framework, I redefine my old Ebenezers as the Do-Good Ebenezers and my old Babbitts as the Shiny Babbitts. The Shiny Babbitts were the subject of many novels, such as Sloan Wilson's *The Man in the Gray Flannel Suit* and all those stories of life in the suburbs. In contrast, the Do-Good Ebenezers redoubled their efforts to eliminate or at least minimize causes of class and racial disparities; they were the intellectual and emotional followers of Madison and the Bill of Rights, Henry George and the type of thinking advanced by Ebenezer Howard himself with the original social cities, Benton Mackaye's form of regionalism, the various pioneers of the low-income housing programs in the 1920s, John Maynard Keynes and his approach to supporting national income, Franklin D. Roosevelt and his stable of New Dealers, and finally those who espoused the Full Employment Act of 1946 to assure economic opportunities for everyone. The Do-Good designator applies to the postwar attempts to ameliorate distressed communities as one industry after another succumbed to foreign competition or technical change and left rusting factories and dislocated workers in the northeast and central parts of the United States. The Do-Goods in the GI Generation were active in the civil rights movement, especially in regard to racial inequities in the housing markets, and in the Great Society programs of the 1960s. Do-Good Silents pitched in as the staffs of Do-Good organizations and politicians. Do-Good Boomers took up the banners for peace and environmental protections.

The housing markets themselves were also modernizing, helped enormously by the federal government. By 1947, the Housing and Home Finance Agency (HHFA), the penultimate array of related federal agencies, had been created to bring together in a rather awkward fashion three quite different entities with different constituencies: the financial operations of the Home Loan Bank Board, the mortgage certification functions of the Federal Housing Administration, and the oversight activities of the Public Housing Administration. HHFA was instrumental in helping very large projects, virtually all in the suburbs, get authorized and financed. Again Winnick:

> Levittown-size developments, benefiting from mass production, prefabricated parts and cheap rural land, created a huge new stock of inexpensive housing whose monthly carrying burden was additionally reduced through a comprehensive reorganization of the mortgage market: government insurance, low-debt service, and standardized contracts that facilitated the establishment of a national market.[21]

All of this constituted a great subsidy for the middle classes. I must note here that the middle classes at the time, who were primarily white, were being treated to the greatest subsidy of all, the deduction of interest on their mortgages in their calculation of federal and state income taxes. Inner-city renters, increasingly nonwhite as the postwar years went on, thus benefited less than the suburbanizing, primarily white, homeowning classes.

This imbalance in assistance, with far more going to the middle than to the lower end of the housing market, has been the subject of much research and considerable agitation for change in the latter part of the twentieth century; one of the best examinations of this issue I have seen is a long article entitled "The Other Subsidized Housing: Federal Aid to Suburbanization," in the journal published by the National Association of Housing and Redevelopment Officials.[22]

A related issue is also relevant here, the fact that the federal government has always had to provide private builders with the prospect of solid profits before they could be induced to build any housing for anything but the wealthiest clientele they could muster. Winnick, looking back, described this expected but often less than savory aspect of the Shiny Babbitt syndrome:

> Unless private builders were proffered enticing profit lures, which in those pre–tax-shelter years meant a high rate of return on a thin base of cash equity, there would be few takers. On the other hand, experience had shown that generous incentives were susceptible to every imaginable abuse—unconscionable profiteering, wasted resources, and corruption.
>
> Looming over HUD and Congress was the specter of the Section 608 scandals. In that postwar veteran's program the exceedingly liberal investment terms dangled before apartment builders resulted in a huge wave

of financial failures and foreclosures. Congressional investigations disclosed that astute developers were able to contrive mortgages in excess of actual development costs, thereby yielding a handsome profit unrelated to a project's market outcome. The chance to "mortgage out" undermined traditional business standards with respect to location, product quality and effective consumer demand. As one investigator commented, a developer could get rich by "building in the Sahara." Moreover, so tempting were the rewards of "mortgaging out" that bribery and political wirepulling were rampant.[23]

The Shiny Babbitts were in full control of the suburbs, and most of the nation's professionally trained urban planners were actually working for these suburban communities and for various regional or statewide planning agencies typically financed by funds from the federal government flowing through or controlled by the then all-powerful state highway departments.

To many people's surprise, however, both Shiny Babbitts and Do-Good Ebenezers found they could collaborate for a brief moment to help the cities that had been bypassed by the pressures, pent-up since the Depression interrupted America's love affair with the automobile, creating suburbia/utopia. Help was ordained by the surprising passage of the Housing Act of 1949, surprising because conservative senators had long been lobbied very effectively by the suburban real estate and mortgage interests to vote against such initiatives. The leadership of Senator Robert Taft (who was angling to be the Republican candidate for president in 1952 at a moment when Dwight Eisenhower's candidacy was not yet apparent) accounted for the change in votes that assured passage.

The Housing Act of 1949 (Public Law 81–171) was, as usual, an omnibus bill.[24] It established the national housing policy of "a decent home and a suitable living environment for every American family." To implement this broad commitment, it established federal assistance to local communities for slum clearance and redevelopment programs. The act also greatly expanded rural housing programs to include direct and insured loans for homes and farm buildings, rural rental and cooperative housing, and grants for domestic farm labor housing.

In order to understand urban redevelopment, it is important to understand the way in which the urban-type developments that were being put in place to create the suburbia we know coincided with a widespread desire on the part of the business community for greater economic efficiency. As Winnick wrote on this aspect of the situation:

The new geographical lures were similarly seized by masses of business firms seeking to capture the production economies of one-story plants and unblocked deliveries of goods-in and goods-out. For much of manufacturing it also became advantageous to settle nearer to markets and low-cost labor pools rather than, as before, to raw materials, ports or waterways. The urban map of residence and employment everywhere was permanently altered. The response of governments to this basic geographical restructuring was to regard it as a problem soluble through the calculus of economic efficiency. Efficiency was to be optimized by accepting the metropolitan area as the de facto city, adapting master plans, inter-municipal arrangements, transportation and capital investment, regulations and statistical accounting to the larger geographic framework.

Radial roads from center city were increased in number and upgraded in capacity and connecter roads built to link the outlying settlements; cluster zoning was enacted to maximize the efficiency of land use. It was the heyday of the community-builder. . . .

The reclamation of distressed cities and stranded regions was similarly treated, at least at first, in a context of economic efficiency, an exercise in damage control. The city's underutilized infrastructure—its housing, schools, streets, its water and sewer systems—was counted as an invaluable capital asset, to be resuscitated through a battery of urban renewal and redevelopment aids. The country's Appalachians were to be salvaged by luring industry with new highways, subsidized factories and a trained and willing labor force.[25]

At the time I was much involved with what I would now call the "financial efficiency" of redevelopment policy. In the background was the federal income tax, which had been very low before World War II but remained high after its rise to pay for the war effort. One of the major attractions for suburban investor-builders was cheap land, since most of the cost of a project built on such cheap land could be depreciated as an offset to the annual federal tax. In the cities, however, land was much more expensive, and new development ordinarily entailed extensive demolition of old structures, but the cost of land was not depreciable, so higher total project cost and minimal tax advantages in the central cities militated against new construction or extensive rehabilitation of existing buildings there. The remedy in the Housing Act of 1949 was for the federal government to provide funds to the cities to write down the cost of assembling, clearing, and redesigning land.

As of 1969 the federal urban renewal program which I imagine was close to its high point before the full impact of the Nixon administration, had contracts with 1,046 localities for a total of 2,658 projects costing the federal government $8.2 billion.[26] The program involved $7.2 billion in urban renewal projects, $590 million for neighborhood development programs, and the balance for other projects and programs: code enforcement, demolition, interim assistance, certified area, community renewal, and demonstration. Not included were the area redevelopment program for distressed rural communities and the special Appalachian programs.

The continual political battles between the Shiny Babbitts and the Do-Good Ebenezers became manifest as soon as the Housing Act of 1949 was signed. The 1960s saw the split in fights over civil rights, over redistricting to empower the suburbs after the one-person-one-vote decision, and over continued buildup of military-industrial-complex grants to firms in the West and Southeast to the dismay of other areas of the country. The split was also shown in white flight as a reaction to school busing decrees, in the abandonment of downtowns as suburban shopping centers were themselves displaced by even larger regional malls, in the struggles over the Vietnam imbroglio, and, finally, in the emergence of the political right wing in the 1964 Goldwater versus Johnson campaign and its growth to victory in the 1968 Nixon versus Humphrey campaign. The split was obviously a major factor in urban affairs in the years between the end of World War II in 1945 and the takeover by Nixon in 1968 and throughout the complicated times from 1968 to the end of the century.

11
Restructuring Continued
The Fractious Postwar Period

Urban Places and Race

In the 1945–60 period, new patterns for restructuring urban phenomena were put in place, and the first round of building (mostly all-white suburbs, and some new construction inside the cities) got under way. The following 1960–68 period saw incredible amounts of new building all over the land: new interstate and suburban highway construction was, perhaps, the most visible, pervasive, and even invasive form, with great clearances for urban renewal projects a close second.

The Eisenhower administration appeared to be tilted toward the Babbitts, especially in regard to social housing programs for those displaced by urban renewal and highway projects, so John F. Kennedy's candidacy provided short-lived hopes for restoring the balance. Many of the powerful mayors who figured so prominently in Jeanne Lowe's book about urban renewal as a political strategy, *Cities in a Race with Time*, met with Kennedy in Pittsburgh shortly after his nomination to get his support for federal programs focused on the cities rather than the suburbs.[1] Kennedy was said to have replied that the politics of the country no longer justified such a commitment. Indeed, the Census of 1960 was confirming that suburban voters were becoming a majority. The *Baker v. Carr* case to install the one-person-one-vote rule was winding its way through the courts, reflecting decades of frustration on the part of city officials whose state legislatures were dominated by rural voters.[2]

Even so, the 1950s and 1960s were wild and satisfying times for both suburban towns and their central cities and, of course, for most Americans as well. The Shiny Babbitts were busy with countless new private ventures, but they relaxed in automobiles that sported fins and chrome and in backyards where barbeques sizzled. The Do-Good Ebenezers were busy with a variety of new governmental and nonprofit initiatives to make our civilized society fairer and more secure for everyone regardless of race, creed, or color (questions of gender, sexual preference, and disability were not yet on the main agenda). By 1968 there were 400 or more federal programs of assistance to state and local governments; these were all "categorical," meaning that each was directed by Congress to a specific target: preservation of open space, historical preservation, subsidies for the Federal Housing Administration (FHA) 236 program, and so on.

While the urban world of these postwar years was affected, in one way or another, by all the important stories and trends of the day, we have to limit our focus here to the relation between the campaign to build more and better housing for everyone, including the low-income and minority populations in the inner cities, and the civil rights campaign. I am sad that this book will not be able to cover many other newsworthy items that I could manage to show had some relevance to how urban places developed in the twentieth century, but, as compensation, I will merely list a few of them: the continuing "rusting" of many communities that ended up with vacant factories and long-term unemployment, the struggles to locate nuclear energy facilities in urban areas (in the middle of the Cold War battles about atmospheric pollution from bomb testing), the landmark case of *Berman v. Parker* with a majority opinion by Justice William O. Douglas affirming the use of eminent domain powers in urban redevelopment areas to make them beautiful as well as efficient,[3] the uneven career of the factory-built house (even in a massive war plant converted for the purpose),[4] the general satisfaction with an America consuming inordinate shares of many of the earth's resources after the nation avoided the feared postwar recession, the struggles over the Taft-Hartley Act that clipped the power of labor organizing,[5] and, the resounding importance of the publication in 1954 of Rachel Carson's *Silent Spring*.

Meanwhile, the urban development program had its scandals much as the FHA 608 and 207 multifamily programs had. Some came to light relatively early in the program, as investigative reporters discovered how redevelopment projects on the west side of Manhattan had been managed.[6] One of the worst ones, the environmental hazards at the Eastwick project in Philadelphia (said to be the nation's largest urban renewal project, one that would help the city counter the attraction of the suburbs with regard to both employment and housing), only came to light many years later.[7] To slow the whole federal urban initiatives process down a bit, Eisenhower administration officials converted the urban redevelopment program into the more comprehensive but even more complex urban renewal program authorized in the Housing Act of 1954, including its requirement that each community in the program get federal approval of a seven-part workable program.[8] Part of the workable program required creation of a fair housing program capable of handling all the people displaced by redevelopment, renewal, or, ultimately, highway programs. This requirement was obviously related to a spate of activities concerning racial practices.

The question of race is endemic in American history and in American life in the twentieth century. Race, in the context of urban policy, refers, almost without exception, to Americans now called African-Americans, formerly denominated as colored, Negro, and black. Racial antagonisms are more or less important factors in every urban phenomenon and issue that I can think of, including city and regional planning, housing, schools, parks, transportation, health services, poverty, crime, and drug use. We can credit Gunnar Myrdal, whose great work, *An American Dilemma: The Negro Problem and Modern Democracy*, was finally getting published about the same time as race riots were going on in Detroit and other war-impacted communities, for breaking through the wall of silence that severely limited public discussion of these syndromes, and for illustrating and detailing how pervasive the racial question was throughout American life.[9]

I credit Chester Hartman and the stable of learned activists he has brought together under the aegis of the Poverty and Race Research Action Council (PRRAC) with generating much of the scholarly documentation of these manifestations of prejudice. Some of the articles in PRRAC's publications were brought together in a volume called *Challenges to Poverty and Race in America*, a title that reflects the scope of these issues. The topics of particular importance to reformers included:

1. The use of FHA standards, beginning in the 1930s, to keep private, federally insured housing developments racially segregated.

2. The practice, dating from the period at the end of World Wars, of having racial and religious covenants in housing contract; efforts to eliminate this depended upon leadership from the National Committee Against

Discrimination in Housing and ultimately resulted in a declaration by the U.S. Supreme Court in *Shelley v. Kraemer* (1948) that such covenants were legally unenforceable.[10]

3. The use of powers under various housing, urban redevelopment, urban renewal, and highway acts to continue patterns of segregation and, indeed, to eliminate whole low-income neighborhoods with typically heavy concentrations of blacks.

The abstract of an article by Arnold R. Hirsch gives a sense of how deeply such racially motivated activities influenced the manner in which suburbs and central cities were developed:

> The Housing Acts of 1949 and 1954 provided the foundation for slum clearance and urban renewal. Despite efforts to finesse the issue, race remained central on the formation and implementation of public policy. The Racial Relations Service (RRS), an institutional remnant of the New Deal, tried unsuccessfully to prevent local authorities from using the new federal resources to reinforce existing "ghettos." Searching for a "sound Negro policy," the RRS warned housing officials against pursuing such a course and offered bureaucratic resistance to individual projects deemed inimical to minority interests.
>
> The coincidence of demographic and political change in the 1950s, the subsequent dismantling of the RRS, the reaction to the Supreme Court's 1954 decision in *Brown v. Board of Education*, and the passage of the Housing Act of 1954 all contributed to the use of urban renewal to create and sustain racially separate neighborhoods even as the civil rights movement gained momentum.[11]

About this time the National Committee Against Discrimination in Housing was established, and it became part of many local campaigns against blockbusting in lower-middle-income parts of cities and against exclusionary practices in the suburbs.[12]

The long-hoped-for overturn of the invidious *Plessy v. Ferguson* decision of 1896, which permitted separate schools for whites and blacks, was accomplished in 1954 with the *Brown v. Board of Education* decision. Except to note its importance, we do not need to cite here the vast documentation available about the reaction to *Brown*, including busing in the old central cities to obtain equal distribution of racial groups in urban schools, an idea fiercely contested in the South and bypassed across the country by white flight, as well as establishment of private sectarian and nonsectarian schools. Despite many academic studies, no reliable data exist to establish the true (in contrast to the perceived or anecdotal) extent of white flight as a result of busing.

Exclusionary zoning by suburban towns was largely accomplished by mandating minimum lot sizes, beyond the financial capacity of lower-income (often, in fact, black) families wishing to move to that community. Much of the rural or low-density land developable for housing in the United States had not yet been zoned by the mid-1950s, and zoning was never popular among those who resented any form of governmental regulation. And large areas of the nation also remained free of building regulations; no permits were required. The zoning and permitting process only became useful tools for promoting conservation and environmental protection several decades after Rachel Carson's *Silent Spring* stimulated many of the individuals and organizations that worked together to create Earth Day in 1970 and all the environmental laws that followed. But zoning as a tool was not able to simultaneously promote integration in housing and education (and even employment), limit population growth in a community, and open up special areas (such as beaches) to public use, nor could zoning maps qualify as evidence of even a minimum level of comprehensive town planning, nor was it easy to get consistency or effectiveness when planning, zoning, and environmental impact studies were played off against each other. The denouncements of these awkward arrangements did not come, however, until late in the century, as a result of pressures from the far right antiregulation extremists and the progressive environmental groups on the left.

Many groups were active in protesting the extent to which urban renewal and highway building through central cities seemed to be equivalent to what was being called "Negro removal"—the effort to obtain central city locations for higher-income and whiter occupancies than those that were being bulldozed or "gentrified" by renewal and rehabilitation. In response, passage in the Housing Act of 1954 of a set of FHA housing programs, Section 221 for relocation housing and Section 220 for rehabilitation loans, helped some families that had been forced to move. At the same time, the decline and fall of the public housing programs (as discussed in Chapter 8 above) accelerated as administrators attempted to serve populations with very low expectation of moving on in a reasonable period. Unfortunately, the fact that so many of these families were black made it exceptionally difficult to find sites for new public housing projects. Some cities, notably Chicago, resorted to complex strategems in order to avoid placing new projects in white areas, a practice that brought them into court on discrimination charges.

ACTION for Housing

All of this commotion was testing the ability of the nation to house all of its citizens, including those who were not veterans and those whose incomes were preternaturally low. The subject of housing occupied a great deal of attention in the 1950s. A group of business owners (notably building materials manufacturers), publishers, and academicians in 1954 established the American Council To Improve Our Neighborhoods, usually referred to as A.C.T.I.O.N. but as "ACTION" in this book. The Ford Foundation was one of ACTION's major supporters. ACTION's mission was to solve urban renewal problems by increasing the supply of housing. Prof. Martin Meyerson, then at the University of Pennsylvania, was hired to direct its wide-ranging research program (and he hired me as his first research assistant).[13] Again, as always when I have been a participant in an activity, it is gratifying to have that activity subject to retrospection by a truly qualified contemporary expert, in this case the Ford Foundation's Winnick:

> ACTION's then chairman was Major General F.A. Irving, former superintendent of West Point and a confidant of President Eisenhower. Eisenhower had bestowed his blessings upon the organization, several of whose members had been among his ardent political allies as well as supporters of the fulcrum of his administration's urban policy—the Urban Renewal Act of 1954. The thrust of that Act was to recast the urban programs of predecessor Democratic administrations in two respects. One was to turn it away from a fixation on slum clearance to an emphasis on urban conservation. The second was to place the private sector ahead of government on the front line of urban revival, to seek a greater private involvement in *res publica.*
>
> Having so recently itself become just such a seeker, the Ford Foundation did not shut its ears to Eisenhower's clarion. Though a young organization, ACTION was a prestigious figure on the urban scene, and so regarded by Ford. And ACTION's proposal had the proper grandeur. Its declared purpose was "to reduce the economic, legal, production and other impediments to the provision of housing adequate to meet at reasonable cost the needs of all income groups."
>
> The principal barrier to an abundant supply of decent housing was construed to be the technological backwardness of the building industry. Block-

ages in the flow of market information had produced a mismatch between builders' products and consumers' preferences. Equally at fault were the weakened investment incentives, an inefficient mortgage market, obsolete municipal boundary lines and hopeless flaws in urban planning. In short, the root cause of the housing problem was held out to be an inadequate knowledge base, inappropriate customs and obsolete institutions.

These problems were to be addressed through a series of research probes by competent analysts who "would gather all available material on the subject, isolate the fundamental policy issues involved and present a series of evaluated recommendations." To assure a pragmatic dimension in research conducted mainly by academics and *realism* in their recommendations, a committee of practitioners was to be attached to each study. The findings and recommendations were to be disseminated through regional and national symposia and, more broadly, through a nationwide publicity campaign sponsored by the Advertising Council.

ACTION's project was carried out more or less in accord with the terms of the grant. Over the next several years, seven books were published, each dealing with a particular "impediment" and each the basis of a sequence of conferences to hammer out *a policy consensus.* [14] The Advertising Council faithfully fulfilled its publicity commitment; it touched all the media bases—TV, radio, newspapers, magazines, bus, subway placards —broadcasting the message that better housing and neighborhoods were within everyone's grasp were everyone to join in cooperative efforts toward that end.

The ACTION program had a mixed outcome. ACTION, for reasons set forth later, had no success in influencing the volume, unit cost or product mix of the nation's housing output or a reassessment of metropolitan planning structures. On the positive side it added a prestigious bipartisan endorsement to the proposition that rehabilitation of inner-city housing and neighborhoods could be a superior alternative to the New Deal-Truman strategy of slum clearance-cum-redevelopment, a proposition that later was to become the central premise of Ford's urban programs. ACTION's stance, however, did not soothe the conservation v. redevelopment imbroglio. Though, ultimately, conservation won the day (by the Seventies large-scale slum clearance was a thing of the past), it would be helpful to recall some of the issues in a debate that wracked urban policy for years, with Ford's constituents represented in both camps.[15]

But laced within all these racial and political approaches were a host of subtle and not-so-subtle arguments concerning the relative merits of new versus rehabilitated areas. Obviously, urban form would be deeply affected by the outcome of these essentially non-urban-form battles.

Urban Redevelopment or Conservation?

Again, Winnick made perceptive comments on the issue of tearing blighted areas down completely or selectively:

> To be sure, more than a few urbanists, (e.g., Raymond Vernon, who had extensively analyzed the New York region, and Martin Anderson, who had cast a skeptic's eye on federal redevelopment programs), declared that the costs of retrieving the sunk investments of old cities would exceed the likely benefits. They assessed the new geography of location as a rational adaptation to market forces and hence a net national gain. In their view, economics could not deliver what politics demanded; older cities should be left to adjust to altered circumstances with minimal, if any, government intervention and subsidy.
>
> But cost-benefit analysis was then (is still) a rudimentary tool, and the voices of the doubters did not prevail. The federal-municipal slum clearance and urban reconstruction programs widened and deepened.
>
> As that happened, it became ever more clear that the decisive element in urban decline was not just failing places and structures but failing people. The city schools that had performed so well for previous generations of enrollees were still on the same sites but now poorly serving their replacements. As slums were razed, the dislodged families too often transformed the area of resettlement into another slum. Expensive new replacement housing deteriorated into inhabitability; human misery remained human misery whatever the change of locus or physical environment.[16]

And on the subject of redevelopment or conservation, Winnick wrote:

> The alignments in the debate were political and ideological, though not in any simple or straightforward way. Generally speaking, the redevelopment constituency was allied to the Democratic Party, the originators of the New Deal's slum clearance–public housing programs. New Deal legislation had expressly declared its major goal to be the rehousing of those trapped in slum buildings, the latter to be demolished and replaced with public housing.
>
> The forerunners of New Deal policy were the early philanthropic housing reformers who deemed few old tenements and slum blocks worthy of salvage. To them, rehabilitation was an uneconomic waste, a palliative to prolong by a few years the habitability of patently obsolete structures.
>
> Worse than the structures were the site layouts, rendered irredeemable by the gridiron street patterns of old cities—rectangular blocks subdivided into 25′ by 100′ lots on which it was impossible to reconfigure

proper standards of space and density. Their ideal was the superblock because it favored the placement of tall buildings amid ample green space and open areas. [[17]] That ideal could not be achieved without major clearance followed by new construction on reconfigured sites. During Truman's administration the slum-clearance took on a whole new dimension. The Urban Redevelopment Act of 1949, which multiplied the authorized volume of public housing, attached an unprecedented "equivalent elimination" clause; it mandated the demolition of one slum dwelling unit for each new unit of public housing.

The pivotal section of the 1949 Act, however, was its Title I. Title I encouraged municipalities to enact comprehensive slum-clearance schemes, rewarded by generous subsidies to defray the bulk of the costs. The cleared land was resold at heavily discounted prices to public and private redevelopers. Moreover, the cleared land could be rebuilt not just with housing but with any of a wide range of land uses deemed appropriate by local planning bodies—office buildings, shopping malls and convention centers, community facilities, or recreation areas.

The typical re-use, however, was middle- or higher-income housing, stirring angry protests against the ouster of the poor for the benefit of the nonpoor. The second most common outcome of slum clearance was rubble and weeds. Large quantities of emptied-out land found no takers, owing to weak central-city real estate markets, and to legal and political wrangles. The clearance-reconstruction approach was enthusiastically backed by the AFL-CIO, a mainstay of the Democratic Party.

Labor support, especially by the building trades, was based more on bread and butter concerns than ideology: New construction offered the maximum potential of high-wage jobs, for their members. In labor's view, housing conservation and rehabilitation was a catch-as-catch-can activity, scarcely deserving to be labeled an industry. It was dirty, small-potatoes work, dominated by undercapitalized contractors who, unless subject to federal Davis-Bacon rules (which mandated union-level wages), were likely to employ low-paid, often pickup, labor.

Big-city mayors (for many years an influential part of Ford's urban constituency), overwhelmingly Democratic, were also in the redevelopment camp, at least until they were chastised by the intolerable political costs of displacement. Many of these mayors were served by "public entrepreneurs," the superstars of large-scale redevelopment schemes. The most renowned were New York's Robert Moses, New Haven's (later Boston's) Edward Logue, and San Francisco's Justin Herman. The redevelopment camp also included many in the real estate and mortgage lending industry, including those who subordinated Republican Party affiliations to economic interests.

On the preservation side, the dominant voices were an anomalous blend of old-fashioned conservatives and doctrinal radicals. The conservatives viewed slum clearance as cost-ineffective and, worse yet, as an ominous step to socialist land ownership.[18] Large-scale acquisition of private property through condemnation was an insufferable infringement of individual rights. Also in the preservation camp were legions of urban architects and planners, who deplored the loss of urban texture and abhorred the cookie-cutter high-rises and superblocks that epitomized redevelopment areas. Jane Jacobs was their Joan of Arc. Their allies included sundry activists and radicals who had never previously found common ground with establishment viewpoints. The latter construed urban redevelopment as an inverted morality play in which evil triumphs over virtue, a thinly disguised conspiracy of predatory real estate developers enriching themselves by dispossessing the powerless poor. Though by then other forces were also moving in the same direction, ACTION's stirrings abetted the formation (nationally and locally) of public-private civic organizations in support of cities in general and housing in particular.

These civic organizations coalesced with a host of special interest groups (housing producers, mortgage lenders, municipal officials) to forge a national "urban lobby" with links to the White House and Congressional leaders of both parties. One consequence was that even during Democratic regimes rehabilitation and preservation programs were accorded a place on the urban agenda higher than they might otherwise have obtained. And during the Republican regimes, allocations for new housing and urban programs generally fared better than they might have.

ACTION was thus the forger of an "iron triangle," one leg of which was a puissant national urban coalition and whose other two legs were HUD and the Congressional housing and urban committees. That iron triangle exerted a powerful influence in each year's tug-of-war over budget authorizations, assuring that housing and urban programs, whatever the balance between redevelopment and conservation, were not unduly neglected.[19]

Cities in Johnson's Great Society

President Kennedy, while not acceding to the urban mayors' request that he give the needs of the cities top priority, was enthusiastic about housing and urban development legislation. The relevant legislation of the Kennedy and Johnson administrations is listed below. President Johnson, second in that long line of GI Generation presidents and a great subject for biography, was undoubtedly sincere in his attempt to mount a war against poverty as a step on the way to a Great Society; at almost every turn, he faced one or another aspect of the racial question in American society. He put his administration on the line to get the Voting Rights Act of 1964 and, indeed, to get most of the legislation listed below. The list, which is in chronological order, is adapted selectively from *Evolution of Role of the Federal Government*, an indispensable compilation of hundreds of laws relating to housing and community development from 1892 to 1974; the list, compiled for a House of Representatives controlled by the Democrats, ends prophetically four years after President Nixon began to get the federal government to withdraw from such activities indefinitely if not permanently.[20] I have interspersed commentary between some of the entries. My selection of representative items, with my commentary, begins with a modest, understandably conservative, statement of national goals for housing and urban development handed to the incoming Kennedy Democrats by the retiring Eisenhower Republicans.

1. Report of the President's Commission on National Goals: For Housing and Urban Development. The Commission recommended:

a. full range of housing opportunities outside the central cities for minority families and for other low-income families;
b. an adequate supply of suitable housing for low- and middle-income families who need or want to live in central areas;
c. greater volume of investment, private and public, in renewal and redevelopment;
d. effective regional planning and stronger land use controls;
e. incentives for effective planning, land-use control, and strong local government, in all Federal and State programs of financial assistance;
f. responsible programming of local housing requirements; and
g. expansion of the market for new and improved housing and of the range of consumer housing choice. November 16, 1960.

Comment. The statement above is a long way down from the proclamation in the Housing Act of 1949 of a "national housing policy: that the general welfare and security of the Nation require the realization as soon as possible of the goal of a decent home and suitable living environment for every American family."

2. *Area Redevelopment Act:* provided loans and grants for public facilities and commercial and industrial facilities in "redevelopment areas" of substantial and persistent unemployment or underemployment. PL87–27, May 1, 1961.

Comment: This became a particularly useful tool for smaller communities that had been losing factories to the South or overseas.

3. *FHA Sec. 221(d)(3) "Below Market Rate" Rental Housing:* authorized insurance for mortgages at low rates with partial or no premium and with liberalized provisions for payment of insurance claims. Housing Act of 1961.

4. *Open Space Land-Grants:* a new program of Federal grants to assist local public bodies in the acquisition of land to be used as permanent open space. Housing Act of 1961.

Comment. These grants, treasured by local governments, were complemented later by federal outdoor recreation programs.

5. *"Transportation System of Our Nation":* The President sent a message to Congress, . . . He asked for fundamental reforms in the areas of: Intercity Transportation; Urban Transportation; International Transportation; and Labor Relations and Research. April 1962.

Comment. At the beginning, urban transportation was a matter for the housing and urban redevelopment agencies to deal with. In 1968 the urban mass transportation programs were transferred to the new Department of Transportation.

6. *Equal Opportunity in Housing:* President Kennedy, by Executive Order, (a) directed Federal departments and agencies to take action to prevent discrimination in the sale, lease, or occupancy of residential property owned or operated by the Federal Government, or the provision of which is assisted by the Federal Government through loans, grants, loans insured or guaranteed, or Federal assistance to slum clearance or urban renewal projects, and (b) established the President's Committee on Equal Opportunity in Housing to promote the coordination of Federal activities under the Order. Executive Order 11063, November 20, 1962.

Comment. Civil rights legislation including voting rights, was proposed by President Kennedy in June 1963. Kennedy was killed in November 1963, and Lyndon Johnson took over the helm. The 1962 executive orders had gone much further than any moves taken by the Eisenhower administration on these sensitive racial issues.

7. *Urban Mass Transportation Act of 1964:* authorized loans and grants and "required the preparation of an areawide transportation plan as part of comprehensive planning for the development of the urban area." PL88–365. July 9, 1964.

Comment. The required "areawide transportation plans" drawn up by the various local agencies applying for loans and grants stimulated the creation of scores of new intergovernmental metropolitan-areawide planning agencies that came as close as anything before or since to bringing regional planning officially into urban planning practice. Some of the staffs for these new agencies were interested in developing sophisticated mathematical models for their localities in order to make multiyear projections concerning the future location, for very small subareas in their regions, of housing, shopping, manufacturing, office buildings, and public facilities. These models were beloved of members of the Regional Science Association and the Committee on Urban Economics, both dominated by professional economists. Unfortunately, two aspects of these arrangements diminished the effectiveness of this approach to more comprehensive planning: (1) consideration of mass transportation media or methods other than buses tended to be minimal, for the automobile was king, and many of the so-called transportation plans were little more than pasteups of the road-building aspirations of the various jurisdictions that had been joined together into a patchwork intergovernmental area-wide planning agency, and (2) as soon as the grants ran out, or as soon as the regional planners began to introduce nondiscriminatory housing or other racially loaded considerations into the planning criteria, the social glue that had held the several local jurisdictions together seemed to evaporate and the new agencies became either moribund, disfunded, or disbanded.

8. Urban and rural *Community Action Programs* in a number of enumerated fields, including housing. In Economic Opportunity Act of 1964, PL-462, August 1964.

Comment. Johnson was beginning his battles against poverty at this time, and Congress provided 90 percent of the cost of operating a local-area community action program (CAP) owned and operated, so to speak, by the folks from the neighborhood. A key feature of the programs funded under this legislation was that they were beyond the control of local elected officials. Such officials may have been involved in selecting local citizens as members of the board of the new CAP agency, but they did not take kindly to lawsuits and demonstrations on the steps of city halls under the direction of the community organizers employed by the CAP to work on the issues most vital to the neighborhood. The Model Cities agencies (below) got such community activities back into the hands of the mayors.

Additional comment. About this time, some loosening of the regulations on savings and loan associations was instituted, beginning the long march to the crisis of the 1980s, and some attention was given to changes in the familiar grant-and-loan form of federal assistance to local governments —specifically, ideas for revenue sharing and for bundling a collection of related federal grants into a single block grant.

9. President's Message on the Cities, March 1965.

10. Appalachian Regional Development Act of 1965 (for economic development).

11. Department of Housing and Urban Development Act, PL89–174, September 9, 1965.

Comment. Finally, Johnson managed to do what Kennedy could not achieve, getting Congress to establish a new department, the Department of Housing and Urban Development (HUD) or (DHUD). Racial considerations were involved in the long delay, "according to reliable sources," although I am not knowledgeable about the struggle. The first secretary was Robert C. Weaver of New York, an economist with a Ph.D. from Harvard and, happily, a black (as African-Americans were just beginning to be called in place of "colored,") a man with long experience in housing and urban development matters.

12. Demonstration Cities and Metropolitan Development Act of 1966: grants (a) to selected cities for "comprehensive city demonstration program" for entire sections and neighborhoods of slum and blighted areas, and (b) for planned metropolitan development and for urban environmental studies . . . and among many other provisions (c) FHA mortgage insurance for new communities (broadening program for land development). PL 89–754, November 4, 1966.

Comment. It was renamed as the Model Cities Program to eliminate confusion with demonstration for civil rights. A "local governing body" could create or designate a "city demonstration agency" that would prepare a plan to provide low and moderate housing for an "entire slum neighborhood," reduce "social and educational disadvantages, ill health, underemployment and enforced idleness," and "contribute toward a well-balanced city." Simple! All sorts of programs were proposed by these new agencies to be approved, first, by the local governing body, then by HUD. Some 400 new agencies across the nation eventually got themselves wrapped up in the endless screening processes and negotiations established by the review teams at HUD. The Model Cities Program did, in fact, elicit a flock of imaginative ideas, many of them implemented, and did, in fact, create whole cadres of new leadership in minority communities, many of whom remain active in civic life.

When Nixon came into office two and a half years later, many activities in the Model Cities Program were in operation, but many applicants were still enmeshed in getting approval of their plans. Nixon appointed a team, headed by Edward Banfield of Harvard, to review the Model Cities Program and make recommendations. Banfield, long associated with studies of urban policy, had just published *The Unheavenly City*, a book that not only was a slashing critique of almost everything dear to the heart of Do-Good Ebenezers but also stoked his new image as a leading member of the neoconservative band of intellectuals and as a contributor to *The Public Interest*, the house organ of the band.[21] I spent the summer of 1969 as Banfield's research assistant (paid by HUD) for his Model City assignment. He wrote the final report himself after reading stacks of study papers and attending a number of committee meetings, joyfully limiting the report to only a few pages to demonstrate that governmental reports could be short. It included acerbic recommendations to eliminate the elegant planning process and send money instead, in effect letting a hundred flowers bloom and merely making sure at the end that the financial reports of expenditures were accurate. The Model Cities Program was terminated with respect to new commitments on January 1, 1975.

13. War on Poverty announced in *Congressional Record*, March 14, 1967.

14. Civil Rights Act of 1968: Fair Housing.

15. Urban Institute 1968.

16. Housing and Urban Development Act of 1968. Authorized Sec. 235 (of the National Housing Act) to provide Federal assistance to homeownership by lower income families, whereby HUD could make periodic payments to lenders in the amount necessary to make up the difference between 20 percent of the family's monthly income and the required monthly payment under the mortgage for principal, interest, taxes, insurance and mortgage insurance premium. . . . plus Sec. 221(h).

Authorized Sec. 236 (of the National Housing Act) to provide Federal assistance to rental and cooperative housing for lower income families whereby periodic payments were to be made to the mortgagee to reduce the rents required by interest costs on a market rate FHA-insured project mortgage.

17. New Communities Act of 1968: included in the Housing Act of 1968.

Comment. Legislation for new communities was so long in prospect that it did not prove as effective as it might have a generation earlier. A related and equally unsuccessful program at about the same time was Operation Breakthrough, another in a long line of attempts to industrialize building practices.[22] Eight projects were finally approved for funding under the New Communities rubric: Jonathan, Minnesota; St. Charles Communities, Maryland; Park Forest South, Illinois; Flower Mound, Texas; Maumelle, Arizona; Cedar-Riverside, Minnesota; San Antonio Ranch, Texas; and Riverton, New York.[23] All of these were nested in or near fair-sized metropolitan areas. None of them proved to be financially viable.

Two of the predecessors of these communities were: Reston, Virginia, and Columbia, Maryland. Both were completely private-sector operations, although the developers had to work very closely over long periods with the local county authorities before getting useful sets of permits, for, in both cases, the elegant land planning and citing of houses challenged the traditional zoning requirements in those jurisdictions. As a staff member of Arthur D. Little, a major industrial consulting firm, in 1960, I produced some population and employment projections under contract to Bob Simon, the creator and, at that time, sole owner of Reston. In 1969, working for the American City Corporation created by Columbia's owner and creator, James Rouse, I wrote a report on the federal new communities program. Both Reston and Columbia are financially viable and are recognized as specially attractive additions to the suburban reaches of Washington, D.C., and Baltimore.

Talk about state-chartered corporations to build large numbers of new housing units and often the new communities to house them recalls the brief, brilliant rise of New York State's Urban Development Corporation (UDC) and its equally swift and near-disastrous plunge into bankruptcy in 1974, almost bringing both New York State and New York City down with it. Created in 1968 under the aegis of Governor Nelson Rockefeller, partly as a response to the riots following Martin Luther King's assassination, it was given the power to override local authorities as necessary to complete its projects and to finance itself by the sale of tax-exempt bonds not guaranteed by the state or any other agency. Its executive director was the dramatic Edward Logue, known for his urban development achievements in New Haven and Boston. Fortunately for me, I turned down the job he offered me in the summer of 1969 to become his director of public finance,[24] for, in the spring of 1975, UDC defaulted on $104 million of bond anticipation notes, this after launching "about $1.5 billion worth of residential and nonresidential projects including 117 separate housing developments comprising 30,000 dwelling units and three brand new communities—one on an island in the middle of New York City."[25] This default, wrote Martin Mayer, "was what triggered the financial collapse of New York City, very nearly destroying the credit of the state and all its municipalities."[26]

The Transition Begins

As luck would have it, two extraordinarily comprehensive, erudite, and readable government reports were delivered just as the Johnson administration was packing up and the Nixon team was preparing to reign.[27] The first, handed to President Johnson on December 11, 1968, was *A Decent Home*, the Report of the President's Committee on Urban Housing, providing encyclopedic research under the aegis of a blue-ribbon committee headed by industrialist Edgar F. Kaiser. The second, a day later, was *Building the American City*, covering an array of related issues, but with hundreds of equally well-researched recommendations, all created under the aegis of an even more impressive committee, this one chaired by former Senator Paul H. Douglas.

The scope of the Douglas report is suggested by its overall structure: Part I. The urban setting: Population, poverty, race; Part II. Housing programs; Part III. Codes and standards; Part IV. Government structure, finance, and taxation; Part V. Reducing housing costs; Part VI. Improvement of the environment.

Many of the recommendations in these reports assume the existence of the housing finance system erected by the New Deal. As interest rates began to rise after the mid-1960s, partly because of the undeclared war in Vietnam, the housing credit system, which was dependent upon an array of savings institutions supervised by the federal government and offering better mortgage deals than commercial banks, would begin very slowly to fall apart. At the end of this line of troubles lay the savings and loan crisis of the 1980s that figures so prominently in the next chapter.

What the New Deal had done was to create an effective two-tier system for building America: savers put their money into "nonfinancial thrift institutions," receiving below-market interest on their deposits; these institutions provided comparatively low-rate mortgage loans insured by the FHA. The commercial banks, which were technically the only true "financial institutions," could offer only punitively low rates on time deposits but were allowed to make business and construction loans that had no federal guarantees or insurance. When the commercial banks were permitted to issue certificates of deposit (CDs) at market rates, consumers took their money out of the savings banks (a process called "disintermediation") in order to buy commercial-bank CDs, initiating the cycle that ultimately destroyed the system. Credit-card debt had not yet become a factor. Under the now-repealed Glass-Steagall Act, commercial banks could underwrite full-faith-and-credit municipal bonds while investment banking firms could handle all the less-than-full-faith-and-credit revenue bonds.

The year 1968 was difficult for the Do-Good Ebenezers. The year included the deaths of Robert Kennedy and Martin Luther King Jr., the riots in the cities, and the disarray of the city-building and housing programs that had been so important a part of the Truman, Kennedy, and Johnson eras. All sorts of complex arrangements to get housing built for low- and moderate-income families were being threatened by the Nixon team. It is still instructive to understand the doleful effect that the Section 608 program had, first, in shoehorning into towns and cities a number of poorly built projects and, second, in making many of the housing initiatives slightly suspect, in the same way as the myth of the welfare queen helped turn legislators against a basically good program in 1996. By this point, however, what Winnick called a "confection of new housing programs" had been authorized. Here are Winnick's parting thoughts on the endemic problems in government-assisted housing in the era following the Section 608 scandals:

> Congress and the Housing and Home Finance Agency (HHFA, HUD's antecedent) feared a reprise of that unsavory episode. To assure the probity of the new programs, they sought to enlist maximum cooperation of not-for-profit sponsors. They alone offered a safeguard that public benefits would be passed through to tenants rather than skimmed away. The most liberal mortgage terms and easiest access to subsidy funds were reserved for such sponsors. The harsh truth was that few nonprofit organizations—most of them church or community affiliated—possessed sufficient competence or working capital to make effective use of the newly presented opportunities.
>
> It was not too much to say that many were feckless amateurs, bumbling in their dealings with public agencies and vulnerable to fleecing by contractors and suppliers. Understandably enough, church-based groups tended also to be ruled by heart rather than head, to weigh their clients' needs more than financial realities. They were notoriously prone to shun hard choices.[28]

Upon his election in 1968, President Nixon decided to make some of those hard choices by himself, and thus the middle third of the century fades into history.

12
Destructuring America, 1968–2000

The Winds of Change

All of this brings us breathlessly to the third part of the twentieth century, with 1968 as a sharp dividing point between it and the world we knew in the previous thirty-five years. A mere listing of a few of the ways in which the systems and ideas prevailing in that 1933–68 period have been changed in the 1968–2000 end-of-the-century era is enough to suggest the ideas that need to be incorporated into the chapters that follow.

1. Keynesian economics and the Employment Act of 1946 replaced by neoconservative and supply side concepts.
2. Institutionalization of the military-industrial complex.
3. Disestablishment of or reduction in many federal housing and home mortgage programs for low- and moderate-income families.
4. The later deregulation of the banking and home finance industries, which led to unwarranted developments and the eventual meltdown of the savings and loan industry (which ultimately cost the federal government $600 billion); the story of this imbroglio is recounted in the appendix.
5. Avoidance or repeal of environmental and conservation laws affecting urban regions and reflected in the rightist "sagebrush rebellion" and "wise use" movements that challenge public land policies and regulation (discussed later in this chapter).
6. Various forms of tax revolt at the level of the states, beginning with California's Proposition 13, leading to widespread fiscal crises at century's end.
7. The suburbanization and virtual dissolution of political parties, leading to lack of political leadership, almost entropy, in both

national and state legislatures, a process that reinforces the impact of campaign finance on our democracy.

8. Globalization of business, with the assistance of U.S. and international agencies, resulting in overseas production but abandoned factories and lower incomes for families in America.
9. Foreign policies that support corporate power in our society.
10. Consolidation of communication and publishing facilities in the age of computers and the Internet.
11. A trend away from governmental programs that protect the poor and disabled in our society and that enhance our civil liberties.

All of these changes meant that, at the end of the twentieth century, we found ourselves with a new set of conditions for life in our urban and rural environments; those conditions are the starting point for the future story of how we as a nation will deal with life in the first century of the new millennium, just as 1900 was the starting point of our story to date.

The end of Strauss and Howe's Great Power Cycle, to my mind, came with the loss of the Vietnam War and the first great interruption in our ability to import oil. At the same time, we were living through the decline of America's union-wage economy, the creation of the Rust Belt as production of iron and steel moved overseas, the passing of the age of ocean shipping and railroads and the vast increase in air and automobile travel and the growth of footloose industries and major transfers of industry to lands below the Mexican border and to Asia.

Strauss and Howe give the name Millennial to the cycle following the Great Power one, and it thereby encompasses the remaining active years of the GI and Silent generations and the best years of the Boom, Thirteenth, and Millennium generations. As they outline this array:

The Boom Generation is, unsurprisingly, denoted as Idealist by Strauss and Howe. Included among the Boomers are the idealists who shamed the self-satisfied GI and Silent generations by joining the Peace Corps, traveling to the South to support the civil rights campaigns, demonstrating against the Vietnam imbroglio, and embracing environmentalism, feminism, and New Age and nondiscrimination practices. Their midlife self-absorptions, according to Strauss and Howe, were accompanied by the culture of narcissism and me-ism, high divorce and drug-use rates, and a low birth rate/late marriage syndrome.

My own thought is that these sociological trends affected city life in many different ways: one divorced partner often fled to the city from the suburb, increasing demand for small apartments, even as white families were fleeing to the suburbs to escape both crime and busing. Smaller houses and more consumer goods generated the demand for acres of storage lockers. Higher incomes and the laws requiring seat belts eventually led to large recreational vehicles despite the nation's difficulty in finding cheap oil to import. As they approached their fifties, many individuals and most Boomer families had to find multiple jobs to make ends meet. During the Reagan and G.H.W. Bush years, they hardly noticed that the savings and loan institutions were costing the federal government half a trillion dollars while the federal debt climbed to unprecedented levels, but they joined in the general feeling of relief as the Union of Soviet Socialist Republics came apart in 1989 and the hiatus in Cold War machinations began. But again, Boomers hardly noticed the first Bush's First Gulf War, being too busy, along with their seniors, with a new round of suburban building, this time of gated communities noticeably away from central-city woes.

The Thirteenth Generation (so named by Strauss and Howe because it did not have a distinct personality when they wrote in 1991) was the thirteenth since the U.S. Constitution was adopted). Members of the Thirteenth Generation would be expected to be Reactive—like the Lost Generation before them—that is, reacting to the efforts of the Boomers to improve the world. Thirteenth Generation people, in fact, spent their college years looking for majors that would lead to good jobs. Being a risk-taking generation, they flocked to the new corporations of the computer age, vaunted their skills, bathed in stock options, built big houses, and splurged on fancy cars. As the twentieth century came to a close and stock values plummeted, they were, for the first time, confronting economic and social realities familiar to earlier generations but which Thirteenthers believed had been transcended.

Strauss and Howe could only speculate, as they finished their 1991 opus, about the Millennial Generation that began in 1982. Since every generation has its own crisis, their cyclic reasoning led them to suggest that the new generation would become Civic in personality. Many Millennials, in fact, do seem to be deeply concerned with the impact of globalization and the effects of the triad of institutions created at the end of World War II: the World Bank, the International Finance Agency, and the World Trade Organization that grew out of GATT, the General Agreement on Tariffs and Trade. And, with respect to the subject of this book, they do seem to be somewhat more urban than suburban in their interests. How they will end up voting and how they will restructure existing institutions when the crisis for their time occurs is beyond anyone's ken; Strauss and Howe suggested that such a crisis could be expected in the 2003–25 period, but perhaps the aftermath of the terrorist attacks on New York and Washington on September 11, 2001, will constitute crisis enough for the Millennials.

I hope these formulations about generations make sense. Other definitions of successive generations, and other characterizations of the differences between the generations, may prove more enlightening than the ones I have taken from Strauss and Howe. The point is that some set of people in the generations now alive will be dealing with the urbanized America of 2000 that emerged step by step from the America of 1900, and some generational characteristics seem more supportive of the general welfare than others. So here is what I see.

Takeover by the Neoconservatives

The Nixon administration represented the triumph of the Shiny Babbitts over the Do-Good Ebenezers. In retrospect it also appears to have been the actual beginning of the campaign by the right to return America to late nineteenth century sociopolitical policies.[1] The year 1968 featured, among other events, riots, assassinations, the impact of George Wallace's campaign on the unions and the Democratic Party, the rising influence of neoconservatives, and consciousness-raising among feminists, gays and lesbians, and environmentalists. The states that gave Nixon their electoral votes contained the plants of the new high-tech companies, which often had defense contracts, for electronic and aviation gear and services. Nixon's victory was assured when the southern voters who were unhappy with the Democrats' racial policies joined the parade.

Many of these states enjoyed warmish climates toward which the first generation of pensioners was gravitating. These pensioners tended to be relatively conservative both socially and economically, a class that had been created during New Deal days in the 1930s by the Social Security system and by pensions in union contracts. They were living on fixed incomes and did not like paying taxes for Great Society–type programs. Many of them were World War II veterans much in favor of the Vietnam War. Collectively, these military-industrial complex folks and pensioners lived in the new cities and vast retirement communities of the Southeast and Southwest.

Many Boomers, children of the GI Generation, joined Shiny Babbitt conservatives in being against the Equal Rights Amendment for women, against abortion, in favor of individual property rights as supporters of the "wise use" and "sagebrush rebellion,"[2] and in favor of minimalizing unglamorous but essential governmental operations and supports. At the time, few of us realized the extent to which the New Deal and the Great Society had generated an opposition so fanatically dedicated to dismantling all those programs and to establishing Shiny Babbittry as the epitome of the American Way, with an ever rising standard of living to be measured by upper-middle-class consumer preferences.

The rightist opposition was politicized by Barry Goldwater in the 1964 campaign and further inflamed by George Wallace in 1968. Among its cultural manifestations, besides infatuation with Ayn Rand's works, was a 1963 book, *Beyond the Melting Pot* by Daniel Patrick Moynihan and Nathan Glazer[3] which seems in retrospect to have been part of the neoconservative's intellectual campaign to gain acceptance for the idea that many racial, ethnic, or cultural groups in the United States had not been able to become fully "assimilated" into middle-class America, nor could they expect to do so, nor, indeed, did all of them even wish any longer to have their separate identities extinguished. At the University of Chicago, especially in its law and economics faculties, this same intellectual movement was linked to European thinkers such as Claude Lévi-Strauss, Michel Foucault, Martin Heidieggei, and Friedrich Hayek. In Cambridge and New York, the movement attracted folks like Edward Banfield, Daniel Patrick Moynihan, Martin Anderson, and Stephen Thorstrum, all writing in *The Public Interest* to publicize their ideas.

Thus began a process that continued almost without interruption for the last third of the twentieth century. Nixon, Ford, and to some degree Carter, Reagan, G.H.W. Bush, and certainly Clinton contributed to a major shift away from a prevailing structure of federalism that called for strong federal programs and a responsive, collaborative, coordinated, reciprocal relationship with state and local government bodies. Gone by the end of the century was the concept of a strong, guiding, supportive role for the federal government to make sure that there would be full employment at fair wages, protection for old-agers and small children, medical services for all, and a safe environment (and even national housing goals).

The Nixonites, moreover, felt they had been handed a housing mess that demanded immediate attention; Nixon, tired of the struggles by

1973, imposed a moratorium on all federal housing programs. As Winnick describes the situation:

> What precipitated a rethinking of priorities was a pervasive and ubiqui-tous series of housing failures affecting the entire low-income housing sector—HUD's assisted private and public housing units and the much larger non-HUD stock of the inner city as well. The nature of the housing problem was in tumultuous flux. The more critical needs were not a lim-itless stream of additional housing but a greater capacity to preserve and manage the vastly larger stock of housing already in place. HUD's tribu-lations were in part the consequences of an unprecedented volume of new assisted housing that flooded the engines of its beneficiaries, beyond their effective ability to absorb.
>
> That occurrence was a stunning shock. It upset the conventional wis-dom that the gulf between housing need and housing supply was, for all practical purposes, infinite, that any and all low- and moderate-income housing would be instantly and fully occupied by a grateful tenantry. Instead there was a manifest oversupply, accompanied by financial fail-ures, foreclosures, and scandals. From the last years of the Sixties, and at a faster tempo in the Seventies, assisted housing came onto the market in record numbers, at an annual rate of between 300,000 and 600,000 sub-sidized units. That level approached President Johnson's commitment in the waning years of the Great Society to produce six million units over the 1968–78 decade.[4]

The changes were accompanied by a variety of events that could not have been anticipated and that changed the political landscape—for in-stance, the fracas about Watergate in 1972 leading to Nixon's resigna-tion and the oil crisis precipitated by OPEC. In the middle of these supervening events, however, Congress initiated a lengthy set of hear-ings on the problems, especially financial and fiscal stresses, resulting from urban growth and on the implications of some of the methods used to control such growth. Congress passed and Nixon signed the path-breaking National Environmental Policy Act (NEPA) of 1969, but Sena-tor Henry "Scoop" Jackson of Washington was unsuccessful in getting Congress to require states to engage in comprehensive land use plan-ning. And destructuring of the federal system that had been developed between 1930 and 1968 proceeded more or less along the following lines (in addition to all the activities on housing and housing finance that led to the savings and loan debacle):

1. A new western and southeastern establishment from new suburbanized places replaced the north and central old-city power brokers.
2. Block grants for federal programs replaced categorical grants, changing the internal politics of cities and states that were thereafter required to risk political troubles in the process of allocating a single pot of money among competing grant seekers instead of having the targeted groups do the political work of securing the separate pots under the highly focused categorical grant system.
3. The National Environmental Policy Act (NEPA) and the new state environmental acts had the effect of overwhelming and obfuscating the old struggles among planning, zoning, and redevelopment agencies, generating the complicated procedures that enflamed developers and property-rights advocates.
4. Steady increases in interest rates during the 1970s and early 1980s encouraged speculative, large-scale construction to generate higher profits, affecting the role of the Federal Reserve, the flow of investment funds (including those from Japan), and the stability of the American banking and thrift systems.
5. The changes wrought by large corporations in their industrial processes were manifest in the rise of the Rust Belt, which led to a further decline in union membership and diminished a locality's ability to resist continued transfers of jobs overseas.
6. An economic system characterized by strong independent regional industries and banks faded away, even as the Democratic Party shifted to the right and espoused both the globalization of business in general and the North American Free Trade Association (NAFTA) bill, which was anathema to local communities and unions.
7. The "urban industrial complex" described by Robert Goodman in *After the Planners* did well, with more roads, more stadia, and more condominiums being built, but, back in the central cities, low-income families were hurt by the flight of affluent white families to the suburbs (a move that reflected to some unmeasurable extent the prevailing set of racial antagonisms in the United States). Poor families were harmed further by limitations on property taxes (led by Proposition 13 in California in the 1970s) that have curtailed financial support of the public

schools and public health-and-welfare services in urban areas. Ever increasing expenditures on the drug war and the symbiotic criminal justice system appear to have absorbed revenue needed for those traditional governmental services.

On a more positive note, Winnick at the Ford Foundation was able to write in the late 1980s that the nation was clearly better off than in 1890.

Today's 240 million Americans, arranged in 90 million households, are manifestly better sheltered than the 63 million people and 13 million households of 1890. With isolated and diminishing exceptions, indoor toilets, running water, and central heating are taken for granted. The urban housing inventory comprises twice as many rooms as people; severe overcrowding as measured on the persons-per-room scale is the unfortunate lot of a small proportion of households. The gross physical deficits and dwelling densities that once impaired the health of occupants and communities are not the plight of the great majority of Americans, not even its poor. For the most part, they affect left-behind segments, many of them concentrated in rural areas, and others, more visibly, within the inner city slums. And even there, the housing problem is primarily deteriorated structures rather than the excessive neighborhood densities or overcrowded dwellings that were once both the main manifestation and cause of slumhood.

The population density of today's poverty concentration is strikingly lower than that of the 1900s and still declining; between 1960 and 1980 the population (within fixed boundaries) of the worst areas in seven cities fell by half.

These achievements notwithstanding, certain facets of the housing problem have intensified. In addition to the increasing spatial concentration of the underclass, they include a rising incidence of homelessness, and an unfavorable relation of housing costs to income. At the core of the residual problems are two deep-seated adversities, one social, the other economic. The social problem derives from the changing nature of poverty, a subject that threads through several chapters in the study and need not be further elaborated here. It concerns the emergence of segments of population burdened by deficiencies in behavior as much as by deficiencies in income, perhaps more so. They are confined to geographical enclaves that can neither be cleared nor, as long as drugs, crime and vandalism are rampant, comprehensively and dependably rehabilitated.[5]

Many subtle changes beyond those mentioned by Winnick occurred within metropolitan areas during the last third of the century. As a result, the 1960s effort to create a better intergovernmental framework for metropolitan area governance seemed to have lapsed in the last few decades of the century after various creative ideas were instituted in a few locales; for example, major city governments were consolidated with their county governments in Miami and San Francisco; elsewhere, "fair share" programs were allowed to spread subsidized low-income and "affordable housing" evenly over the metropolis; and systems of "tax base sharing" were installed in a few places to reduce the economic disparities between rich and poor communities.

In recent years, the major apostle of sound policy analysis of a given metropolis's social, economic, and political condition has been Myron Orfield of Minneapolis. He has written and lectured on the woeful condition of the typical American metropolis, trying to go beyond the usual treatments of "sprawl" and the fiscal impacts of new development. The litany of woes he discerns includes: concentrated poverty, racial segregation, fiscal stress and high developmental costs on the fringe, and difficult environmental and transportation conditions. The following comments are typical of Orfield's general findings as he observed the situation in a number of metropolises around the nation; I abstracted them from his report, titled *Seattle Metropolitics: A Regional Agenda for Community and Stability in the Puget Sound Region,* to the Institute for Washington's Future in May 1999 (the italics are mine):

> Social and economic polarization threaten the future of the Puget Sound region. . . . The mythic dichotomy of urban decline and suburban prosperity holds that social and economic decline stops neatly at the central city borders. Nothing could be further from the truth. . . .
> . . . [Although] as in most metropolitan areas of the U.S., social need is relatively high in the central city, *poverty and social instability are also pronounced in older working class and middle income satellite cities and their suburbs* . . . [which lack] the strong central business district vitality and resources, high-end housing market, parks, culture and amenities that the central city has; and often without a large police department and social service agencies to respond to growing social stress; the schools in these communities become poor faster, and the local commercial and residential values are simply not sufficient to keep taxes affordable and to deal with increasing social pressures.
> Second, in a related pattern, *growing middle-income communities,* dominated by smaller homes and apartments, developing without sufficient property tax base to support schools and other public services, are beginning to

experience increases in their poverty and crime rates. These fiscally stressed communities could well become tomorrow's troubled cities. . . .

Third, upper-income communities . . . *are capturing the largest share of regional infrastructure spending, economic growth and jobs. As the tax base expands in these affluent communities and their housing markets remain closed to most of the region's workers, these communities . . . become both socially and politically isolated from regional responsibilities. . . .*

While these *affluent, high tax base communities* have resources, they often *cannot, by themselves, control the pace of development* that takes them every day toward a scenario of rapid residential and commercial growth and unbearable levels of traffic congestion—a scenario that they may not want.

Only through a strong, multi-faceted, regional response can social and economic polarization and wasteful development patterns be countered. To stabilize the central city neighborhoods and satellite cities and to minimize unplanned outward development there are three areas of reform that must be achieved on a metropolitan scale:

1. greater fiscal equity among jurisdictions of the region,
2. smarter growth through better planning practices, and
3. structural reform of metropolitan governance to allow for fair and efficient implementation of the other reform measures.[6]

These policies are interrelated and reinforce each other substantively and politically. I maintained earlier that the only proper way to think about the American city at the end of the twentieth century is in the context of the metropolis,[7] and I think both Winnick and Orfield are basically correct: most Americans are better housed and situated than they were a hundred years ago, and most metropolises are engaged in a process that spreads poverty and congestion across the whole area and that will not grant immunity even to the residents of lovely high-income gated communities. This is a true di-lemma, two lemmas without a satisfactory resolution of the problem in sight; this is where the pundits left us at the beginning of this new Millennium, and it is not going to be easy to work ourselves out of the box, as we must!

Changing Cityscapes and the Savings and Loan Debacle

No question but that this last third of the century witnessed a truly tremendous expansion of America's metropolises as the automobile came to dominate our lives. Much of the building was at the margins of cities, in the areas between the old city and the new interstate highway exits. While America boomed unevenly but dramatically in those three decades, most of the highways had been finished, and, at virtually every major interchange across America, there appeared an appropriate blossoming of gas stations and motels. Some very rural interchanges got only a single facility—a welcome break in a featureless landscape for high-speed travelers. The approaches to even small cities, however, began to feature a collection of business establishments, and over the decades each type was magnified—their motels grew from twenty or thirty units to several hundred in multistoried edifices, and gas stations became travel centers with restaurants and stores. Where there had been one or two retail franchises, now there were a score of national names.

Between cities, along the interstate corridors appeared a new kind of retail center, congeries of "outlets" of branded goods of all types. At the same time, central cities across the nation lost their preeminent or flagship status as retailing centers because wave after wave of suburban shopping centers, malls, and regional mercantile centers, each larger than the earlier ones, were created to serve the automobile-endowed suburban consumers who would no longer venture into town.

Despite the social, economic, and political problems of each city's "inner city," one central city after another managed to rebuild its downtown areas, and, at one time in the 1970s, I thought it would be fun to get a grant (but I never succeeded in getting one for this purpose) to study how much of this activity took place on land cleared under Title I of the old federal urban renewal program.[8] All cities, even dying ones, have seen tall buildings arise in the last few decades, creating little urban skylines. In the 1970s and 1980s, a vast number of high-rise projects soared into view, some certainly within urban renewal boundaries and built to implement municipal hopes for a renaissance. Some of these skyscrapers provided far more space than could reasonably be expected to be absorbed by the market in the then foreseeable future, so far as my quite extensive experience as an analyst of local economic and real estate conditions suggested, but they were built anyway. One reason for their construction was certainly a lack of better investment opportunities (this in the years of little growth in the stock market and long before the high-tech and then the dot.com explosions), even in major cities of enormous size.

So let us grant that America looks better built, shinier, faster, and more efficient for the Babbitts.[9] And the suburban places of business and manufacturing are often gorgeous, landscaped creations. And the architects have often rendered impressive service in creating fascinating (in the original meaning) environments. And in the late 1980s and 1990s a vast wave of new enterprises based on computer technology emerged—they may have originated in garages, but they surfaced in huge new industrial edifices erected in former suburban grasslands adjacent to highways. The popular conception is that their executives were largely Thirteenth Generation folks (born between 1961 and 1981, according to Strauss and Howe) who were determined to earn a great deal of money in order to replace their old houses with grand mansions, often settling, however, for the "McMansions" that were filling up large chunks of undeveloped land in the suburbs, utterly transmogrifying the landscape.

At the same time, during the 1970s and early 1980s, the federal government, the states, and their local governments were expressing their rising concern about long-term neglect of the basic infrastructure of the metropolis, such as bridges rotting away and even collapsing.[10] My observation of discussions of this problem in King County (Washington) was perhaps typical in that the list of needed infrastructure investments compiled by local officials in response to these federal initiatives featured a collection of new and additional roads and bridges to accommodate more traffic in the new suburbs. Only a few projects were designed to preserve and renew sunk investments in the older areas of the metropolis.

The transcontinental drive my wife and I took in 2001 provided some confirmation of these changes in the layout and functioning of cities in the automobile age. No one should underemphasize the impact of the interstate highway system on American life, although I have yet to see any analysis of Census 2000 data that specifically addresses how communities that are not close to an interstate highway have lost population and economic activity and, the converse, how population and the local economy have blossomed in towns that ended up astride an interstate. Of course, many interstates completely replaced old roads by using their rights of way or bypassing them entirely, in the process making parts of our twentieth-century history obsolete, as somewhat dolefully reflected in a brochure from Oklahoma's Route 66 Museum:

> From its official beginning on November 11, 1926 through the heyday of auto travel in the 1950s and '60s, Route 66 was explored by families, vagabonds, dreamers and untold others—fueling thousands of restaurants, hotels, motels and tourist attractions along the way.

U.S. Highway 66 stretched from Chicago, Illinois, to Santa Monica, California. Some 2,400 miles coursed through eight states and three time zones, influencing lifestyles and spawning a culture that earned it the nickname "Main Street of America."

The Road for Dreamers

Route 66 was more than a cross-country passage for early auto travels. It exemplified the open road, beckoning adventurers with the promise of freedom. It carried people through bustling cities and into neon-lit small towns in the heart of America, and to places where telephone poles and train tracks were all that broke the scenery for miles. Scattered in between were mom-and-pop stops, roadside diners and motor courts with refrigerated air.

During the Great Depression of the 1930s, it became the road to a new beginning for many down-on-their-luck farm families who abandoned drought-ravaged homes and headed west in search of a better life. Their plight was made famous by John Steinbeck's novel (and later the motion picture) *The Grapes of Wrath*. The intrigue and allure of The Mother Road inspired dozens of other books, songs and even a television series.[11]

Examples of highway-oriented urban growth that may well be typical of conditions across the nation appeared during our automobile trip back and forth across the county in 2001:

1. In La Crosse, Wisconsin, a complete new town was developed, replete with residential enclaves, schools, shopping malls, and industrial buildings, between the interstate highway and a well-refurbished old town five or six miles down along the banks of the Mississippi River. Apparently this and other small well-located cities have become magnets in the past few years for young couples who simply did not want to work and bring up their families in larger places.

2. Birmingham, Alabama, is another case of an old part of the city appearing to have quieted down while much of the area's "urban" life takes place along the many miles of suburban development that run past the interstate interchange and along state highway 280, all within the actual boundaries of the city.

3. Jackson Hole, Wyoming, and Seneca Falls, New York, are typical of many places that are becoming cities dedicated to tourism and recreation. Jackson Hole itself has been built up with

countless stores and ski lodges, while only a few miles away are "villages of condominiums" for all-year-round vacationing. Seneca Falls is a well-built modern vacation area at the center of New York State's nineteenth-century canal system in the Finger Lakes region, with an impressive national park installation commemorating the emergence of the women's movement in 1848.

4. Cascades of shopping centers, gated residential communities, tall office buildings, and clusters of high-rise hotels near constantly expanding airports and suburban centers greet travelers on the completed highway systems of all of the major metropolises north and south, east and west.

Investment in new structures is considered by economists to create "real" rather than paper wealth. In Figure 12.1, I portray the record of new, private, residential, and nonresidential construction in constant 1996 dollars for the nation from 1960 to the end of the century, together with the average interest rate on mortgages at the end of each year. The interest rate, with measurable effects on the banking system, climbed steadily from the early 1960s until it peaked in the early 1980s, falling equally steadily until 2000. The relatively steady growth of construction in constant dollars reflects both a growing population and a generally strong economy. Changes in the interest rate on mortgages ordinarily have a profound impact on the amount of new, private, residential construction put in place in any given year, and this truism stands out clearly in Figure 12.1, most dramatically in the early 1980s. Private nonresidential construction is a little less responsive to such changes in interest rates; and it is such construction that changes the face of urban America.[12]

The basic assumption for those of us who work as consultants and teachers in the field of community economic development is that the rate of new construction in a given location is intimately tied to the growth of the local economy. Two professional colleagues and I had an opportunity to test this assumption in the late 1980s when the Department of Commerce made available for the first time the detailed reports on all types of private new construction submitted every month from some 17,000 building-permit offices in the United States. These data could then be matched with the only consistent and reliable set of economic analyses for local areas available, a series produced and published by NPA Data Services, Inc, a well-known private firm.[13]

Figure 12.1   **Construction in the United States, 1960–2000** (by year)

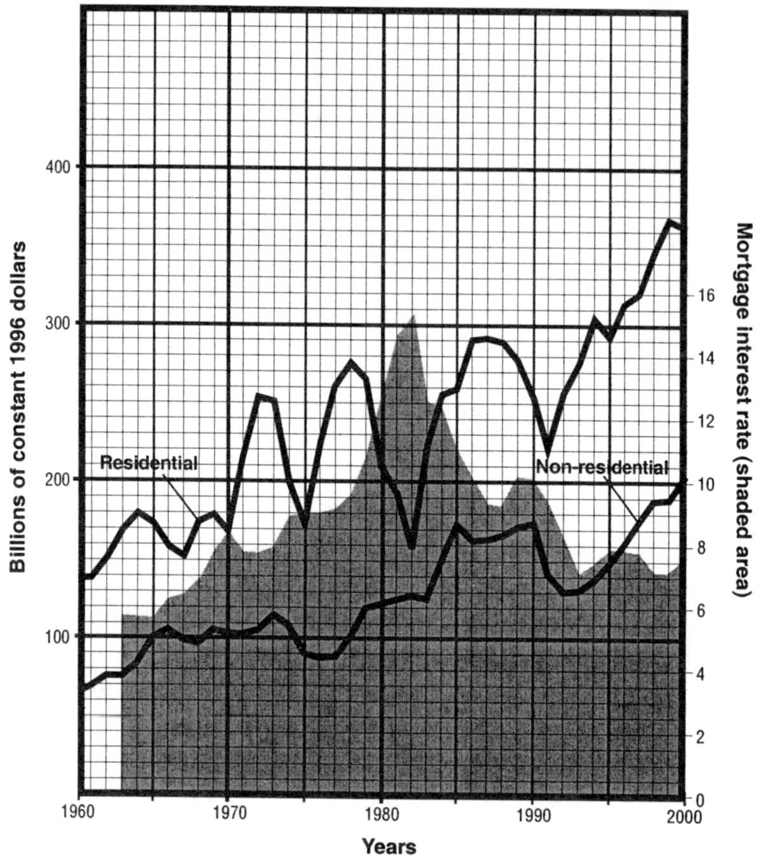

Source: *Economic Report of the U.S. President* (Washington, DC: GPO, 2001), Tables B7, B18, and B73.

We used the Department of Commerce's Bureau of Economic Analysis's array of 183 "economic areas" as an excitingly meaningful new way of dividing up the entire nation. Only fourteen of these economic areas did not have a census-defined Metropolitan Statistical Area within their boundaries, and since we had data for all the counties in the nation, we did not have to leave out of our analysis any counties that might be related to but not formally included in an officially defined metropolis. The question we wanted the data to be able to answer was whether "real investment" in a given locality bore any reasonable and stable relationship to facts about the local population and trends in the local economy. The following section is abstracted from our report.

Although economic areas differ in their size, location, resource base, and the range of their economic activities, they have many characteristics in common. The challenge is to discover whether their differences can be described in such a way as to provide a basis for predicting the amount and kind of new construction that is most typical of the given area. We started out with a mass of detailed construction permit data that had not been available before: the annual tapes created by the Bureau of the Census for 17,000 reporting places.[14] We then related the data to the economic geography of the 183 economic-area construction markets.

We used statistical cluster analysis to enable us to split the whole group of 183 economic areas into a small number of relatively homogeneous groups using as few distinguishing variables as possible.[15] Then we matched the construction data for these 183 market areas with economic data (supplied by NPA Data Services, Inc.) for population, employment by type, personal income, and other categories and with housing data from the Census of Population. We found very strong relationships between levels of residential and nonresidential construction on the one hand and growth in population and in employment in the same markets on the other. Total per capita dollars for all categories of construction were generally greater in the metropolitan portions of the economic areas than in the nonmetropolitan portions, and new housing units as a percentage of 1980 stock were also higher in the metropolitan portion.

Then, for each economic area, we compared the projected trend values to actual total construction for each year of the 1980–87 period and, of course (for the first time ever), actual permits for all residential and nonresidential categories in that area. Lastly, the statistical program we used produced clusters of economic areas that seemed to have similar characteristics as markets for new construction. The first three clusters contained (a) the nation's fastest growing economic areas: Dallas, Orlando, Austin, Las Vegas, Anchorage, (b) Los Angeles as a unique place, and (c) Houston, Denver, Salt Lake City, Reno, Grand Junction. Cluster (d) contained nineteen areas all in the West or Southeast, cluster (e) contained sixty-one slightly slower-growing areas, cluster (f) was New York by itself, cluster (g) contained the old elephants: Chicago, Philadelphia, San Francisco, Boston, and Detroit, and cluster (h) had the remaining eighty-six relatively smaller and more heterogeneous areas.

We did not realize when we were analyzing the data for all these places that these were the years when the savings and loan system was foundering. No one has a clue, so far as I know, about how much of all the construction in Figure 12.1 was financed by the savings and loans confraternity, but the importance of this strange episode in our national life is that it marked the tragic end of decades of work that Democrats and Republicans alike had put into creating a financial system that could support the efforts of developers as well as of aspiring homeowners and working families saving for their old age.

I looked over a cartload of books devoted to the situation, some contemporaneous with the events, most written later, but none was as well researched or reflected as great a sense of outrage as the situation deserved (outrage that has never been forthcoming from either the federal government or the defrauded taxpaying public) as a small book with an appropriately big title, *Big Money Crime: Fraud and Politics in the Savings and Loan Crisis,* by Kitty Calavita and Henry N. Pontell at the University of California (Irvine) and Robert H. Tillman at St. John's University (Jamaica, New York).[16] The excellent little history they compiled as background for the astounding and true tales they tell is largely unknown to the general public, and it is a privilege to set it forth in full in the appendix, "A Short History of S&Ls." It illustrates how political dogma that insists on dismantling basic regulations in an industry set up to serve the public can, wittingly or unwittingly, end up not only disserving the public but sending it a half-trillion dollar bill in addition.

The book, extensively covering dollar crime in the capitalist system, goes into considerable detail to explain how the operators managed to perpetrate their games of fraud and deception.[17] Of course some apologists said that the troubles were the fault of bad governmental policies, or unanticipated falls in real estate values, or misguided or inept lending practices, or inflation, or excessive risk-taking behavior. Not at all, say Calavita and company, as they list and describe various types of fraud: Your bank is about to fail, but pay large dividends anyway. Give a loan to a borrower who then invests in your own project. Cozen your appraisers so they will provide the needed high appraisals. Sell stock in your new bank and use the proceeds to pay interest and dividends, otherwise known as a Ponzi scheme. Make loans that are contingent on some other action by a borrower. Pay exorbitantly large bonuses to officers, board members, and employees. Engage in "land flips" by selling the same property back and forth between friends at ever increasing prices. And use something called a "daisy chain." Calavita's team felt that the Resolution Trust Corporation (RTC), set up by the federal government to resolve the crisis, and the congressional inquiries into the RTC's efforts hardly scratched the surface about the fraud inherent in the industry.[18]

I hardly imagined a situation like this that could end up costing the federal government at least $500 billion (and create so many private fortunes when the RTC sold off its inventory of distressed thrift institutions) when I was writing my own book only a few years earlier; that book, *The Real Estate Gamble*, covered many instances of greed and stupidity in the real estate investment industry between 1925 and 1980, a period reasonably free of such collusive behavior.[19] Nor were my colleagues and I thinking about arrant fraud when, from 1981 to 1983 we were publishing a monthly economic letter, *The State of the Region*, about economics in the five northwest states and found that data about the region's thrift institutions that we had been receiving in a timely manner from the local branch of the Federal Home Loan Bank Board began to arrive late and then not at all, just when the bad times were coming in earnest. *Big Money Crime* is thus a most welcome look at what was really going on behind some scenes.

The savings and loan disaster marks the end of the GI Generation's suzerainty. In the late 1990s, the Whitewater investigators laid bare all the detailed comings and goings of scores of people connected in one way or another with President Clinton and the case. It was the first time the public had been given a full case study about how one institution invested its funds as an example of how those hundreds of billions of dollars had been invested before similar institutions went bankrupt. A few of the Bush family were involved in similar cases, but little was made of them in the press of the day. The exquisite torture inflicted on Bill Clinton, the first U.S. president from the Boom Generation, on the participants, and on the reading public during the investigation produced only a few penalties for minor infractions, and then the matter was laid to rest.

While the lesson may be that regulation of the mortgage industry is not such a bad thing for the general public after all, many of the egregiously large residential and commercial construction projects of the 1975–90 period might have been built anyhow as well-to-do Americans continued to demand a range of ever more capacious, exciting, and comprehensive facilities and services at places near and far, indeed sometimes far from the places where more conservative investors were building. Notwithstanding the characteristically high interest rates of the late 1970s and 1980s, the venture capitalists of the day, including major Japanese investors, competed with one another to satisfy the perceived demand for fancy new facilities. It took real estate markets a long time to absorb the inventory of projects built (or half built) before the collapse of the savings and loan binge of the early 1980s.

But by the 1990s, life in the new suburbia, life in the central cities, and life along the interstates all began to suffer from congestion and to show visible evidence of unpleasant changes in both natural and human-made environments. The time had come for some serious evaluation of urban growth now that it had occurred.

The Rise of New, Smart Desprawling Ideas

The popular format for discussing the American metropolis these days is most emphatically not the comprehensive Orfield model discussed above but merely something called "sprawl," which becomes the object of various remedies advanced to cure it. These approaches include "smart growth" and "new urbanism." My instinct is always to try to evaluate those approaches in the context of the basic changes in governance that might encourage higher levels of "comprehensive planning and redesign" for an entire metropolis. I have not had an easy time keeping track of the work of the pioneers of these approaches, despite the continually growing pile of professional and popular pamphlets, periodicals, books, and newspaper articles I have collected on the subject. Naturally, before writing anything about this emerging field, I looked for definitions and reports of the first appearance of these techniques. To my delight, I found the following in the Oxford English Dictionary:

> *Sprawl* [from Old English and Frisian]. . . . The act of sprawling, an awkward or clumsy spreading out of the limbs. . . . A struggling array or display of something . . . [as an intransitive verb:] To move the limbs in a convulsive effort or struggle; to toss about or spread oneself out; in later use, to be stretched out on the ground, etc., in an ungainly or awkward manner; . . . to crawl from one place to another in a struggling or ungraceful manner.

This definition reminds me of much of the rhetoric of both European and American town and country planners in the 1950s describing urban conditions in terms of human anatomy, with avenues becoming arteries, the central city as the heart of the metropolis, and parks and open spaces being lungs (just as Frederick Law Olmsted had suggested a century earlier). Now we have the suburbs as limbs scattered awkwardly around the landscape and forcing suburbanites to crawl from place to place in a struggling, ungraceful manner, surely as good a description of traffic congestion as any I've read.

So far as I can discover, the word "sprawl" began to be applied to suburban America only in the 1960s, by which time much of the suburban infrastructure put in place during World War II and the decades immediately following had made it easier for massive amounts of real estate development to occur. Closely associated with such development are the twin phenomena of fiscally impaired local governments and crowded highways. Sprawl rose higher in consciousness with the publication in 1974 by the Council on Environmental Quality, U.S. Department of Housing and Urban Development, and the Environmental Protection Agency (EPA) of *The Costs of Sprawl: Environmental and Economic Costs of Alternative Residential Development Patterns at the Urban Fringe*, a work that David Bollier says "remains seminal and entirely relevant theoretically to contemporary sprawl."

Bollier put together an important guide into these topics, *How Smart Growth Can Stop Sprawl* for the Sprawl Watch Clearinghouse.[20] Since I touch only lightly in this book on the prescriptions being advanced currently for unscrambling one or all of American metropolises, I offer the table of contents of Bollier's guide as an example of the broad range of more or less familiar topics that get explored together as the context for serious work by the leaders of the antisprawl movement.

I. The Hidden Subsidies and Long-Term Costs of Sprawl
   A. The Subsidized Supremacy of the Automobile
   B. Twin Pathologies: Urban Disinvestment and Suburban Sprawl
   C. How the Tax System Encourages Sprawl
   D. Sprawl Fuels Racial Polarization and Social Inequity
   E. How Residential Segregation and Sprawl Are Linked
   F. The "Spatial Mismatch" Between the Urban Poor and Suburban Jobs
   G. City/Suburban Inequalities in Public Education
   H. The Vast Environmental Harm Caused by Sprawl
   I. The Elimination of Farmland and Open Spaces
   J. Sprawl and the Loss of Community and Quality of Life
   Conclusion: Creating New American Myths
II. Strategies That Can Revitalize Cities and Arrest Sprawl
   A. The Benefits of Regionalism

Bollier ends his book with a useful list of fifty-three organizations and Websites of philanthropic foundations and a list of sixty-one books and reports covering the political, economic, environmental, racial, transportation-related, agricultural, urban design, and architectural aspects of American urban sprawl. With the exception of two items concerning sprawl in Europe and elsewhere and five other books published before 1990, the bibliographic selections were all written in the 1990s. The five oldies are classics in the field: Kenneth Jackson's *Crabgrass Frontier* (1985), Jane Jacobs's *The Death and Life of Great American Cities* (1961), Christopher Alexander's architectural guide *Pattern Language* (1979), David Burchell and David Listokin's anthology *Energy and Land Use* (1982), and the aforementioned EPA-HUD report, *The Costs of Sprawl* (1974).

I think I need to say an extra word here about that definitive book that Kenneth Jackson wrote about the rise and future of the suburbs in America. His descriptions of the experiences of many developers and a few utopians in creating suburbs on the "crabgrass frontier" around most of the major cities in the nineteenth century show how accustomed Americans were to the idea, but the reality, as he also shows, was that the suburbs served primarily very well-to-do families and the working families required to provide for their comfort, while efforts to make houses affordable to the entire range of economic classes and to lease instead of sell building sites to rich families were equally unsuccessful. Jackson's only reference to Ebenezer Howard is in connection with the building of the New Deal's greenbelt cities in the 1930s. Jackson's strong conclusion in 1985 was that suburbanization would continue to conquer the urban world, but I could not find either the word "sprawl" or any discussion of methods for ameliorating the effects of sprawl.

I am sorry that Bollier does not mention the intense activity in local town halls and city councils across the nation that had been engendered decades ago, first as a result of the publication of solid research concerning the true cost of new developments to suburban municipalities and then as a result of applying fiscal-impact fees based on such studies, the latter topic, of course, encouraging law suits by developers.[21] Nor, for that matter, have contemporary writers on sprawl yet evaluated the usefulness of the environmental impact statements that were mandated in the 1970s to anticipate and prevent some of the bad effects of sprawling.

At the same time, I have no doubt that the proponents of the smart-growth approach know and appreciate these intellectual and political foundations of their field, and so I have come to believe that the main contribution that the smart-growth folks and new urbanists are making to our American life is not in the creation of entirely new ideas, for virtually all the basic ideas have been around for some time, but in forging a political will to allow some changes to be made. Advocates of better and saner policies may not have made great political progress since the 1970s when states adopted state environmental policy acts as required to support the National Environmental Policy Act (NEPA), which began the environmental-impact assessment process across the land, and when some states, such as Oregon, went further and adopted "urban growth" legislation. But perhaps the smart-growth partisans should be given the credit for assuring that all the platforms for the 2000 presidential election adopted by the major political parties were forced to deal with sprawl as one of the public's most pressing issues, and the smart-growth people can also take some of the credit for popularizing a better understanding of the extent to which sprawl has largely been created by governmental subsidies to middle-income homeowners and car owners. Over the coming decades, governmental leaders will be pressed to find political will to make the various deep changes required to create more sensible metropolises.

Some useful distinctions need to be made between smart-growth and new-urbanism platforms. Bollier writes

> What distinguishes smart growth from sprawl, according to the U.S. EPA's Smart Growth Network, is its ability to "make the link between development and quality of life." Smart growth recognizes that how buildings are built and where development takes place are the factors that make development either a community asset or liability. Smart growth advocates seek growth and development where it will build community, protect environmental amenities, promote fiscal health and keep taxes low, maximize return on public and private investment, and encourage economic efficiency. Smart growth, it should be added, tries to achieve these goals by focusing on market structures, public subsidies and other signals and incentives that affect development and land use.[22]

Frankly, I had been under the impression throughout the last fifty years or so of my professional life that all such smart-growth goals were exactly what city and regional planners were trained to do in their role as public employees charged with protecting the public interest. But perhaps the onslaught of the Reagan administration changed the nature of the planning profession more than I realized, making the profitability of a private-public developmental partnership the model for municipal action more impelling than protecting the public interest in all those goals listed for smart-growth action. Most progressive planners have remained dubious about the new-urbanism model.[23] Many planners, however, have been participants in a process that forfeited much respect for local government decisions that seemed to give developers relatively free rein to build and build some more while the municipality was forced to raise taxes in order to supply the necessary roads and other public services for the community and to fulfill its end of the bargain with the developers. So the smart-growth folks can be complimented on their diligence and optimism in taking a new, much needed, and properly comprehensive view of the steps that we can take to work ourselves out of the present set of impasses.[24]

At this point, now that the Boom Generation constitutes the leader-ship cadre and the Thirteenth and Millennium generations are in the line of succession, I am tempted to say that the operative distinctions be-tween Shiny Babbitt and Do-Good Ebenezer that seemed useful in deal-ing with life in the first few postwar decades are no longer really valid. Perhaps the most important reason is that the range of politically likely alternatives has narrowed now that most of the slums have been razed or gentrified, now that most of the inner-city families who wish to migrate to the suburbs have gotten there (aided by the creation of private schools where public schools do not satisfy), now that most people want and may already have the kind of houses and suburban amenities that were the goals of the Shiny Babbitts, and, sadly, now that the issues of racial discrimination, elimination of poverty, overcrowding for some poor people, and homelessness for others, are all now dominated by federal and state legislation that is largely beyond the influence, much less con-trol, of any set of local officials or advocacy groups.

I believe that most people share common goals with regard to im-proving the quality of life in both suburb and central city, but some are harder of heart and less willing than others to pay taxes for the public goods and services that only taxes can support. Assuming that both smart-growth advocates and new urbanists are among those willing to support public initiatives, a fair distinction is that the smart-growth advocates seem to be more interested in designing at the scale of the metropolis than the new urbanists, who tend to be the architects of specific residen-tial developments that are said to have community-building characteris-tics. Here is how the new urbanists describe their movement:

> New Urbanism is an urban design movement that burst onto the scene in the late 1980s and early 1990s. New Urbanists aim to reform all aspects of real estate development. Their work affects regional and local plans. They are involved in new development, urban retrofits, and suburban infill. In all cases, New Urbanist neighborhoods are walkable, and contain a diverse range of housing and jobs. New Urbanists support regional plan-ning for open space, appropriate architecture and planning, and the bal-anced development of jobs and housing. They believe these strategies are the best way to reduce how long people spend in traffic, to increase the supply of affordable housing, and to rein in urban sprawl. Many other issues, such as historic restoration, safe streets, and green building are also covered in the Charter of the New Urbanism, the movement's semi-nal document.[25]

A famous article, "Home From Nowhere" by James Howard Kunstler (one of the authors in Bollier's list), which appeared in the September 1996 issue of the *Atlantic Monthly,* caused something of a sensation in municipal planning offices across the nation.[26] Kunstler showed, and it is undoubtedly true, that practically none of the new-urbanism ideas can be put in place if traditional regulations (mostly outside of the broader scope of "planning" and closer to architectural standards) were followed; what "planning" is all about at the current time is the subject of much thought in other circles.[27] Kunstler showed explicitly in words and pictures how difficult, if not impossible, it would be for the new-urbanist kind of community to be built under typical zoning regulations that were responsible for the contorted, unsightly, inefficient shape of our urban areas and that led to the smart-growth movement. These regulations lie in wait for developers and builders wanting permits and prevent realization of most of the new-urbanist concepts.

Under the typical set of existing regulations, there probably can be no stores near residences, no sidewalk cafes, no curbside trees or parallel parking, while the requirement for off-street parking makes site planning unnecessarily difficult. Moreover, large-lot zoning regulations for single-family houses require houses to be larger and farther apart and set further back than called for by new-urbanist designers, streets must be wider, miniparks are not allowed (only large open spaces), there can be no business uses in houses, and so on. And Kunstler notes, with regard to an oft-mentioned side effect of satisfying the American dream,

> It is no small irony that during the period of America's greatest prosperity, in the decades following the Second World War, we put up almost nothing but the cheapest possible buildings, particularly civic buildings. Compare any richly embellished firehouse or post office built in 1904 with its dreary concrete-box counterpart today. Compare the home of a small-town bank president of the 1890s, with its massive masonry walls and complex roof articulation, with the flimsy home of a 1990s business leader, made of two-by-fours, Sheetrock, and fake fanlight windows. When we were a far less wealthy nation, we built things with the expectation that they would endure. To throw away money (painfully acquired) and effort (painfully expended) on something certain to fall apart in thirty years would have seemed immoral, if not insane, in our great-grandparents' day.[28]

The fact is that the cities and towns in which our great-grandparents lived, circa 1900, were transmogrified into the urban sprawl of 2000 by millions of people building one project at a time under the regulations and economic realities that prevailed at that moment. My guess is that the world envisaged by the smart urbanists of the present time will get created, if allowed to happen at all, by the same types of small increments repeated millions of times in tens of thousands of places. Perhaps the saving grace is that much of the flimsy construction of the postwar period, what songstress Malvina Reynolds called all those ticky-tacky boxes, can be replaced in due time without too much trouble on land laid out to encourage better community-wide relationships with more suitably designed structures.[29]

Practically everyone admits that suburbanites have more cultural, shopping, and employment opportunities nearby than before but, at the same time, have found it more difficult to move around and park in recent years. Yet "we like it" is a prevailing sentiment.[30] What is going on to correct whatever can be corrected? Presumably urban planners will be involved—and what they might say is currently a matter of speculation in the profession.[31]

Positive change, if/as/when it happens, will probably be in accord with the planning philosophy of "disjointed incrementalism"[32] and may well consist of many small changes, some at the level of the individual family and its patch of land, some the result of "smarter" architecture, and "smarter" decisions by city and town zoning and planning boards and legislative bodies.

The open question for those of us who consider ourselves "progressive" in attitude is whether the smart-growth movement is dealing adequately with the nation's growing racial and economic divide, with "the urban problem," with "the ghettoization of the central city," and with the parlous condition of our health and education systems, all problems that used to concern the nation. The answers to that question may be lurking somewhere in the way in which the nation will address the disarray of the believers in a New Economics in the first few years of the new millennium, and not least in the way Congress will legislate suitable amendments and improvements (or even repeal of the 1996 Temporary Assistance to Needy Families Act), and, lastly, in the way the urban scene changes as a result of the September 11, 2001, terrorist attacks.

V

Looking Onward

13
The Metropolitan System in Gear

Aspects of Metropolitanism

Today's America can be visualized as a collection of conurbations, together with some less-populated metropolises and a few economic areas where nature has inhibited significant settlement by humans. The incoming generations must take this array of inhabited places as a given and change them as they can. My intent in this penultimate chapter is to consider the present conditions by which such changes might be induced. Thus the topics below include a look at the implications of our present condition—that the metropolis has come to dominate the city and that the metropolis must deal with the globalization of the economy—together with some thoughts on likely scales and rates of change within the metropolis.

The metropolis has replaced the central city as the focus of any serious attention given to the urban sector of the nation, and, to a large extent almost everywhere, the central city itself is no longer the dominant member of the metropolis's community of local governments. At this early stage, my guess is that there is a fairly low probability that those diverse local governments will have either the political will or the technical ability to work together to implement, with enthusiasm and resources, the ideas of the smart-growth-new-urbanism movements, although those movements may bring some important and positive ideas to the present set of activities that are shaping the metropolises of the nation. Positive change is our only hope, but we must also assume that many familiar processes for making decisions for the metropolis will continue in effect. Those decisions will have measurable effects on the various population groupings and multitudinous minor civil divisions in the typical metropolis.

I also suspect that the metropolises will need to tap their own fiscal resources far more than ever before to the limit permitted by state laws. The federal interest in cities specifically and, more broadly, in the structure, efficacy, and equity of the American federalist system as a whole seems to have been dissolved in the mists of "devolution" following the incursions wrought by the U.S. Congresses elected in 1994 and thereafter. Where our bookshelves were full of federal studies of urban problems and prospects in the 1960s and 1970s, together with the enlightened work of the U.S. Advisory Commission on Intergovernmental Relations and the associated committees in Congress, little of the sort has been added in recent decades and no such inquiries are in the offing at this writing.

The metropolises themselves are often described as "networks" now, rather than central places out of which spokes lead to suburbs. Effective oversight of the American metropolis as a cohesive entity, much less real accountability for its governing bodies, is literally unknown. In a few instances, major cities have been merged with the county of which they are a part, and, in most metropolises, some kind of formal collaborative mechanism exists to provide a meeting place for the scores or hundreds of autonomous general governments and special-function governmental entities in the area, but I know of no effective metropolitan-wide governing body anywhere in the nation. As a result, decision making in the urban sector is diffuse to the point of entropy, a condition in which there are so many conflicting points of view, so many political considerations, so many dimensions to any question, that the system is too full of dispersed energies, "noisiness," and, in the dictionary definition, "randomness, disorder, and chaos," for any kind of consistent policy making to be implemented. Indeed, the lack of fair, equitable policy making for our metropolises is, I believe, the most serious of all our urban problems, for almost all the urban problems of our society demand metropolitan-wide solutions (with or without financial assistance from higher levels of government) rather than citywide ones.

In similar fashion, where the voice of the power elite used to be accepted as the voice of the community rather than just as the voice of the elite of the private sector, the members of that leadership group, notably the community's bankers, mercantile captains, and major industrialists, have left town or are now involved in global rather than local concerns. The voice of the people in the metropolitan community, however, is muffled, so that important questions of social equity and of respect for different cultures may not get to the table where the elected officials and the powerful sit. The resultant need for capable leaders is considered in the next chapter.

We Americans are still in the age of the automobile and the scatteration it causes, so all programs that involve the construction of major facilities must pander to the existing array of automobile users. Almost unendurable pushes and pulls among the interested parties must be expected if our metropolises are to begin to balance total pandering to the car-users with some addition to the local mass transportation facilities (and I note here that mass transportation facilities were not in evidence in the cities my wife and I drove through and described in Chapter 12 above). While New York's wonderful mass transit networks justify and are supported by high-density projects (making reconstruction of the World Trade Center somewhat simpler), no high-density development whose occupants would have to rely on transit can be imagined, at this writing, in any metropolis not already well-served by mass transit (meaning many intersecting lines and maximum five-minute waits) unless the development also provides ready access by automobile and a bountiful, convenient supply of parking.

Impact of Globalization on the Metropolitan Economy

The World Trade Center (WTC) that collapsed in the attack on New York on September 11, 2001, enjoyed its stature as the epitome of high-density edifice-building, but it was also the working home of countless participants in the globalizing economy that affects every aspect of urban America.

Concern about the globalization that was affecting the thousands of workers on the streets of Seattle during the 1999 protests against the World Trade Organization (WTO) reflected the basic economic issues that had bedeviled the cities of the United States during the Great Depression, when it was painfully clear that the collapse of international trade was a prime cause of the long lines of the unemployed lining the streets of America. President Franklin D. Roosevelt led the parade away from the gold standard that had dominated world trade in the twentieth century to that point, but it was not until the end of World War II that the victorious nations dealt with the question directly. They established the International Monetary Fund (IMF), the International Bank for Reconstruction and Development (the World Bank), and the General Agreement on Tariffs and Trade (GATT, out of which came, years later, the WTO), a triad of institutions to deal with some of the critical aspects of international cooperation in monetary affairs, economic development, and trade.

After World War II we helped rebuild the economies of Germany and Japan, enabling them to obtain modern industrial facilities able to compete more successfully than we had imagined with the aging, obsolete iron and steel and other factories of what came to be called America's Rust Belt. The Rust Belt, in the middle of the country, contained factories that closed as cheaper products piled in from new sources and new factories abroad, a process that continues at this writing. As a result, all through the 1950s and 1960s, city and regional planners worked to find new sources of employment for cities and towns in the Rust Belt, work that was paralleled by the efforts to bring the communities of Appalachia into the mainstream by building roads into the mountains. Vigorous but ultimately unsuccessful efforts were made to enable local workers to buy going businesses or branches of major corporations that were scheduled for departure from communities where they had been for generations; the classic case is that of Youngstown Steel in the 1970s.

By the 1970s and 1980s, attention had shifted to the steady drift of U.S. factories from stateside locations to the border with Mexico and to Asia, and to the steady growth in imports of agricultural produce and both consumer and industrial goods from plantations and manufacturing plants in underdeveloped former-colonies-become-nations. American consumers were buying such foreign-made goods with abandon because their prices were so much lower than those of goods made and produce grown in the United States, but many local communities mourned the absence of local employers who had picked up and left, sometimes without saying proper good-byes, taking with them even such incorporeal items as the pension funds that local families had been relying upon.

The relatively strong unionization of the workforce in the Rust Belt states and the relatively strong environmental laws passed by the federal and state governments in the 1970s and 1980s encouraged American firms to seek ways of moving production offshore. America's growing trade deficits, the value of imports exceeding the value of exports in any given period, were merely exacerbated by the willingness of the U.S. government's Export-Import Bank to make low-cost loans to foreign governments and airlines to enable them to buy airplanes made in America by unionized companies. A major objective of the Reagan administration, I believe, was to drive the American union movement as far into oblivion as it could, beginning with the destruction of the air

controllers' union early in Reagan's first term. The National Labor Relations Board was made increasingly unhelpful to union organizing efforts thereafter. Reagan's love affair with rigidly applied Laffer-curve
supply side economics and Friedman-type monetary policies marked
the effective setting aside (with no attempt to relegislate) of the national
goals and methods expressed in the Full Employment Act of 1946. Mag-
nification of the gaps between rich families and working families in
America was only exacerbated by the "reforms" in the 1996 Tax Act.

The drive by a Democrat in the White House to get Congress to ap-
prove the North American Free Trade Agreement and to enable a president to sign trade agreements that would thereafter have a fast track to
Congressional approval with only a minimal amount of review was a
sign that the unions were no longer able to play as significant a role in
American political life as they had in the days of the Wagner Labor
Relations Act of the 1930s; the postwar Taft-Hartley Act and the later
activities of the conservative (or George Wallace) wing of the union
severely weakened the union movement.

The long-term decline in the proportion of the nation's work force
employed by manufacturing enterprises was certainly part of the reason
why less and less concern was directed to the plights of factory workers,
unionized or not. Part of the increase in the service sector is attributed to
the development of computers and the so-called information industries.
Computerized operations were steadily replacing workers on the factory
floor with highly trained technicians at computer consoles. Factories themselves were changing character, fashioning high-value, small-sized, low-
weight objects where once they were making large, heavy, capital
equipment and bulky objects in the form of both industrial and consumer
goods. In the distant past of the 1960s, the lovers of cities speculated
about the coming of a postindustrial society featuring pollution-free manufacturing, decentralized offices connected with computers in the homes,
and large amounts of leisure time devoted to cultural and recreational
activities and adult education.[1]

In 1983, Jane Jacobs wrote a most intriguing book, *Cities and the Wealth
of Nations* (cited earlier), which provides a still-fresh perspective on all
these issues.[2] She observed, first, that most of the productive activities in
the world were occurring in a limited number of metropolitan areas. The
profits from activities in these areas were being siphoned off by national
governments and redistributed to the less dynamic areas of those nations,
to the detriment of those living in the productive metropolises and of sub-

optimal benefit to those outside the boundaries of these fortunate places. Her analysis of this situation led her to conclude that the productive metropolises of the world had manufactured their own luck by steady attention to acquiring capital by abstaining from reliance on imported goods, reinvesting their surplus profits in new capacity, and finding export markets for their products. Those markets tended to be primarily in other metropolises around their own country and abroad that were performing in a similar manner. Thus nation-states themselves, she said, had become functionally obsolete and could be abandoned.

The world would be composed thereafter of productive metropolises linked together by trade, and the key to uplift for all the areas left out of the original band of high-productivity metropolises was a program quite opposed to the neoliberal type promoted in country after country by the World Bank and the IMF. The program that Jacobs hoped each such lagging area would adopt would require it to, first, stop exporting its raw materials and importing consumption goods, second, start making its own consumer goods and industrial equipment even though the quality at the beginning would be much lower than its citizens were accustomed to, all in order to acquire capital by minimizing purchases of high-cost consumer goods from elsewhere; until, third, it could use its new store of investable capital to create its own self-sustaining economy with a reasonable volume of export goods, thus joining the confraternity of viable metropolises.

What was actually happening in the U.S. urban world? For the last decade or so (and even more so as the economy finally drifted officially into recession in 2001), I have felt that the result of all the changes in industry and commerce, domestically and internationally, had to be that family incomes would be downsized as union salaries were replaced by fast-food-restaurant wages while families maintained their levels of consumption by increasing credit-card debt. Eventually those levels would fall and, as a result, the ability of consumption outlays to sustain the general economy of the U.S. would be seriously impaired.

In any case, in addition to losing basic manufacturing and department stores, cities were losing bank branches and locally owned newspapers and other media, while city residents were getting used to importing most of their food from factories and farms a thousand miles away from their tables as a result of the merger of local food producers into national corporations. A spate of neoliberal economists promised a golden era if "free trade" could take over and free markets flourish. A far more grounded set of observers held out for "fair trade" that would respect the rights of labor and the right to a sensible, safe environment for all people, and for a "fair economy" that closed the yawning chasms between rich and poor, providing "jobs with justice," strong "safety nets," good educations and health services for all citizens, and a better "social contract" than that promised by the free-traders.

In the process, little attention was paid to what used to be called the urban problem, nor were there congressional hearings of the sort common in the 1960s and 1970s. Perhaps the problems were not urgent enough to get the nation excited; perhaps the situation in the inner cities was not quite as dire as I had come to believe. In any case, the nation seemed to tear through the 1990s as though high-tech industries (created by Boomers and many in the Thirteenth Generation) would be sufficient to support our whole economy, with the rest of us somehow fitted into whatever niches were left over after the world economy became globalized. Presumably our urbanized economy could prosper in the age of a wireless Internet and broadband communication systems.

The protests in Seattle at the time of the WTO meeting notwithstanding, the problems of inner cities were hardly mentioned, if at all, in the 2000 presidential campaign, and the fact that family incomes in the metropolises might be blasted by too much free trade serving neoliberal global-scale corporations was not admissible in the debates. The candidates did agree that the problems of middle-income suburbs, where most of the potential voters lived, were of concern to the nation, for voters did not like sprawl, loss of open space, or traffic congestion. None of the candidates, however, showed any sign of being able to imagine an American metropolis where a family with children could live without one or more automobiles, nor could any one imagine the American people "willing to sacrifice" in order to eliminate our dependence on and love for the individually owned automobile and its dependence on foreign oil.

Note on Likely Scales and Rates of Metropolitan Development

In the globalized world, the WTC itself was the epitome of high-order business-oriented planning as it was performed in the second half of the twentieth century, and now the question is whether that kind of megalithic activity will be repeated as New York rebuilds.[3]

The WTC was as big, awesome, unnerving, and posh as anything built in the United States in the twentieth century, but I am on the side of those who think that it should not be rebuilt in the same fashion and that at least part of it should be reconstituted as a memorial not only to those who died but to the passing of the kind of megalomania that makes nations compete to have the highest building in the world. The discussion on this subject on public radio a day or two after the attack featured a landscape architect who hoped to see thousands of trees planted on the spot, one for each of the people who died there. Others felt that the soul, or certainly the ego, of the United States was wrapped up in rebuilding to show that nothing can daunt us.

The ways that sites in major cities change over time in response to external changes are endlessly fascinating to observe and are also critical inputs in framing development strategies. New York provides an interesting context for the discussion of such change. In 1900 the shoreline west of New York's financial district was used for shipping, with a full complement of public wharves, berths for great ocean liners, warehouses, and ferry terminals. At the Battery was Castle Garden, built in 1807 as a fort, later turned into a theater and opera house that hosted the Marquis de La Fayette in 1824 (he had been a major general in the American Revolution) and a few years later P.T. Barnum's Jenny Lind (a famous Swedish soprano), then, from 1855 to 1889, serving as the immigrant landing depot through which some 8 million immigrants (including my father and his parents) passed before all that activity was transferred to Ellis Island out in the bay; then, until 1939, housing the aquarium that I visited as a boy growing up in Manhattan; and finally, having narrowly avoided complete destruction when the Brooklyn-Battery Tunnel was built, becoming a national monument and serving as the southerly anchor of the waterside developments that included the WTC.

Massive redevelopment of that mile of waterfront, after New York City officials in the 1950s determined it was a "blighted area" as required for inclusion in New York's slum clearance and redevelopment program and thus qualified for federal assistance under the Housing Act of 1949, demanded the attention of the kings of the financial industry who worked in what were then considered tall buildings around Wall Street. As a project, or rather what turned out to be a series of projects, the redevelopment represents something of an all-time pinnacle in the arts of central city rebuilding as masterminded by members of the GI Generation. This set of projects transcended the earlier sketches for redevelopment under the control of New York's redevelopment czar, Robert Moses, a member of the Lost Generation.[4] The leadership role was given to (or perhaps taken by) David Rockefeller, Ph.D., head of the Chase (and soon to be Chase-Manhattan) Bank, and his committee of leading citizens. A similar brand of strong leadership, in this case involving many of the same institutions that combined their effort in the 1960s, will certainly be required to reach agreement on whatever change or reconstruction occurs hereafter on top of and near the sad remains of the massive foundations of the old WTC.

C. Wright Mills, author of *The Power Elite,* and Robert and Helen Lynd, authors of *Middletown* (it turned out the model was Columbus, Ohio), described how a small group of influential business and social leaders holds the real power of decision making in the typical city or town.[5] In New York City in the 1960s, the city planners and even the legislators on the city council were, to a large extent, in the service of such an elite group. Only the Port of New York Authority could have managed to build the WTC in the face of opposition from the major real estate moguls in town, who objected strenuously to having so much vacant office space thrown on the market at one time by a public body.[6] The Port Authority, being an interstate compact approved by the U.S. Congress, stood above such criticism and was responsible only to an unelected board of directors appointed by the governors of New York and New Jersey, who were de facto members of the power elite that inhabited Manhattan's financial center. Since the early 1920s, the Port Authority, in fact, had been exploring the limits of being an autonomous governmental body; it had used its powers of eminent domain and sold revenue bonds to build bridges and tunnels between the two states and, after the original costs of the projects had been recovered, kept tolls high in order to keep on receiving large revenues; these surplus revenues were then bankrolled to build and operate new projects for ships, trucking and warehousing firms, and all the motor vehicles and airplanes operating in the New York area.

In 1940, plaintiffs in an important lawsuit claimed that the Port Authority was actually a for-profit company in disguise.[7] The success of the Port Authority in getting the courts to declare that it was really a form of government and not a private corporation had a major ripple effect by encouraging a number of states in the postwar period to establish such authorities, using their capacity to sell "revenue" bonds that were usually not backed by the state's full faith and credit and that were exempt from federal and state income taxes in order to assist in the building of toll highways, airports, college dormitories, and industrial facilities.

Whether, in this first decade of the twenty-first century, any public authority anywhere in America, even the Port of New York Authority, would be able to muster public confidence so that it could erect office buildings for rent to private firms on a scale that would rattle the owners of all the real estate for miles around is unclear, even with the backing of a local power elite. American life before September 11, 2001, had acquired an antigovernment claque with influence out of proportion to its numbers, and whether those critics would suppress their dislike of such governmental operations in the aftermath of such a terrorist attack is a question. In any case, the power elites have absented themselves from their roles as the kingpins of the municipalities of the country. Locally owned banks, department stores, and industrial companies that were important voices for a myriad of localities in development programming in the 1960s and before are typically now branches of national or international firms that have no particular attachment to place and possibly more affinity for suburban malls and office parks than for central city downtowns.

My own experience suggests the idea that the age of large central city urban renewal programs in the United States is pretty much over (replaced by many small-scale developments in smaller centers dispersed across the metropolis), and I continue to have my doubts whether the events of September 11 will cause a reversal in the long withdrawal of public favor for (or just acquiescence to) such massive changes in land use and occupancy as occurred during the 1950s and 1960s when urban redevelopment and highway programs ripped into and through the cities and towns of the nation. My own career was actually heavily involved with all those programs. In the mid-1950s in New York, after a year at ACTION that was my introduction to the real world of planning and redevelopment, I worked on the study of New York's economy performed by the Regional Plan Association of New York for the Port of New York Authority. This in turn led to my working on the Bowery Quadrangle project, conceptualized by Abraham Kazan of the great Amalgamated Housing Corporation. Amalgamated, the creator of some 100,000 units of moderate-income cooperative apartments, had been appointed by Robert Moses to be the nonprofit sponsor of the proposed Cooper Square Urban Redevelopment Project under Title I of the Housing Act of 1949. Cooper Square, a very large project in itself, was connected to a proposed major cross-Manhattan highway at Houston Street that Robert Moses had also proposed. Amalgamated included the Bowery Quadrangle project as part of the overall project as a way of providing new, efficient, horizontal industrial space (of a type never to that time built in Manhattan) for a multiplicity of small firms that could employ all those thousands of people who would come to live in the apartments.

The crosstown highway and the Cooper Square-Bowery Quadrangle project died around 1960 as public distaste for the redevelopment process rose and, more importantly for my reeducation, as a progressive group of city planning professionals (Planners for Equal Opportunity [EO], which I joined shortly thereafter) and other lovers of cities began to realize not only that officials were neglecting to listen to the people affected by the urban renewal process, especially lower-income people and racial minorities, but that the planning profession itself was not including a fair proportion of minorities and women in its own ranks.[8] At that time in the late 1950s, many of us were attending meetings convened by Jane Jacobs who was trying to save part of Greenwich Village, an experience that ultimately led to the writing of her most famous book, *The Life and Death of Great Cities.*[9]

All in all, I had gained a fair knowledge of how redevelopment worked and was able to apply that knowledge as a consultant with the community economic development section of Arthur D. Little, Inc., an old-line consulting firm with headquarters in Cambridge, Massachusetts. I worked on economic and urban development studies in scores of cities across the United States, and many of the sponsors of the work were downtown power elites and the local agencies trying to accommodate them, hoping that their companies would not move out of town and hoping to encourage new investment in the community. The tendencies for these power elites to become dispersed and no longer of influence in a given city were vital topics in the early 1960s; over the years large national corporations scooped up smaller firms that had been important parts of local or regional economies, or closed factories in the north and transferred production and workers to the southern states, and, by the end of the century, globalization in all its various roles was the major concern.

So both the politics and economics of urban renewal have changed, it seems to me, since the WTC was begun in the 1960s. When I last walked through the entire riverfront from the Cortlandt Street subway stop to the Battery, a number of residential and office buildings just north of the World Financial Center were still under construction, evidence that the magnificent promenade along the waterfront had become the framework for creating a whole new kind of living in Manhattan. The apartment buildings themselves were bigger than such projects had been in earlier decades, in line with the giant corporations that had come to dominate the global economy. I was assuming, of course, that the WTC was tenanted primarily by such corporations, but, in fact, as analysis of the occupancy of the WTC after the attacks revealed, most of the firms in the buildings were small, although many operated as complements to major firms and considered themselves importantly involved in the care and feeding of the global economy.

Apparently most of the areas around the world that have been devastated by natural catastrophes or wars get rebuilt sooner or later, laid out more or less as before.[10] With regard to the WTC, incredibly complex questions about jurisdiction will have to be settled before any form of reconstruction takes place. For example, is the job the responsibility of the man who had leased the whole project from the Port Authority? The insurance companies want to know whether the attack was one event knocking down two towers and thus entitling the lessee to one check in compensation, or two events each justifying compensation. What roles should local and state governments, their politicians, and business and banking groups play in the decision making and financial arrangements hereafter? What should be the roles for the churches and labor unions who are ordinarily to be found on the side of any proposal (anywhere in the nation) that offers employment to their members? And where do "people in the community" (including those in mourning for family members lost in the rubble of the WTC) and a wide range of community or nongovernmental groups fit into such discussions and negotiations?

Most elusive of the conundrums will be discovering whether, as a result of the terrorist attack and subsequent exposure to terrorism, the federal government will become more interested in America's metropolises, their central cities generally and in New York City in particular. My guess is that only on very rare occasions in the future will the governments in the federal system subsidize urban redevelopment projects or enable private developers to create megaprojects. Whatever transpires in the inevitable remaking of significant portions of America in the twenty-first century will probably be on more modest scales than were common in the heyday of urban renewal in the century just past. On the other hand, if a metropolis does get the power to pull itself together under the kind of enabling legislation that I said on the first pages of this book was required, I have to admit the possibility that some Very Large Project Areas might get established and redeveloped, but, again, I do not think it likely that the federal government will be subsidizing such a program as was done with urban redevelopment and renewal under the Housing Act of 1940.

14

Remaking America in the Twenty-first Century

The twentieth century was full of irreversible human-made changes in both cityscape and landscape. The end of that century was notable for the well-celebrated beginning of a new millennium on December 31, 1999 (or was it 2000?), but I believe that the terrorist attacks of September 11, 2001, on New York's World Trade Center and Washington's Pentagon marked the beginning of significant changes in how we will rebuild America in the twenty-first century, and that, therefore, that day of infamy marks the change from the old century to the new one more clearly than the brouhaha about "Y2K" and the potential disarray of our computer-dependent capitalist society. Whether it will also mark the time when we work together on creating a less racist, more equitable society remains problematic.

But now "all other things being equal," the qualifying term in economic formulas and prognostications, has been expanded to include the possibility of damage to metropolitan America from overt terrorist acts as well as from major disasters. More changes to our system of making decisions about metropolitanization are inevitable, and they will come with whatever degree of guidance we have the will to get the system to deliver. If we are going to make any progress along the lines I recommended at the beginning of this book, we will need an informed public and strong but democratic leadership, but the well-entrenched processes discussed later in this last chapter will probably continue to shape the ways we make decisions about the built environment, unless we can figure out ways to replace them with better processes. And, despite the need for strong leaders and their visions, the need is even greater to protect our civil liberties from autocratic architect-builders such as are portrayed by Ayn Rand in *The Fountainhead*, a book that is lauded by the political right wing as the proper way to build a city.[1]

An example of the danger of having autocrats in charge is seen in *Metropolis,* a famous silent film made by Fritz Lang and Thea von Harbou in Germany in 1926, which I watched just before writing the early draft of these last two chapters. The setting is a city with tall buildings somewhat like the World Trade Center, all connected with skyways for automobiles that foreshadow both Norman Bel Geddes's influential depiction of the future for the General Motors exhibit at the 1939 New York World's Fair and the narrow urban canyons through which spaceships fly in science fiction movies made later in the twentieth century.[2] My film guide says the movie "details the horrors of a mechanized Utopia" that becomes a battleground for labor and capital.[3] The film opens with shots of hundreds of workers, dressed somewhat like those confined a few years later in Nazi concentration camps, shuffling off to their day-shift occupations. By the end of the film, the workers have destroyed the city but made peace with the "capitalists" who created the terrible working conditions and the dreary city spaces. The movie is redolent of the current struggle between the global capitalists operating the levers of power in international organizations such as the World Trade Organization and the collectivity of churches, labor unions, and environmentalists opposing them. The continuing struggles between Babbitts and Ebenezers are happily of a milder type.

From the turn of the century around 1900 until the mid-1960s, visionaries explored what the city of the future might look like and how it would feel to live in it and how such a city could be part of a possibly lovely society. I had not realized how early some of the famous books had appeared: Samuel Butler's *Erewhon* in 1872 and Edward Bellamy's *Looking Backward* in 1888. Then came Ebenezer Howard and his "social city of 1898," the garden city folks of 1902 who adopted only the nonsocietal part of his ideas, and, of course, the work of some of the twentieth century's great designers: Frank Lloyd Wright's Broadacre City and his Mile-High City, Norman Bel Geddes's General Motors exhibit at the New York World's Fair of 1939, and Le Corbusier's horizontal cities, to name a few, and we should remember all the learned disquisitions by my mentors after World War II as to the different forms and shapes that the emerging American metropolises could achieve with appropriate public policies and investments. America's two most promising post-war contributions to this art form were two "new towns," Robert

Simon's Reston, Virginia, and James Rouse's Columbia, Maryland, both of which were privately sponsored and financed. Only at the end of the mid-century's visionary period did President Lyndon Johnson bring forth his Great Society vision of the city without poverty and a metropolis with at least a few of his "new communities."

Since 1968 we have used up many of our form-giving options. Our metropolises have fewer relatively low-density or even never developed parcels of land where new housing, new business parks, and new malls might be located and fewer areas where parklands and pastures should remain. Redesigning, rezoning, and otherwise increasing density in single-family districts are conceivable but politically hazardous strategies almost everywhere in suburban America. New housing for the expected increases in population will undoubtedly make further inroads at the outer edges (euphemistically called "edge cities") in order to find suitably cheap land for development or be shoehorned into more central areas, but our utopian visions (and possibly our hopes for ecological protection) may have drifted out of sight.

As I searched for other people's visions, even as the Boom Generation took the helm of our society and might have spoken inspirationally to the Thirteenth and the Millennial generations, its juniors waiting in the wings, I was struck by how very few visions of the cities of the future got into print in 1999 on the eve of the 2000 millennium. The great task now as my Silent Generation passes into true silence is for new leadership to formulate new visions for the metropolises my generation is leaving behind.

In the previous chapter, I wrote that the day of the megaproject may have passed, but less grandiose projects still require adroit leadership. So does the effort to encourage good, environmentally sound design in building practices. On the leadership required to organize and implement major urban development programs, these typically spicy words spoken in 1966 by Robert Moses (famous in his own right as an autocrat) are still pertinent:

> Water supply, sewage and waste disposal, roads, parking, schools, hospitals and health, all are in the same category of works requiring an honest, factual, fearless approach and attack by officials with at least a thirst for martyrdom as well as an instinct for the jugular.
>
> Where are such leaders to be found in sufficient numbers for the tasks? Search me. I'm no Houdini. All I can say, based on my own not necessarily persuasive experience, is that we shall have to go back to plain, tough, old-fashioned, dedicated leadership to meet these challenges, and not to

gadgets of reform, efficiency systems, mechanical inventions, technological advances, psychiatric and diagnostic clinical analyses, quaint electronic devices, super duper regional planning and administrative bodies,
sociological abracadabra, and the lingo, patois and passwords of slick
promoters.

When a war breaks out the public is ready to turn to exceptional men,
respected but not popular, to save the day, men who promise victory only
at the expense of sweat, toil and tears. Some of the challenges of our time
are those of at least cold wars and the remedies are the same. In emergen-
cies the cry is always for leadership. City calls to city, state to state and
land to land "Show us your man."[4]

It is hard for any of the individual cities and towns in our hard-to-
govern metropolises to get strong leadership, but the next round of significant changes will be under the direction of individuals who are
members of generations just coming into their prime. I read with delight
Professor Ely's thoughts on the subject (in Chapter 7 above), and I have
no wish or need to speculate further about characteristics or qualifica-
tions for effective leadership in the future. But future leaders of whatever degree of power and influence will undoubtedly use procedures
and processes that the reader has seen evolving in the twentieth century.
Many of these processes seem to be still viable in our society and are
reviewed in the next section.

Processes That Need to Be Changed

When four social scientists in the National Academy of Sciences were
asked in the early 1970s to define what "urban processes" were at work,
they wrote perceptively about economics, politics, and social relations,
with some focus on the situation of blacks and whites in society.[5] Nobelist
Kenneth Arrow (economics, Harvard) wrote about failures of the price
system to assure justice in cities or to limit "externalities" imposed when
one part of a population is not being charged the full cost of the public
services it consumes. James G. March (social sciences, University of
California-Irvine) opined that "the city" in America was "in serious political trouble" as a place for community and citizenship. James S.
Coleman (sociology, Johns Hopkins) was concerned that various groups
in the population were withdrawing trust and confidence in the way in
which the economy distributed its largesse and were thus threatening
the legitimacy of our political institutions. Finally, Anthony Downs (then

at Real Estate Research Corp, currently at Brookings Institution) expressed his concern that President Nixon's hopes would actually be realized: Nixon recommended that nothing more should be done than we have done in the past "to stop deterioration or counteract deprivation in central-city ghettos, or to encourage dispersal [to the suburbs]."

I do not believe the situation has changed significantly in the last thirty years, except that a succession of presidents and a succession of federal laws have turned the nation into a meaner place. These laws devolve federal responsibilities to the states and tend to leave cities and low- and even moderate-income citizens relatively worse off with regards to housing, health, and income security. But the basic processes continue, and these must be redirected if progress is to be made along the smart-growth lines. Only a confident, socially progressive, citizenry can assure the kind of metropolises we want, but important changes in our politics and government will have to occur if America is to provide a healthy, sane environment for all people and decent education for the young, and get citizens to share equitably in the financial burden.

A tactical game plan to effect such changes, however essential, is beyond the scope of this book. To implement any such plan requires that fair-minded Americans resist the elements in our society who seem determined to continue their work of destructuring the set of programs and institutions that were created to deal with the Depression and two world wars. I prefer to assume that the do-gooders are actually superior in number to their opponents, even though unnervingly reluctant to go to the polls, and are equally determined to reestablish progressive policies regarding health, education, welfare, environmental protection, fair and affordable housing, a fair tax system, and an end to racist or discriminatory patterns in society. A meaningful contest between the destructors and the do-gooders will, I believe, have to focus on the six challenges outlined below, challenges that seem to me to be most worthy of serious attention at this juncture in the future history of our urbanized society.

1. We need to improve current methods of forecasting population movements.

We could use better ways to prepare for population increases in given localities. Willy-nilly, some 100 million or more souls will be added to the U.S. population in the next century or less. As urbanists have come to realize, projections of population for the nation are subject to major revisions when the actual rates of births and deaths change for whatever reasons of economic fear, different modes of social behavior, wider use of new methods of birth control, and improvements in medical practice, and when actual rates of internal migration and immigration from other lands are factored in. Moreover, the U.S. will no doubt continue to have great difficulty limiting immigration, legal and illegal, despite any anti-immigrant or antiterrorist laws that may be passed.

Demographers may not be able to produce more reliable estimates than in the past of future populations for particular localities, for small-area projections are especially vulnerable to errors in estimates of internal migration (for decades we, especially me, underestimated movements of population from east to west and from central cities to their suburbs) and errors resulting from the inability to predict the extent to which the incremental populations will actually end up residing in more densely built housing on whatever raw, redeveloped, or infill parcels are made available by changes in local regulations. But implementation of all sorts of ideas for smart growth would certainly be easier and more effective if we had better tools for anticipating and even inducing migration into and within our metropolises.

2. We could use better ways to take advantage of the process of physical deterioration of our housing stock and local infrastructure.

Ineluctably, time has a way of making the present obsolete or obsolescent, so it is reasonable to assume that some "nontrivial" share (to use economists' lingo)—say, 1 percent per year—of the existing housing inventory will be used up, and researchers are busy at this writing in adding up the impressive percentages of existing housing that would therefore be expected to need replacement at such a rate in the first two or three decades of this twenty-first century. Millions of ticky-tacky or not-so-tacky housing units built since 1950 are the inventory. One question, for instance, is whether any of their replacements could possibly be located in New Towns on the British model or even true Ebenezer Howard "social cities." More likely those that are not simply rebuilt in place will end up in a scatteration of neotraditional garden apartments or new-urbanism projects, or in fairly large multifamily or cluster projects in the inner and inner-ring cities (or their old "gray areas" or contemporary "brownfields") or understandably in more standard, sprawly, single-family developments.

And, while we are busy thinking about housing in the metropolis, we also need to think about the ways in which electricity is used in the new houses (even if increasingly generated by solar energy), for the nation's infrastructure of electricity-generating facilities including nuclear plants and hydroelectric dams will be deteriorating as well, demanding the highest level of attention on the part of the metropolises' leaders and ratepayers to assure a sufficiency of energy to their larger populations.

Deterioration also happens to automobiles. The process of replacing them may provide opportunities for building carefully designed housing areas and business parks where systems of buses, jitneys, monorails, and guided highways might be installed to complement or supplement new fuel-cell-driven noncarbonaceous automobiles.

3. We need to encourage smallness and simplicity (again).

The idea that "small is beautiful," originally articulated by E.F. Schumacher in the 1960s, remains a guiding principle for all right-thinking people.[6] However, the reality is that almost everything that sustains urban life in America is involved in some mysterious process that makes it more complicated than it used to be. Every new or rebuilt public facility is made larger than the one before it in order to handle more traffic. The stated reasons for this ineluctable trend to greater complexity, primarily related to so-called economies of scale, leave me unconvinced.

As it is, urban form and urban life are negatively impacted every day. Supersized stores have replaced almost all the mom-and-pop-sized enterprises. Airports keep reinventing themselves to handle larger airplanes, more parked cars, and millions more passengers. Highway travel gets a boost with the introduction of electronic passes to get through tollgates, but this technology creates the possibility of merging the record of drivers' highway usage with records emanating from their use of credit cards, Social Security and health benefits, bank machines, telecommunications, and the Internet, thus raising the specter of a Big Brother government or private entrepreneur able to monitor everyone's entire life, to the horror of civil libertarians. Day after day, all across the country, multistoried and gated residential complexes and office buildings replace smaller structures and parking lots.

The trend is simply exacerbated by other sorts of technological change, such as those that require a householder to install additional telecommunications lines or channels to accommodate new gadgets that tend (in ways that follow something akin to Gresham's law in economics about bad money driving out good money) to drive out old technologies. Only real optimists think this process will abate, but we should recognize how much more difficult is the job of creating stable relationships and interactions in such artificially induced conditions of change.

4. Each metropolis will need to concoct ways to help stabilize employment in its region, given the facts of globalization.

The cities of 1900 were built around the needs of relatively small-scale manufacturing, shipping, retailing, agricultural, and resource-extraction operations. Much of their output was consumed locally in the days before refrigeration and faster transportation methods were introduced. Almost all these basic activities have been transmogrified, with well-known consequences in the present and unmeasurable implications for the future.

Much of the twentieth century was dominated by what the institutional economists called finance capitalism, whereby the investment houses on Wall Street obtained almost irresistible power to create great agglomerations in manufacturing, creating such corporations as General Motors, General Electric, General Foods, which eventually, over recurrent cycles of merger-mania, absorbed or displaced thousands of smaller, regional, family owned companies and their workers.

By this time, we have obviously moved to a different stage in which global corporations tilt for power with and over nation-states. An essential element in this process is clearly the computer. The effect these mega-corporations will have on the size and shape of retailing and manufacturing in our metropolises, and the extent to which telecommuting will replace daily face-to-face interactions, will be the most tangible of the impacts that might be forecast by local planners. A more subtle but even more cogent influence will be how production of basic commodities and finished goods is allocated by the global corporations to other countries; the challenge to the United States is to develop different sources of income-producing employment and different sources of income for its people. Without steady jobs in real-wealth-creating occupations and without income from exports, no metropolis can have a viable economic base for long.

Perhaps, dealing effectively with such economic processes, especially as we move toward sustainability in the metropolis at the level of both household and community, is the most critical of all the challenges cited here.[7]

5. We need to return to appropriate concepts of good government and public finance.

It is of critical importance for America that people have confidence in their government and accept the fundamental ideas underlying such terms as "the general welfare," "the public interest," and "merit goods" (specifically public education, public health and safety, and "safety nets" for all poor people). For governments to work fairly, we may have to deemphasize our notions of efficiency and economy in order to achieve equity. Fairly ungrudging acceptance of the positive role of good government on the part of taxpayers is also necessary, the critics say and I agree, before we will get either sustained actions and interventions by government or progress in our attempts at redressing the social, environmental, and economic costs of the long retreat from the New Deal/Great Society norms to the drastically lower levels for government suggested by Barry Goldwater in the 1964 presidential campaign and implemented in successive waves by all presidents since Richard Nixon.

Many of us know that there is a causal link between government-supported programs, such as school busing and "fair housing" that fight racial discrimination, and the flight of white families to suburbs imagined to remain forever free of crime, poverty, and the kind of schools they left behind in the inner city. The links are genetically resistant to quantification at academically acceptable standards, so causation cannot be proved, nor can we prove that resistance to such governmental initiatives is a proximate cause of the loss of confidence in government and of willingness to pay taxes.

In any case, a long series of such social upheavals has upset the idea of balancing the distribution of federal, state, and local responsibilities in "public finance" along the lines promoted at midcentury by the much missed U.S. Advisory Commission on Intergovernmental Relations (USACIR). USACIR's work was fundamental to many of the analyses in my doctoral dissertation and in my professional life thereafter. The USACIR theory of public finance was based upon identification of appropriate uses of income and sales taxes, fees for service, and charges from special-purpose authorities at all levels of the federal system. In recent years, the existing suboptimal fiscal systems at the state and local level have become even more unbalanced, reflecting at least rising anger by local property owners against property taxes, thus severely affecting state and local budgets for schools and transportation agencies; the right wing's campaigns for reduction of government in general and taxes in particular; and the reliance by pusilanimous state legislatures on revenues from lotteries and gambling for maintenance of important programs.

Vice president Al Gore was in charge of a "reinventing government" task force in the Clinton administration. Stabilizing the finances for essential public services was not a major item, as I recall, in that agenda, but such stabilization, together with appropriate growth in actual dollars, will be necessary in order to make reasonable progress in improving education, housing, health, transport, and economic conditions in both "inner" and "outer" parts of the nation's metropolitan areas.

Election of a refreshingly different form of political leadership may be necessary here. Such leadership, unafraid to tackle the real cultural and institutional impediments to creating a fair, multicultural society, can be elected only if the reapportionment of legislatures based on the decennial census of 2000 provides a framework for fair representation of all groups in the population; if election process reforms prevent donnybrooks like Florida's presidential election in 2000; if campaign finance reforms at both federal and state levels minimize the undue influence of contributors, for, as Louis Winnick observed, "The calculus of the special interest group is such that a benefit obtained for itself, however modest, will outweigh a cost to the general public, however great";[8] and, most importantly, if a vastly greater percentage of eligible voters exercise their franchise than has been seen in recent decades.

6. We need to question the appropriateness and propriety of each proposed "public-private partnership."

As Professor Ely noted in 1902, the last thing business leaders in the community wanted was "good government" if that meant giving up the impressive power they exerted on the formulation, passage, and implementation of public policies that used the public's tax revenues for the interests of business or that regulated the business owners' ability to operate and build freely. Alas, we have changed only in technique but not in substance in the ensuing ten decades.

Not that great efforts were not made to halt the simple bribery, combined with the restriction of the vote largely to white males, that prevailed in 1902. A flock of reforms did come to pass during the years, including further development of the civil service, introduction of voter initiatives and referenda, the expansion of the franchise to women, the Voting Rights Act of 1964, and the one-person-one-vote decisions. The biggest change, in my opinion, was the increased reliance by political campaigns on high-cost television, thus generating the demand for plain and fancy methods of filling campaign coffers and, by centralizing campaigns around television advertising, destroying the local neighborhood or ward organizations that had long functioned as the source of a family's political information. The rise of "special interests," partly as a result of governmental programs that created a class of voters eager to have such programs continue and able to make significant financial contributions, has been instrumental in converting the word "public" to mean "capable of supporting a particular group in the population."

One correlative to such conversion in the meaning of "public" was the building-up of the notion that the "public-private partnership" was the optimal relationship between the private sector and the public sector. In turn, with regard to city and town planning, that meant that the role of the planner working for the local public regulatory agency was subtly shifted from the original "enhancing the public interest" to "helping private developers or homeowners work their way through the system as quickly as possible with the least obvious damage to the public interest." Accordingly, in reality, land-use planners were often persuaded by their politician employers to allow private objectives to take precedence as the public-private partnership for a given real estate development was forged. The development community, including land-use planners, urban designers and architects, the real estate and banking organizations, and the related public officials, have much work ahead of them if the general public's confidence in their decisions is to be restored.

Coda

And so I write this coda, defined in my abridged Oxford English Dictionary as a musical term meaning a passage added after the natural completion of a movement, so as to form a more definite and satisfactory conclusion. This coda is intended to illuminate how improving the processes reviewed above might affect the spider's web of interacting factors that characterize the metropolitanized system we are all familiar with as the twenty-first century continues on its way.

Let us begin with the implication of an increasing population. In and out of the metropolis, people must have income to live, so the system will need to offer more jobs or create broader uses of job-sharing and wealth-sharing. As it is, I've been amazed at the ability of the U.S. economy to maintain itself, even (so far) avoiding long-term recessions. I worry about the widening income gap between upper and lower strata in the population, and I find it probable that globalization will lower innumerable working families to near poverty levels.

A variety of "public" and "merit goods" are required to make a metropolis work. The forecast is for a continuing crimp in local budgets, and thus physical infrastructure and public services will become increasingly inadequate for both existing and larger populations. A major thrust of programs for rebuilding the nation's infrastructure to create both work and income (along Keynesian lines) is improbable but desirable (and still sometimes suggested). In any case, the Keynesian focus on the power of consumer expenditures to support our economy is still the basis for expectations about economic conditions. As for the reliance by the conservatives on "free markets" around the world, their credibility is considerably weakened by President George W. Bush's call for protective tariffs for the nation's steel industries, not to mention the diminished credibility of major corporations afflicted with deceptive accounting and operating policies.

Despite such budgetary pressures, localities will be grappling with propositions concerning sprawl, urban growth controls, smart-growth programs, and environmental restitution and protection, to name a few approaches. We must accept the idea that most people do like sprawl, with its fairly low density of housing, but they do not countenance the traffic congestion that ensues. One important question is whether smart growth and new urbanism, ideas advanced by a fortunate few, are solutions capable of helping the many. Much more analysis of those concepts needs to be done to resolve the issues involved.

Such analysis is rare, but the nature and scope of one of the major challenges here are outlined in the best piece that I have found to date, a commentary on how smart growth became San Diego's Trojan horse, threatening the lot of lower-income residents because, as city planner Nico Calavita describes the situation,

> with the false promise of a comprehensive regional approach to the problems of growth, [smart growth] opens the door to wholesale gentrification through the densification and infill of already urbanized communities . . . such a strategy is based on an assumed, but mistaken, capacity of the existing infrastructure and public facilities to accommodate additional development. Without adequate public facilities, densification would worsen existing conditions and deepen the urban/suburban divide at the metropolitan level. It is possible that most cities considering densification are confronted with a situation akin to that of San Diego and Los Angeles, where urban neighborhoods are saddled with huge public facilities deficits. . . . One after another, single family neighborhoods were invaded by multifamily buildings . . . and community facilities were overwhelmed by the onslaught of newcomers.[9]

Calavita reviews the ways in which San Diego not only failed to implement plans to finance facilities such as schools, libraries, parks, and streets by fees on developers but committed its fiscal resources to the construction of a ballpark instead (as has been well reported, other cities also have used up large parts of their available fiscal and political resources on fancy new stadia for professional teams). Even without further research, I am clear that "comprehensive regional approaches" are even scarcer than financing for infrastructure and public facilities, for at least two reasons: programs for small parts of a metropolis can be neither comprehensive nor regional, and no metropolis that I know of has a governmental structure that is empowered to design, much less finance, a broad-reaching approach for dealing with major increases in population while saving both the cities and the environment at the same time.

The critical issues of additional jobs and new occupations are hardly mentioned in the current literature about urbanism and smart growth (not to mention even deeper questions of race and income distribution). The nineteenth century idealists visualized communities where families lived in close proximity to both their work and their means of producing food. Ebenezer Howard had similar aspirations for his social cities, and most of the communities actually built in the New Town movements in England, Scotland, and the United States were designed so that most jobs needed by the populace could be situated in the town itself or very close by in order to minimize commuting and the resulting strain on transportation facilities. Unfortunately, such aspirations have almost never been realized to the extent hoped, and even in the age of computers and more work done at home, the need for central places where people can meet and work face-to-face remains. The advantages of job-sharing and shorter workweeks are not attractive in an era when Social Security and pension arrangements are threatened.

The dreams of a postindustrial era (when people would have more leisure, increasing demands for more parks, libraries, recreation, and adult education opportunities) faded about the time that the oil crisis of the mid-1970s brought the United States back into the real world of scarce resources. The state of the metropolis in this post–September 11 world is also one of scarce resources. As a nation we do not seem to have reconciled ourselves to erasing the existing deficit in public facilities, much less providing expanded capacity for increased populations. Although both projects and individual buildings may end up smaller than they might have been in, say, the 1990s, more land in urban areas will be required. Possibly a good deal of land for development can be obtained by redeveloping old areas, including buildings built in the 1950s and 1960s, rather than taking arable or forest lands for new residential developments, but land-use controls of all sorts will be under stress. Into the mix we might also add the pressure for additional land for office buildings outside of central cities if there are strong desires for dispersion as an antiterrorism measure. Having grown up in a city with a forest of 1920–scale skyscrapers, I was always surprised that so many of them could be scrapped during the building boom of the 1970s and early 1980s so that even larger buildings could be erected on the cleared downtown sites at prices that seemed astronomical compared to the typical $2-per-square-foot rock-bottom price for central-city land in the urban redevelopment projects (financed under Title I of the 1949 Housing Act) of a decade earlier. What happens during the twenty-first century to all those never-fully rented 40-, 50-, and 60-story office buildings built in the late twentieth century in cities large and small across the nation will be an important part of the story to be written a hundred years from now.

The key, as ever, may be in our ability to deal with transportation problems in the metropolis. So far, almost every place in the nation has successfully avoided putting major resources into even one (much less a larger number) of the flock of transportation proposals that have been around since at least the 1960s. Included in the list are promising programs involving more buses, trolleys, guided rails, jitneys, monorails, light rail systems, and bicycles, to name a few, plus techniques for administering differential pricing for peak and off-peak use of highways, not to mention higher prices for gasoline. All of these ideas require large amounts of both public willpower and public money, both being perhaps the scarcest resources of all.

Each generation active during the twentieth century brought something different to the work of urbanizing our society. Not everyone has envisaged a metropolitan-suburban society that is equitable, nonracist, crime-free, environmentally protected, and beautiful, nor have enough people worked to create that kind of society, so I came to the conclusion that we need to encourage the emerging generations to have the same kind of benign and generous visions of people and places as Ebenezer Howard had. By 2012, even the youngest member of the Boom Generation will be fifty years old, and, by then, members of succeeding generations will be full participants in the debates about how to make the metropolises of their time and place as livable for all citizens (and other residents) as possible. I hope this portrait of how previous generations dealt with the wide range of issues involved will simply make these emergent generations a little more Ebenezer than Babbitt.

Appendix
"A Short History of S&Ls"

To understand the S&L crisis, it is important first to know some history. The federally insured savings and loan system was established in the early 1930s to promote the construction of new homes during the Depression and to protect financial institutions against the kind of devastation that followed the panic of 1929. The Federal Home Loan Bank Act of 1932 established the Federal Home Loan Bank Board (FHLBB), whose purpose was to create a reserve credit system to ensure the availability of mortgage money for home financing and to oversee federally chartered savings and loans. The second principal building block of the modern savings and loan industry was put in place when the National Housing Act of 1934 created the Federal Savings and Loan Insurance Corporation (FSLIC) to insure S&L deposits.

Until 1989 the FHLBB was the primary regulatory agency responsible for federally chartered savings and loans. This independent executive agency was made up of a chair and two members appointed by the president. It oversaw twelve regional Federal Home Loan Banks, which in turn served as the conduit to individual savings and loan institutions. The district banks provided a pool of funds—for disbursing loans and covering withdrawals—to their member institutions at below-market rates. In 1985 the FHLBB delegated to the district banks the task of examining and supervising the savings and loans within their regional jurisdictions.

Reprinted with permission from: Kitty Calavita and Henry N. Pontell (University of California-Irvine) and Robert H. Tillman (St. John's University, Jamaica, New York), *Big Money Crime: Fraud and Politics in the Savings and Loan Crisis* (Berkeley: University of California Press, 1997), pp. 9–16.

The FSLIC, also under the jurisdiction of the FHLBB, provided federal insurance on savings and loan deposits. In exchange for this protection thrifts were regulated geographically and in terms of the kinds of loans they could make. Essentially, they were confined to issuing home loans within fifty miles of the home office. The 1960s brought a gradual loosening of these restraints—for example, the geographic area in which savings and loans could do business was extended and their lending powers were slowly expanded—but this did not significantly alter the protection/regulation formula.

A number of economic factors in the 1970s radically changed the fortunes of the savings and loan industry and ultimately its parameters. Thrifts had issued hundreds of billions of dollars of thirty-year fixed-rate loans (often at 6 percent), but they were prohibited from offering adjustable rate mortgages (ARMs). Thrift profitability thus declined rapidly as interest rates climbed. By the mid-1970s the industry was insolvent on a market-value basis (i.e., based on the current market value of its assets rather than on their reported book value). With inflation at 13.3 percent by 1979 and with thrifts constrained by regulation to pay no more than 5.5 percent interest on new deposits, the industry could not attract new money. When Paul Volcker, head of the Federal Reserve Board, tightened the money supply in 1979 in an effort to bring down inflation, interest rates soared to their highest level in the century and triggered a recession. Faced with defaults and foreclosures as a result of the recession and with increased competition from high yield investments, given the hikes in the interest rate, S&Ls hemorrhaged losses. By 1982 the industry was insolvent by $150 billion on a market-value basis and the FSLIC had only $6 billion in reserves.

Coinciding with these economic forces, a new ideological movement was gathering momentum. Since the early 1970s, policy makers had been discussing lifting the restrictions on savings and loans so that they could compete more equitably for new money and invest in more lucrative ventures. But it was not until the deregulatory fervor of the early Reagan administration that this strategy gained political acceptance as a solution to the rapidly escalating thrift crisis. Throwing caution to the wind and armed with the brashness born of overconfidence, policy makers undid most of the regulatory infrastructure that had kept the thrift industry together for half a century.

They believed that the free enterprise system works best if left alone, unhampered by perhaps well-meaning but ultimately counterproductive government regulations. The bind constraining the savings and loan industry seemed to confirm the theory that government regulations imposed an unfair handicap in the competitive process. The answer, policy makers insisted, was to turn the industry over to the self-regulating mechanisms of the free market. In 1980 the Depository Institutions Deregulation and Monetary Control Act (DIDMCA) began to do just that by phasing out restrictions on interest rates paid by savings and loans. This move to the free market model, however, was accompanied by a decisive move in the opposite direction. At the same time that the law unleashed savings and loans to compete for new money, it bolstered the federal protection accorded these "free enterprise" institutions, increasing FSLIC insurance from a maximum of $40,000 to $100,000 per deposit. . . . This selective application of the principles of free enterprise —spearheaded in large part by members of Congress with ties to the thrift industry—laid the foundation for risk-free fraud.

When the industry did not rebound, Congress prescribed more deregulation. In 1982 the Garn-St. Germain Depository Institutions Act accelerated the phaseout of interest rate ceilings. Probably more important, it dramatically expanded thrift investment powers, moving savings and loans farther and farther away from their traditional role as providers of home mortgages. They were now authorized to increase their consumer loans, up to a total of 30 percent of their assets; make commercial, corporate, or business loans; and invest in nonresidential real estate worth up to 40 percent of their total assets. The act also allowed thrifts to provide 100 percent financing, requiring no down payment from the borrower, apparently to attract new business to the desperate industry. On signing the fateful bill, President Reagan said, "I think we've hit a home run." The president later told an audience of savings and loan executives that the law was the "Emancipation Proclamation for America's savings institutions."

The executive branch joined in the "emancipation." In 1980 the FHLBB removed the 5 percent limit on brokered deposits, allowing thrifts access to unprecedented amounts of cash. These deposits were placed by brokers who aggregated individual investments, which were then deposited as "jumbo" certificates of deposit (CDs). Since the maximum insured deposit was $100,000, brokered deposits were packaged as $100,000 CDs, on which the investors could command high interest rates. So attractive was this system to all concerned—to brokers who made hefty commissions, to investors who received high interest for their money, and to thrift operators who now had almost unlimited access to funds—that brokered deposits in S&Ls increased 400 percent between 1982 and 1984.

In 1982 the FHLBB dropped the requirements that thrifts have at least four hundred stockholders and that no one stockholder could own more·than 25 percent of the stock, opening the door for a single entrepreneur to own and operate a federally insured savings and loan. Furthermore, single investors could now start up thrifts using noncash assets such as land or real estate. Apparently hoping that innovative entrepreneurs would turn the industry around, zealous deregulators seemed unaware of the disastrous potential of virtually unlimited new charters in the vulnerable industry. Referring to this deregulatory mentality and the enthusiasm with which deregulation was pursued, a senior thrift regulator told us, "I always describe it as a freight train. I mean it was just the direction and everybody got on board."

The deregulatory process was accelerated by the fact that federal and state systems of regulation coexisted and often overlapped. State-chartered thrifts were regulated by state agencies but could be insured by the FSLIC if they paid the insurance premiums, which most did. By 1986 the FSLIC insured 92.6 percent of the country's savings and loans—holding over 98 percent of the industry's assets. The dual structure, which had operated smoothly for almost fifty years, had devastating consequences within the context of federal deregulation. As the federal system deregulated, state agencies were compelled to do the same, or risk their funding.

The experience of the California Department of Savings and Loans (CDSL) is a good example of this domino effect of deregulation. Beginning in 1975 the CDSL was staffed by tough regulators who imposed strict rules and tolerated little deviation. California thrift owners complained bitterly, and when federal regulations were relaxed in 1980, they switched en masse to federal charters. With the exodus, the CDSL lost more than half of its funding and staff. In July 1978 the agency had 172 full-time examiners; by 1983 there were just fifty-five.

The California Department of Savings and Loans learned the hard way that if it was to survive (and if state politicians were to continue to have access to the industry's lobbying dollars), it had to loosen up. On January 1, 1983, the Nolan Bill passed with only one dissenting vote, making it possible for almost anyone to charter a savings and loan in California and virtually eliminating any limitations on investment powers. As a savings and loan commissioner for California later said of the deregulation, "All discipline for the savings and loan industry was pretty well removed." Spurred on by consultants and lawyers who held seminars for developers on how to buy their own "moneymaking machines," applications for thrift charters in California poured in. By the end of 1984 the CDSL had received 235 applications for new charters, most of which were quickly approved.

Some states, such as Texas, already had thrift guidelines that were even more lax than the new federal regulations, but those that did not quickly enacted "me-too" legislation. By 1984 thrift deregulation was complete, except, of course, that the industry was now more protected (by federal insurance) than ever before. *Business Week* pointed out the discrepancy: "In a system where the government both encourages risk taking and provides unconditional shelter from the adverse consequences, excess and hypocrisy can be expected to flourish in equal measure."

Deregulation was heralded by its advocates as a free market solution to the competitive handicap placed on thrifts by restraints on their investment powers and interest rates. But the cure turned out to be worse than the disease. Deregulating interest rates triggered an escalating competition for deposits, as brokered deposits sought ever higher returns. One commentator attacked the logic of the deregulation frenzy: "[It can] be summed up by saying that, beginning in 1980, the thrift industry was turned loose to its own devices to find its own way out of its difficulties by taking in more highpriced deposits and lending them out at better than the historically high rates then prevailing. As an article of financial wisdom, this ranks with the notion, held by some, that it is possible to borrow one's way out of debt."

It was worse than that. Deregulation not only sunk thrifts deeper into debt as they competed for "hot" brokered deposits, but more important, it opened the system up to pervasive and systemic fraud. With federally insured deposits flowing in, virtually all restrictions on thrift investment powers removed, and new owners flocking to the industry, deregulators had combined in one package the opportunity for lucrative fraud and the irresistible force of temptation. L. William Seidman, former chair of the Resolution Trust Corporation, which was responsible for managing the assets of failed thrifts during the bailout, blamed the S&L crisis on the combination of deregulation and increased deposit insurance (which he called "a credit card from the U.S. taxpayers"). He underlined the possibilities for fraud that this combination opened up: "Crooks and high flyers had found the perfect vehicle for self-enrichment. Own your own money machine and use the product to make some high-odd bets. We provided them with such perverse incentives that if I were asked to defend the S&L gang in court, I'd use the defense of entrapment."

Business Week struck a warning note as early as 1985 with its tongue-in-cheek description of the "Go-Go Thrift": "Start an S&L. Offer a premium interest rate and watch the deposits roll in. Your depositors are insured by Uncle Sam, so they don't care what you do with their money. And in states like California, you can do almost anything you want with it. Add enormous leverage—you can pile $100 of assets on every $3 of capital—and you've built a speculator's dream machine."

Losses piled up. In 1982 the FSLIC spent more than $2.4 billion to close or merge insolvent savings and loans, and by 1986 the agency itself was insolvent. As the number of insolvent thrifts climbed, the FSLIC was forced to slow the pace of closures. The worse the industry got, the more likely its institutions would stay open, as the FSLIC was now incapable of closing their doors and paying off depositors. As the zombie thrifts churned out losses, the price tag for the inevitable bailout mounted.

As we write this, Charles Keating has been released from prison, his federal conviction thrown out on the grounds of jury misconduct. Although this judicial decision says nothing of the merits of the case against Keating, it inevitably provokes speculation that the role of criminal misconduct in the savings and loan crisis may have been exaggerated by prosecutors and a scandal-hungry media: If even this poster boy of the S&L crisis cannot be successfully prosecuted, perhaps thrift crime was not so rampant after all. In the face of such speculation, it becomes even more critical to reexamine the record of the thrift debacle and the role of fraud in the industry's collapse. It is critical not only for our understanding of the dynamics of this sort of white-collar crime, but to put in place policies that will prevent such financial disasters in the future.

Notes

Chapter 1

1. Corroboration for my guesstimate is in a study by United Nations demographers—"Accordingly, in the next 50 years America will grow by 100 million people"—as reported by Ben J. Wattenberg in his op-ed piece, "It Will Be a Smaller World After All," *New York Times*, March 8, 2003.

2. In *The Calvin and Hobbes Tenth Anniversary Book* (Kansas City: Andrews and McMeel, 1995, p. 54), Bill Watterson writes: "Calvin's transmogrifier sums up the spirit of the strip. A cardboard box becomes a series of great inventions with a little imagination. The transmogrifier shows the kind of kid Calvin is, and it added a new dimension to the strip's world." My thanks to my daughter Marli for telling me about Calvin and his box.

3. Rachel Carson, *Silent Spring* (Boston: Houghton Mifflin, 1962); see also George Perkins Marsh, *Man and Nature; or Physical Geography as Modified by Human Action* (London: S. Low, Son and Marston, 1864); the definitive study of this extraordinary man is David Lowenthal's *George Perkins Marsh: Versatile Vermonter* (New York: Columbia University Press, 1958), reprinted with the subtitle "Prophet of Conservation" by the University of Washington Press in 2000.

4. Quoted from "Hidden Spirit of the Wilderness" by Stuart Schneider, in "Sand Dunes Breezes," Colorado: Great Sand Dunes National Monument, 2000–01.

5. See: James Bryce, *The American Commonwealth* (London and New York: Macmillan and Co., 1888, 3 vols.), and President's Research Committee on Social Trends, *Recent Social Trends in the United States* (New York: McGraw-Hill, 1933).

Chapter 2

1. Ebenezer Howard, *To-morrow: A Peaceful Path to Real Reform* (London: Swan Sonnenschein, 1898).

2. Ebenezer Howard. *Garden Cities of Tomorrow* (London: Swan Sonnenschein, 1902). There are scores of books since 1902 on "garden cities" and the impact of Ebenezer Howard's ideas; the most recent is Kermit C. Parsons and David Schuyler, eds., *From Garden City to Green City: The Legacy of Ebenezer Howard* (Baltimore: Johns Hopkins University Press, 2002); see also Robert Beevers, *Urban Utopias in the 20th Century* (New York: Basic Books, 1977), and Clarence Stein, *Toward New*

Towns in America, introduction by Lewis Mumford (Chicago: Public Administration Service, 1951).

3. Quoted from Peter Hall and Colin Ward, *Sociable Cities: The Legacy of Ebenezer Howard* (Chichester and London: John Wiley, 1998), p. 3.

4. See Adna Ferrin Weber, *The Growth of Cities in the Nineteenth Century* (Ithaca, NY: Cornell University Press, 1963; originally published in 1899 for Columbia University by Macmillan).

5. How the Ford Foundation in the 1960s helped establish the Committee on Urban Economics (CUE) is discussed in Chapter 9.

6. *Progress and Poverty: An Inquiry into the Cause of Industrial Depressions and of Increase of Want with Increase in Wealth: The Remedy* (New York: Doubleday and McClure, 1898), p. 431. The first edition came out in 1879. Millions of copies of its various editions have been sold, according to the *Columbia Encyclopedia*.

7. Ibid., p. 396. Wallace Stegner, in his retrospective account of the growth at the end of the nineteenth century of his hometown in the Great Plains, *Wolf Willow* (New York: Penguin, 2000), p. 252, observes that the major landowner discovered that he would be the one to pay most of the taxes and thus had to make sure that his neighbors did not install a single tax system.

8. Ray Thomas, "Howardian Economics and the Future of London," in "One Hundred Years of *To-morrow*," Special Supplement to *Town and Country Planning*, October 1998, p. 9ff.

9. Colin Ward, "Howard, Kropotkin and the Decentralist Vision," in "One Hundred Years of *To-morrow*," Special Supplement to *Town and Country Planning*, October 1998, p. 4.

10. The most explicit examination of how capitalism creates inequities in the metropolis is probably *Social Justice and the City* by David Harvey (London: David Arnold, 1973). See also Manuel Castells, *The Urban Question* (Cambridge, MA: MIT Press, 1977).

11. Thomas, "Howardian Economics," pp. 9–11.

12. G.E. Cherry, ed., *Pioneers in British Planning* (London: Architectural Press, 1981).

13. Hall and Ward, *Sociable Cities*, p. ix.

14. Peter Hall, in "One Hundred Years of *To-morrow*," Special Supplement to *Town and Country Planning*, October 1998.

15. Interlaken Gardens in Eastchester, New York, was built by the Fred F. French Investing Companies a few years before World War II and was said, by William Flanders of that company, to be one of the earliest of the middle-income projects under that section of the housing acts.

16. H. Peter Oberlander and Eva Newbrun, *Houser: The Life and Work of Catherine Bauer* (Vancouver, BC: UBC Press, 1999), pp. 230–32. The authors incorrectly (as happens too often) ascribe the 1898 date, which relates to *To-morrow*, rather than the correct 1902 date, to the relatively toothless *Garden Cities*.

17. The 1962 Census of Governments was one of the first U.S. Census "products" to be available in what was then called "machine readable form." I purchased the tapes and hired a programmer to prepare them for publication, the first time such a list had ever been seen in its entirely. The one-inch-thick book's catalogue entry is Alan Rabinowitz, *Directory of Special Districts: Based on Information Compiled for the U.S. Census of Governments, 1962* (Boston: Urban Survey Corporation, 1964).

18. The first master's degree in city planning was offered by Harvard as of 1928, beginning a march toward professional status for practitioners. Eventually, in the 1980s, the American Institute of Planners (home of the professionals) merged with the American Society of Planning Officials (ASPO, home of planning commissioners and other interested people) to form the American Planning Association with its affiliated American Institute of Certified Planners (AICP, a new home for the trained, experienced planner, including this book's author).

19. See William H. Wilson, *The City Beautiful Movement* (Baltimore: Johns Hopkins University Press, 1989) (with reference to my great-grandfather Abraham Gottlieb's tilt with Daniel Burnham, p. 56).

20. Elaine D. Engst and H.T. Nickerson, *Urban America: Documenting the Planners* (Ithaca, NY: Department of Manuscripts and University Archives, Cornell University Libraries, 1985), p. 5.

21. The basic text here is Mel Scott's *American City Planning Since 1890: A History Commemorating the Fiftieth Anniversary of the American Institute of Planners* (Berkeley: University of California Press, 1971). Ebenezer Howard is mentioned in connection with his garden cities, not his social city, and no mention is made of urban design, a concept associated with the leadership of Kevin Lynch at MIT to get planners and architects to think responsibly when operating on larger-than-project terms.

Chapter 3

1. Quote from *Babbitt* (New York: Bantam Books, 1998), pp. 188–92, with an excellent introduction by John Wickersham.

2. William Strauss and Neil Howe, *Generations: The History of America's Future, 1584 to 2069* (New York: William Morrow, 1991).

3. Alan Rabinowitz, *The Real Estate Gamble: Lessons From 50 Years of Boom and Bust* (New York: AMACOM [American Management Association], 1980).

Chapter 4

1. My newly born father arrived in Manhattan from the Ukraine in 1884 and had a career in New York real estate from 1903 to his death in 1973; a few events in his extraordinary career appear in the pages below. My mother's forebears had all arrived in Illinois in the middle of the nineteenth century.

2. See Richard Hofstadter's *Social Darwinism in American Thought* (Boston: Beacon Press, 1955), and also Ann Douglas's *The Feminization of American Culture* (New York: Knopf, 1977). Also of relevance to this book are Hofstadter's *Age of Reform: Bryan to F.D.R.* (New York: Knopf, 1955) and *The Progressive Movement 1900–1915* (New York: Simon and Schuster, 1986).

3. Example: Morton Horowitz, *Transformation of American Law, 1780–1860* Cambridge: (Harvard University Press, 1977).

4. 11 Peters 420 (1837). See Carl Brent Swisher, *Historic Decisions of the Supreme Court* (New York: Van Nostrand, 1958), p. 40.

5. Program on Corporations, Law and Democracy (POCLAD), "Contesting the Authority of Corporations to Govern," a project of the nonprofit Council on International and Public Affairs, P.O. Box 246, South Yarmouth, MA 02664.

6. Among many midcentury writings on the subject, see Wallace E. Oates, *Political Economy of Fiscal Federalism* (Lexington, MA: Lexington Books, 1977).

7. See, for example, Anwar H. Syed, "Sovereign or Vassal," in *The Politics of American Local Government* (New York: Random House, 1966). See also C.E. Jacobs, *Law Writers and the Courts: The Influence of Thomas M. Cooley, Christoper G. Tiedeman, and John F. Dillon upon American Constitutional Law* (Berkeley: University of California Press, 1954).

8. The late nineteenth and early twentieth century saw a number of tracts and treatises on the virtues or disadvantages of municipal ownership of local utility services. Only a few localities still own such utilities. The complex history of privately owned public utilities in the era of "finance capitalism" is interestingly described from a conservative's viewpoint by N.S.B. Gras in *Business and Capitalism* (New York: F.S. Crofts, 1947). I note that, at times of stress such as the electric power crisis in California in early 2001, even modern conservatives advance schemes for reregulation of the private utilities and possible state ownership.

9. Alan Rabinowitz, "Municipal Debt/Intergovernmental Fiscal Relations: A Study of Options and Guidelines in the Financing of Local Public Goods and Services" (Ph.D. diss., Massachusetts Institute of Technology, 1969).

10. Many of the comments in the next few paragraphs are based on Carter Goodrich, *Government Promotion of American Canals and Railroads, 1800–1890* (New York: Columbia University Press, 1960), with a fine map, p. 34.

11. Ibid., pp. 53–55.

12. See, for instance, John Fairlie, "Municipal Development in the United States," in *A Municipal Program* (New York: National Municipal League, 1900).

13. For instance, Lewis Mumford, *The City in History* (New York: Harcourt, Brace, 1961).

Chapter 5

1. Alfred Thayer Mahan, *The Influence of Sea Power Upon History, 1660–1793* (New York: Little, Brown and Co., 1942).

2. Or, as euphemistically described in U.S. Department of Commerce, U.S. Bureau of the Census, Population Division, *Population of States and Counties of the United States 1790–1990*, comp. and ed. Richard L. Forstall (Washington, DC: GPO, March 1996), p. 42: "Hawaii was an independent nation prior to ceding its sovereignty to the United States in 1898; it was made a territory in 1900." Cited hereafter as *Population of States and Counties*.

3. U.S. Department of Interior, Bureau of Land Management, *Public Land Statistics* (Washington, DC: GPO, 1976), Tables 1, 2, 3, and 7.

4. See, for instance, Donald McCaig, "The Bozeman Trail: In the 1860s, the Lakota and Their Allies, Led by Chief Red Cloud, Closed an Immigrant Route and Made It Stick," *Smithsonian Magazine*, October 2000, p. 88ff.

5. Much of the following commentary, except as otherwise noted, is based upon an excellent article, "Indians in Contemporary Life," *Encyclopaedia Britannica, 1973* printing of the 14th Edition; vol. 12, p. 75ff.

6. *Population of States and Counties*, p. vi.

7. The land my wife and I purchased in the 1950s on the island of Martha's Vineyard provides a perfect example of the process in the years before the reserva-

tion system was established. The English claimants of New York and New England made grants to prospective settlers. The island's settlers thereafter, about 1643, made agreements with the Indian sachems. The land in possession of the Indians could not be officially registered at the courthouse in an individual's name until 1828; parcelization of Indian common lands to individual Indians was mandated by the state after adoption of the post–Civil War amendments to the U.S. Constitution; eventually most of these parcels were sold to non-Indians. The full story is found in Charles E. Banks, *History of Martha's Vineyard, Dukes County, Massachusetts*, vol. 1 (Boston: George H. Dean, 1911).

8. Alexis de Toqueville, *Democracy In America* (New York: Vintage Books, 1954 Vol. 1), p. 363 (also quoted in the *Encyclopaedia Britannica* article cited above).

9. John Echohawk of the Native American Rights Fund is in charge of the case brought by the Indians: *Elouise Pepion Cobell, et al. v. Gale Norton, Secretary of the Interior, et al.*, F. Supp. 2d, 2002 WL 100136 at 1*, May 17, 2002. See also Brian Brasel-Awelhali and Silja Talvi, "The BIA's Multi-Billion Shell Game," *Z Magazine*, April–May 2002, pp. 40–46.

10. Turner's ideas were first expressed in his 1893 address to the American Historical Association, titled "The Significance of the Frontier in American History."

11. See, for instance, the well-known book by Mark Sullivan, *Our Times: The U.S., 1900*–1925 (New York: Scribner, 1926).

Chapter 6

1. See Thomas Beer, *Mauve Decade: American Life at the End of the 19th Century,* 1926 (reprint, New York: Vintage Press, 1961).

2. Reported in "Predictions from 1900: some listed, some not," John Hanchetter, *Home News Tribune*, East Brunswick, NJ, December 31, 1999.

3. Reported in an article by Dennis McCann, "Looking back at predictions from eve of 1900," *Milwaukee Journal Sentinal*, Milwaukee, WI, December 22, 1999.

4. Reported in Charles Perry, "Back to the Future," *Los Angeles Times*, December 26, 1999.

5. Reported in "Looking back at predictions from eve of 1900," Dennis McCann.

6. Reported in John M. Mcguire, "Back to the Future: In 1900, the 20th Century Promised Long Life and Unimaginable Change," *St. Louis Post-Dispatch*, St. Louis, MO, December 26, 1999.

7. Citations from Enhanced Transcript, "Anything Seemed Possible," Part IV of *America 1900*, 1999 *PBS/Online/WGBH*.

8. Reflections in Chapter 8 on the data in Table 8.4 (Land Area and Population Per Square Mile in Selected Standard Metropolitan Areas, 1960) are the foundation for this calculation.

Chapter 7

1. See, for example, John Rogers Commons, *Institutional Economics: Its Place in Political Economy* (New York: Macmillan, 1934), and his *Legal Foundations of Capitalism* (New York: Macmillan, 1924).

2. Richard T. Ely, *The Coming City* (New York: Thomas Y. Crowell, 1902).

3. Ibid., pp. 16–19.

4. Jane Jacobs, *Cities and the Wealth of Nations: Principles of Economic Life* (New York: Random House, 1984). Her ideas in this book are discussed further in Chapter 13; she has written several books on economics and cities.

5. Ely, *The Coming City*, p. 25.

6. For example, "Land in the neighborhood of a town gives a greater rent than land equally fertile in a distant part of the country. . . . it must always cost more to bring the produce of the distant land to market. . . . Good roads, canals, and navigable rivers, by diminishing the expense of carriage, put the remote parts of the country more nearly upon a level with those in the neighborhood of the town. . . . They are upon that account the greatest of all improvements." Excerpt from *An Inquiry into the Nature and Causes of the Wealth of Nations*, by Adam Smith, LL.D, edited, with extensive commentaries, by James E.T. Rogers (Oxford: Clarendon Press, 1880), 2nd ed., Vol. I, Book I, Chapter XI, p. 156.

7. *The Economist*, December 23, 2000, p. 17. But planners' actual experience during the twentieth century with state-level and certainly small area projections was that long-range migration estimates, say for ten or twenty years into the future, even those done by the most elegant of methods in the most prestigious offices of government, academia, and the private sector, usually turned out to be notoriously, sometimes embarrassingly, inaccurate.

8. Ely, *The Coming City*, p. 26.

9. Ibid., p. 28.

10. Ibid, pp. 40 and 57.

11. Ibid., p. 61.

12. Ibid, p. 63.

13. Ibid, pp. 64–69, and see Richard Hofstadter, *The Age of Reform: Bryan to F.D.R.* (New York: Knopf, 1955).

14. Ely, *The Coming City*, p. 69.

15. Ibid., p. 109.

16. The role of the settlement houses was revisited by Robert A. Woods about 1915, who noted that the pressure for acculturation that immigrants felt at the settlement houses often led to a move from their culturally comfortable, in-city neighborhood to suburbs that were culturally rather sterile. His earlier work was *City Wilderness* (1898, no publisher listed in the Library of Congress records) followed by *Americans in Process: A Settlement Study by Residents and Associates of the South End House* (Boston: Houghton Mifflin and Company, 1902); his writings were reinterpreted by Sam Bass Warner at the MIT-Harvard Joint Center for Urban Studies in *The Urban Wilderness: A History of the American City*, (New York: Harper and Row, 1972). Warner is also noted for his *Streetcar Suburbs: The Process of Growth in Boston 1870–1900* (Cambridge, Harvard University Press, 1962).

Chapter 8

1. William Cronan, *Changes in the Land: Indians, Colonists, and the Ecology of New England* (New York: Hill and Wang, 1983).

2. There is an interesting contrast here to the colonization of Australia by the English late in the eighteenth century. They asserted that the land was "unoccu-

pied," a doctrine known as *terra nullius*; hence the Aborigines living there officially did not exist and did not need to be consulted or paid. This doctrine was repudiated by the courts only in 1994.

3. See Brian J.L. Berry and Allen Pred, *Central Place Studies: A Bibliography of Theory and Applications*, Bibliography Series No. 1 (Philadelphia: Regional Science Research Institute, 1965).

4. The best explanation of Christaller (and other theorists such as August Lösch and Johann H. Von Thunen) I know of is in Edward L. Ullman's *Geography as Spatial Interaction*, edited by Ronald R. Boyce and with a foreword by Chauncy D. Harris (Seattle: University of Washington Press, 1980). In the introduction to Ullman's "classic" article, "A Theory of Location for Cities," Boyce writes: "Theories about central place were published initially by Walter Christaller in 1933 in Germany. Edward Ullman introduced Christaller's work to an English-speaking audience, extended and clarified it, and coined the phrase 'central place theory'." The U.S. Department of Commerce's economic areas prepared by its Bureau of Economic Research are based on these theories and appeared in Alan Rabinowitz, Nestor Terlecky and Terry Brooks, *Markets for Construction*, 1987–87. Washington, DC: MPA Data Services, Inc. 1988, discussed below in Chapter 12.

5. Kenneth Jackson, *Crabgrass Frontier: The Suburbanization of the United States* (New York: Oxford University Press, 1985), p. 20.

6. My wife Andrea's grandfather was an executive of an electrified interurban line in Cleveland, Ohio, that had failed by the time of his retirement in the 1930s.

7. "The Conspiracy Revisited Rebutted," by Louis Guilbault, on the Electric Railway Historical Association of Southern California's Website: www.ERHA. org/plotz.htm (March 2002). Other Website links: www.culturechange.org (for information about the Sustainable Energy Institute's Alliance for a Paving Moratorium; see also, Modern Transit Society (www.trainweb.org.mts/), and www.self-propelled-city.com.

8. For example: Mark S. Foster, *From Streetcar to Superhighway: American City Planners and Urban Transportation, 1900–1940* (Philadelphia: Temple University Press, 1981); Noam Chomsky, *Year 501* (Boston: South End Press, 1993); David James St. Clair, *The Motorization of American Cities* (New York, Praeger, 1985); Bradford C. Snell, *American Ground Transport*, U.S. Senate, Subcommittee on Antitrust and Monopoly of the Judiciary Committee, Washington, DC: February 26, 1974, pp. 27–34.

9. "Taken for a Ride," a well-known fifty-five-minute film by Jim Klein and Martha Olson, New Day Films, 314 Dayton St. #207, Yellow Springs, OH 45387.

10. And see Ann Satterthwaite's *Going Shopping* (New Haven: Yale University Press, 2002).

11. The classic example of in-city rezoning was New York City's down-zoning of hundreds of thousands of parcels about 1960, a successful attempt to make the zoning envelope provide reasonable rather than wildly optimistic opportunities for construction on a given site in a given neighborhood. In contrast in Seattle in the 1970s, Beatrice Ryan, head of the Mayor's Strategic Planning Staff, could do no more than to declare that no higher densities would be allowed in single-family neighborhoods as then zoned.

Chapter 9

1. John Rogers Commons, *Institutional Economics: Its Place in Political Economy* (New York: Macmillan, 1934), and *Legal Foundations of Capitalism* (New York: Macmillan, 1924).

2. See George H. Ellis, "The Fed's First 50 (1914–1964), Supplement to *New England Business Review*, undated reprint of speech delivered June 5, 1964, by Mr. Ellis, the president of the Federal Reserve Bank of Boston).

3. Where I took my MBA forty-two years later. In the 1950s I corresponded with the dean concerning the absence from the curriculum of any mention of real property, mortgage finance, land economics, or community development. By about 1970, a few courses in real estate had been instituted.

4. The case was *Village of Euclid v. Anebler Realty Co.*, 272. U.S. 365, 47 S.Ct. 14 (1926).

5. William Strauss and Neil Howe, *Generations: The History of America's Future, 1584 to 2069* (New York: William Morrow, 1991) p. 217.

6. I now try to think of my great-grandparents as members of the Progressive Generation, my grandparents as members of the Missionary Generation (rather than Victorian), my parents as Lost Generation (rather than Edwardian), and my own as Silent!

7. Strauss and Howe, *Generations*, pp. 217 and 220.

8. Robert Goodman, *After the Planners* (New York: Touchstone/Simon and Schuster, 1971).

9. A good example of support for this view, and discussion of how various interpretations can be given to the term, is found in Arthur M. Weimer and Homer Hoyt, *Principles of Urban Real Estate* (New York: Ronald Press, 1948), p. 10.

10. By "mixed," I mean a kind of social-welfare capitalism with government providing both essential regulation of and essential assistance to the private sector and private individuals. I was taught that city and regional planning has a relatively useful but nonideological role to play in society, unapologetically seeking the general welfare rather than merely instrumenting the inevitable enhancement of the capitalist system. My impossibly naive view is to be contrasted with Manuel Castell's more dramatic Marxist view: "By urban planning, I mean more precisely the intervention of the political in the specific articulation of the different instances of a social formation within a collective state of reproduction of labour power, with the intention of assuring its extended reproduction, of regulating the non-antagonistic contradictions that have arisen and of repressing the antagonistic contradictions, thus assuring the interests of the dominant social class in the whole of the social formation and the organization of the urban system, in such a way as to ensure the structural reproduction of the dominant mode of production" in Manuel Castells, *The Urban Question*, (Cambridge: MIT Press, 1977), p. 432.

11. Coverage of this major topic is in the real estate history section later in this chapter.

12. Benton Mackaye, *The New Exploration: A Philosophy of Regional Planning* (New York: Harcourt Brace, 1928).

13. See *Construction Volume and Costs 1915–1956*, a supplement to *Construction Review*, U.S. Department of Labor, 1956, the first compilation I know of with these data.

14. The first passenger elevators are said to date from 1857, using technology developed by Elisha Graves Otis.

15. One wonders at this point what will be the long-term effect on cities and on city-building of insurance claims in the aftermath of the terrorist attack on the World Trade Center and the consequent devastation of New York's financial section. See Chapter 13.

16. I have not been able to locate (yet) good histories of these various industry associations.

17. Louis Winnick, et al., "Philanthropy's Adaptation to the Urban Crisis," Unpublished manuscript, 1987–1989, Ford Foundation Archives Report #012158. This will be cited hereafter as Winnick, *Ford History.*

18. Winnick, *Ford History*, Ch. II, "Philanthropy's Housing Programs: The Hundred Years from Peabody to Ford," p. 5: Those with deeper curiosity about the early history of philanthropic housing may beneficially consult the following works from which much of this section was drawn: A.S. Wohl, "Octavia Hill and the Homes of the London Poor," *Journal of British Studies* 10 (May 1971), p. 105; Eugenie Ladner Birch and Deborah S. Gardner, "The Seven-Percent Solution: A Review of Philanthropic Housing, 1870–1910," *Journal of Urban History* 7, no. 4 (August 1981); Roy Lubove, *Progressives and the Slums: Tenement House Reform in New York City, 1890–1917* (Pittsburgh: University of Pittsburgh Press, 1962); Robert W. DeForest and Lawrence Veiller, ed., *The Tenement House Problem*, including the Report of the New York State Tenement House Commission of 1900 (New York: 1903); James Ford, *Slums and Housing* (Cambridge: Harvard University Press, 1936); Roger Starr, "Phipps Houses: 75 Years and More of Housing Programs," anniversary report published by the Phipps Foundation, 1981.

19. Winnick, *Ford History*, Ch. II, "Philanthropy Attacking Progress: American Beginnings," pp.18–19, followed by discussion of Veiller's spat with the National Housing Association and government generally.

20. Edith Elmer Wood, *Recent Trends in American Housing* (New York: Macmillan, 1931).

21. For good stories of such holdouts, see William J. Brede's *Skyline Builders* (New York: Early Brothers, 1948).

22. From *50 Years of Amalgamated Cooperative Housing—1927–1957* (New York: Amalgamated Housing Corporation, 1958), p. 7:

In 1929, news of the success of the Amalgamated development reached Franklin D. Roosevelt, then the governor of the State of New York. Aaron Rabinowitz, member of the State Board of Housing representing that body on the Board of Directors of the Amalgamated Housing Corporation, reported to the governor, in glowing terms, of the new method used to solve a portion of the housing problem in New York City. At the urging of Roosevelt, the then Lieutenant Governor, Herbert H. Lehman, and Aaron Rabinowitz volunteered to assist with the financing of a similar project in a slum area of the Lower East Side of the City. Sidney Hillman, encouraged by the results of the development in the Bronx, agreed that an example of cooperative housing on the East Side of Manhattan might pave the way for the rebuilding of the slums of the City by others. The Amalgamated Union therefore became the sponsor of the new cooperative.

A square block of 60,000 square feet was acquired and a limited-dividend company was set up under the name of Amalgamated Dwellings, Inc. Lehman and Rabinowitz agreed to help finance the construction until all the apartments were subscribed for. They also agreed to set up a fund to assist prospective cooperators who could only invest 50% or more of the required $500 equity per room. The average carrying charges were set at $12.25 a room per month. The development was completed in November 1930.

In the beginning, the project was rather disappointing. The early effects of the depression and the lack of understanding of the cooperative idea were obstacles almost too difficult to cope with. Gradually, however, these difficulties were overcome and the building was fully subscribed and occupied.

23. Alan Rabinowitz. *The Real Estate Gamble* (New York: American Management Association, 1980).

24. This situation required tens of thousands of pages of testimony before the Congress shortly after Franklin Roosevelt took office. Eventually the courts took over the now-bankrupt mortgage issues and appointed proper trustees for them. My father, Aaron Rabinowitz, spent much of his time from the mid-1930s to the late 1940s as one of three trustees appointed by Judge Alfred Frankenthaler to nurse Series F-1's hundreds of properties back to health for the benefit of thousands of irate bondholders who had made their investments in the 1920s. My understanding is that Series F-1 was eventually liquidated at a profit for those bondholders.

25. French's life and career appear in Eugene Rachlis and John E. Marqusee's *The Landlords: An Informal History—from Astor to Zeckendorf—of the Men Whose Adventures in Real Estate Changed the Face of America* (New York: Random House, 1963), and in *A Vigorous Life: The Story of Fred F. French, Builder of Skyscrapers* by his son John W. French (New York: Vantage Press, 1993), and many other places. Tudor City, Knickerbocker Village, and 551 Fifth Avenue are among the many French projects that appear regularly in architectural surveys of New York or histories of housing.

26. Werner Hegemann, *City Planning Housing: Political Economy and Civic Art* (New York: Architectural Book Publishing, 1937), vol. 2, pp. 274–77.

27. Marc A. Weiss, *The Rise of the Community Builders: The American Real Estate Industry and Urban Land Planning* (New York: Columbia University Press, 1987); Leo Grebler, *Experience in Urban Real Estate Investment* (New York: Columbia University Press, 1987).

28. Marc A. Weiss, "Real Estate History: An Overview and Research Agenda," *Business History Review* 63 (Summer 1989): 241–82.

29. Adna Ferrin Weber, *The Growth of Cities in the Nineteenth Century* (New York, Macmillan, 1899). Hurd's book was published in New York by the *Record and Guide*.

30. My own contribution in this category is a book, *Land Investment and the Predevelopment Process* (Westport, CT: Quorum/Greenwood Press), 1989.

31. Weiss, "Real Estate History," p. 255.

32. Ibid, p. 257.

33. Typical of the literature are the following: L.A. Dougharty, *Forces Shaping Urban Development: The Property Tax* (Santa Monica, CA: Rand Corporation, 1973); Edwin S. Mills and Wallace E. Oates, eds., *Fiscal Zoning and Land Use Controls: The Economic Issues* (Lexington, MA: Lexington Press, 1975); and George R. Zadrow, *Local Provision of Public Services: The Tiebout Model After Twenty-five Years* (New York: Academic Press, 1983).

34. One of the few studies on the subject is Robert E. Shultz, *Life Insurance Housing Projects* (Homewood, IL: Richard D. Irwin, 1956).

35. Exemplified by David Harvey, *Social Justice and the City* (London: David Arnold, 1973).

36. Alan Rabinowitz, *Municipal Bond Finance and Administration* (New York: John Wiley, 1969).

37. After working for the F.F. French Companies since 1950, I joined the four students already in residence—at the Institute for Urban Land Use and Housing Studies: Louis Winnick, David Blank, John Runnels, and Chester Rapkin—all of whom went on to meritorious careers as urban economists. In November I was recalled to active duty in the United States Naval Reserve, a year after the Korean War began. By the time of my return to civilian life two years later the Institute was closing down; Greber and Fisher were instrumental thereafter in creating more viable university-connected centers that led to the pioneering contributions later made by Marc Weiss, described above.

38. Winnick, *Ford History*, Ch. III, "Urbanizing America's Universities: The Elite Universities," p. 12, primarily Harvard, MIT, Princeton, Columbia, University of Chicago, Johns Hopkins, and Northwestern. I spent much of the 1960s in and around the Ford-funded MIT-Harvard Joint Center for Urban Studies and was awarded a V.O. Key Fellowship for 1968–69 in support of my dissertation writing.

39. The economics profession tended to look with some scorn on "urban economics," deeming the study of national and international situations more important than local or metropolitan situations. A useful resource is Irving Hoch, *Progress, in Urban Economics: The Work of the Committee on Urban Economics 1959–1968 and the Development of the Field* (Washington, DC: Resources for the Future, Inc., 1969). Urban economists, on their part, looked with some scorn on urban planners not schooled in mathematics, although the members of the Regional Science Association were usually accepted as colleagues. Planners, on the other hand, often considered the urban economists deficient in understanding the real-life physical and design aspects of urban life.

40. Fred Bosselman and David Callies, *The Quiet Revolution in Land Use Control*, prepared for the council on Environmental Quality, (Washington, DC: Supt. Docs., GPO, 1972). See also Richard Babcock and F.R. Bosselman, *The Contest for Public Control Over Land Development: A Rough Intergovernmental Game for the Seventies* (Los Angeles: Institute of Government and Public Affairs, University of California, 1970). The Council on Environmental Quality has continued in the executive office of the president.

41. The state of the law at the end of the century is recounted in many books and conference proceedings; among the best are R. Meltz, D. Merriam, and R. Frank, *The Takings Issue: Constitutional Limits on Land Use Controls and Environmental Regulation* (Washington, DC: Island Press, 1999); David Callies, ed., *Takings: Land Development Conditions and Regulatory Takings after Dolan and Lucas* (Chicago: Section of State and Local Government Law, American Bar Association, 1996); Harvey M. Jacobs, ed., *Who Owns America? Social Conflict Over Property Rights* (Madison, WI: University of Wisconsin Press, 1998) and the 4th edition of *Land-use Planning: A Casebook in the Use, Misuse, and Reuse of Urban Land* by Charles Haar and Michael Allan Wolf (Boston: Little Brown, 1989).

42. The quotation about the Lucas case (*Lucas v. South Carolina Coastal Council*, 505 U.S. 1003, 112 S. Ct. 2886, 1992) comes from the amicus brief prepared by the American Planning Association et al. (see www.planning.org/amicusbriefs/pdf/

tahoesierra.pdf) in the case of *Tahoe-Sierra Preservation Council v. Tahoe Regional Planning Agency* (Decision No. 00–1167), a case whose origins went back to controls instituted in 1981. The quotation from the Community Rights Counsel, which had also filed an amicus brief, is from its May 2002 newsletter at www. communityrights.org.

Chapter 10

1. After September 11, 2001, White seemed to have been eerily prescient; the full quotation from his book *Here Is New York*, reissued with introduction by Roger Angell (New York: The Little Bookroom, 1999; original Harper and Brothers, 1949), p. 54, goes on as follows: "A single flight of planes no bigger than a wedge of geese can quickly end this island fantasy, burn the towers, crumble the bridges, turn underground passages into lethal chambers, cremate the millions. The intimation of mortality is part of New York now: in the sound of jets overhead, in the black headlines of the latest edition."

2. William Strauss and Neil Howe, *Generations: The History of America's Future, 1584 to 2069* (New York: William Morrow, 1991), p. 257.

3. Ibid., p. 261.

4. Ibid., pp. 293, 281, and 283. Although the Korean conflict was not a declared war, I was called back for it for two years of active duty.

5. *Evolution of Role of the Federal Government in Housing and Community Development: A Chronology of Legislative and Selected Executive Actions, 1892–1974*, U.S. House of Representatives, Committee on Banking, Currency and Housing, Subcommittee on Housing and Community Development, 94th Cong., 1st sess., (Washington, DC: GPO, October 1975), p. 2: (hereafter cited as *Chronology*). The Emergency Relief and Construction Act of 1932 permitted the RFC to make loans to corporations to provide housing for low-income families or to reconstruct slum areas, as stated in Chapter 7 above. Fred F. French's Knickerbocker Village was the result of one of two such loans made.

6. Ibid. At the time, such institutions included building and loan associations, savings and loan associations, cooperative banks, homestead associations, insurance companies, and savings banks.

7. Louis Winnick, et al., *Philanthropy's Adaptation to the Urban Crisis*, Unpublished Manuscript, 1987–1989 Ford Foundation Report #01458, Ch. II, "Philanthropy's Housing Programs: "Housing for the Working Poor," pp. 1–2.

8. See C. Lowell Harriss, *History and Policies of the Home Owner's Loan Corporation* (New York: National Bureau of Economic Research, 1951), published as part of NBER's Urban Real Estate Finance Project, which included three previous works: Miles L. Colean's *The Impact of Government on Real Estate Finance in the United States*, Ernest Fisher's *Urban Real Estate Markets: Characteristics and Financing*, and R.J. Saulnier's *Urban Mortgage Lending by Life Insurance Companies*.

9. See one of my very favorite documents: *Our Cities: Their Role in the National Economy*, Report of the Urbanism Committee to the National Resources Committee (Washington, DC: GPO, June 1937); see also the massive *Report on National Planning and Public Works in Relation to Natural Resources, and Including Land Use and Water Resources* compiled for the National Resources Board (Washington, DC: GPO, December 1, 1934).

10. Abstracted from *Chronology*.

11. "Public Housing Legislation: How It Evolved," *Journal of Housing*, special issue celebrating the fiftieth anniversary of the National Association of Housing and Redevelopment Officials (formerly the National Association of Housing Officials), (September/October 1984): 147.

12. Elaine T. Ostrowski, "Managing Public Housing: The Impact of the 80s," *Journal of Housing* (March/April 1984): 40–41. See also "Public Housing Legislation: How It Evolved."

13. And see *Public Housing Design: A Review of Experience in Low-rent Housing* (Washington, DC: Federal Public Housing Agency of the National Housing Agency, GPO, June 1946).

14. Ostrowski, "Managing Public Housing," p. 41.

15. See *report on National Planning and Public Works in Relation to Natural Resources* cited above.

16. See, for instance, *Report of Project East River*, Part V, "Reduction of Urban Vulnerability," prepared under Signal Corps Contract No. DA-49–025–SC-96 (New York: Associated Universities, Inc., 1952) (Associated Universities included I believe, MIT-Lincoln Laboratories); see also R.W. Lotchin, ed., *The Martial Metropolis: U.S. Cities in War and Peace* (New York: Praeger, 1984).

17. A number of organizations were concerned with resources in the years just after World War II, including the president's Material Policy Commission in the 1950s; see *Resources for Freedom; a report to the President*, 1952, and *Towards a National Materials Policy: Basic Data and Issues*, Report of the U.S. Commission on Materials Policy (Washington, DC: GPO, 1972).

18. Gunnar Myrdal, *An American Dilemma: The Negro Problem and Modern Democracy* (New York and London: Harper., 1944) (written with the assistance of Richard Sterner and Arnold Rose).

19. Winnick, *Ford History*, Ch. I, "Introduction and Conspectus," pp. 4–5.

20. Ibid. p. 5.

21. Ibid. p. 6.

22. T.H. Hanchell, "The Other 'Subsidized Housing': Federal Aid to Suburbanization," *Journal of Housing* (January/February 2001): 19ff.

23. Winnick, *Ford History*, Ch. II, "Philanthropy's Housing Programs: From Action to Action," pp. 37–38.

24. See *Chronology*, p. 150.

25. Winnick, *Ford History*, Ch. I, "Introduction and Conspectus," 6–7.

26. Urban Renewal Directory, *U.S. Department of Housing and Urban Development* (Washington, DC, December 31, 1969).

Chapter 11

1. Jeanne Lowe, *Cities in a Race with Time: Progress and Poverty in America's Renewing Cities* (New York: Random House, 1967). An important book with somewhat larger scope is Martin Mayer's *The Builders: Houses, People, Neighborhoods, Governments, Money* (New York: Norton, 1978).

2. *See, for instance, Problems of Legislative Apportionment and Districting after* Baker v. Carr: *A Subject Bibliography* (Trenton: New Jersey Law and Legisla-

tive Reference Bureau, 1966), and Philip B. Kurland, ed., *The Supreme Court and the Constitution: Essays from the Supreme Court Review* (Chicago: University of Chicago Press, 1965).

3. *Berman v. Parker*, 348 U.S. 26 (1954).

4. See "Homebuilders and Prefabrication in the Postwar Period" in Alan Rabinowitz, *The Real Estate Gamble* (New York: American Management Association, 1980), pp. 106–12.

5. See, for instance, Sumner H. Slichter, "The Taft-Hartley Act," *Quarterly Journal of Economics* (February 1949): 1–31. Slichter was the professor of labor relations at Harvard Business School at the time.

6. See, for instance, Fred J. Cook and Gene Gleason, "The Shame of New York," *Nation*, special issue, October 31, 1959.

7. See Guian A. McKee, "Liberal Ends Through Illiberal Means: Race, Urban Renewal, and Community in the Eastwick Section of Philadelphia, 1949–1990," *Journal of Urban History* 27 (July 2001): 547–93.

8. Section 701 of the 1954 Housing Act established a program to assist all communities, especially smaller ones, to engage trained city planners. Over the years, the 701 Program, something of an employment act for planners, generated a few superb planning reports and tons of pot boiler plans.

9. Gunnar Myrdal, *American Dilemma: The Negro Problem and Modern Democracy* (New York: Harper, 1944); for the story of the difficulty in getting Myrdal's book out, see Alan Pifer, *Philanthropy in an Age of Transition: The Essays of Alan Pifer* (New York: Foundation Center, 1984).

10. See various articles by Arnold R. Hirsch (University of New Orleans): "'Containment' on the Home Front: Federal Housing Policy from the New Deal to the Cold War," *Journal of Urban History* 26, no. 2 (January 2000): 158–89; "Choosing Segregation: Federal Housing Policy Between *Shelley* and *Brown*," in John F. Bauman, Roger Biles, and Kristin M. Szylvian, eds., *From Tenements to the Taylor Homes: In Search of an Urban Housing Policy in Twentieth-Century America* (University Park: Pennsylvania State University Press, 2000), pp. 210–25.

11. Arnold R. Hirsch, "Searching for a 'Sound Negro Policy': A Racial Agenda for the Housing Acts of 1949 and 1954," *Housing Policy Debate* 11, no. 2, pp. 393–439 (Washington, DC: Fannie Mae Foundation, 2000).

12. See, for instance, "Burbs, Blockbusting and Blacks: Morphesis of the Postwar American City," essay by Matthew Jalbert for John's course at University of California Berkeley, "Economy and Culture of the Western City," Fall 1993, available at www.rut.com/mjalbert/burbs.

13. The structure of a full-scale research program (conceptualizing what could be lifetimes of work by an army of researchers and practitioners) was outlined in a seventy-one-page *Summary of Urban Renewal Research Program* written by ACTION's Research Committee, chaired by Reginald Isaacs and sent in October 1954 to Ferd Kramer, ACTION's Chair.

14. Louis Winnick et al., *Philanthropy's Adaptation to the Urban Crisis*, Unpublished Manuscript, 1987–1989, Ford Foundation Archives Report #012158, Ch. II, "Philanthropy's Housing Programs: The Action Program," Note 13, p. 30. The seven books: Edward C. Banfield and Morton Grodzins, *Government and Housing in Metropolitan Areas*; Louis Winnick, *Rental Housing: Opportunities for Private Investment*; Burnham Kelly et al., *Design and the Housing Industry*; William W. Nash,

directed by Miles L. Colean, *Residential Rehabilitation: Private Profits and Public Purposes*; John M. Dyckman and Reginald R. Isaacs, *Capital Requirements for Urban Development and Renewal*; Charles M. Haar, *Federal Government Credit and Private Housing: The Mass Financing Dilemma*; Nelson Foote, Janet Abu-Lughod, Mary Mix Foley, and Louis Winnick, *Consumer Choice and Housing: Present Behavior and Future Expectations*. The series was published between 1958 and 1960 by McGraw-Hill.

15. Ibid.

16. Winnick, *Ford History*, Ch. I, "Introduction and Conspectus," p. 7.

17. Winnick, *Ford History*, Ch. II, "Philanthropy's Housing Programs: Redevelopment or Conservation," pp. 31–34. "The extensive writings in support of such a policy, which go back more than a century, are summarized in James Ford's magisterial *Slums and Housing*. . . . Closer to our time among the most influential authors was Charles Abrams in, among other works, *Future of Housing* (New York: Harper and Row, 1940) and *The City Is the Frontier* (New York: Harper and Row, 1965)."

18. Ibid. "The anti-redevelopment camp was supported by a prodigious literature. Several books were particularly influential. The economic inefficiency arguments are most cogently set forth in Martin Anderson's *The Federal Bulldozer* (New York: McGraw-Hill Book Company, 1967). The urban planners' bible is Jane Jacobs, *The Death and Life of Great American Cities* (New York: Random House, 1970). Jacobs carried her opposition into the streets as well as into the university and converted a whole generation of urban planners to her philosophy. The social planners' case is well made by Herbert Gans, *The Urban Villagers: Group and Class Life of Italian-Americans* (Glencoe, IL: The Free Press, 1962), and Chester Hartman's *Housing and Social Policy* (Englewood Cliffs, NJ: Prentice-Hall, 1975):, cf. James Q. Wilson, ed., *Urban Renewal: The Record and the Controversy* (Cambridge, MA: Massachusetts Institute of Technology Press, 1966)."

19. Ibid.

20. *Evolution of Role of the Federal Government in Housing and Community Development: A Chronology of Legislative and Selected Executive Actions, 1892–1974* (Washington, DC: GPO, October 1975), hereafter cited as *Chronology*.

21. Edward C. Banfield, *The Unheavenly City: The Nature and Future of Our Urban Crisis* (Boston: Little, Brown, 1968).

22. Winnick, *Ford History*, Ch. II, "Philanthropy's Housing Programs: Policies to Contain Housing Costs, p. 110, and also see Winnick's summary of the four major reasons for endemic high costs in new residential construction: burdensome regulations, expensive sites, high interest rates, and industry lagging in productivity gains, Ch. II pp. 101–3.

23. Most authoritative write-up: *Federally Assisted New Communities: New Dimensions in Urban Development*, Landmark Series, Hugh Mields Jr. (Washington, DC: Urban Land Institute, 1973).

24. Instead, I accepted a job as administrator for program planning and finance at the Boston Redevelopment Authority (BRA), which Logue had had created at the end of the 1950s as a superagency with the city's redevelopment and building power. When Logue left BRA in early 1968 to run unsuccessfully for mayor of Boston, many urban renewal projects lacked the necessary federal grants, for the projects had been started before the full federal grants that had been promised were actually in hand, and the Nixon administration was very slow in honoring what BRA be-

lieved were the Johnson administration's contractual obligations. Shortly after I left BRA, I wrote up some impressions of that agency as a planning authority, and the manuscript was published and distributed as *Non-planning and Redevelopment in Boston: An Analytic Study of the Planning Process* (Seattle: University of Washington Urban Planning/Development Series Number Nine, Department of Urban Planning, September 1972).

25. Louis K. Loewenstein, "The New York State Urban Development Corporation —A Forgotten Failure or a Precursor of the Future?" *Journal of the American Institute of Planners*, July 1978, p. 261. With a grant from the Ford Foundation, Loewenstein also has written but not published a most detailed monograph, *The New York State Urban Development Corporation: Private Benefits and Public Costs— An Evaluation of a Noble Experiment*, undated but done in the late 1970s, available from the Ford Foundation's archivist.

26. Martin Mayer, *The Builders: Houses, People, Neighborhoods, Governments, Money* (New York: W.W. Norton, 1978), p. 281.

27. Both reports were ultimately available from the Superintendent of Documents, GPO, Washington, DC. The Report of the President's Committee on Urban Housing, *A Decent Home*, was delivered Dec. 11, 1968 but dated 1973 by GPO. The Report of the National Commission on Urban Problems, *Building the American City*, is identified as a House Document 91–34m 91st Congress, 1st Session but sold by GPO after delivery on Dec. 12, 1968.

28. Winnick, *Ford History*, Ch. II, "Philanthropy's Housing Programs: From Action to Action," p. 38.

Chapter 12

1. This perspective is developed more fully midstream during President G.W. Bush's first term by William Greider in "The Right's Grand Ambition: Rolling Back the 20th Century" (*Nation*, May 12, 2003), but he marks the beginning with Reagan rather than with Nixon or even the earlier 1964 Goldwater election campaign.

2. See, for instance, the Sierra Club's *The War Against the Greens: The "Wise-Use" Movement, the New Right and Anti-environmental Violence*, by David Helvarg (San Francisco: Sierra Club Books, 1994), and John D. Echeverria and R.B. Eby, *Let the People Judge: Wise Use and the Private Property Rights Movement* (Washington, DC: Island Press, 1995); and from the wise use movement on the other side, a task force report edited by Alan M. Gottlieb, *The Wise Use Agenda: The Citizen's Policy Guide to Environmental Resource Issues* (Bellevue, WA: Free Enterprise Press, 1989). Possibly the most profound of the retrospectives on the whole issue is Jean Hardisty's *Mobilizing Resentment: Conservative Resurgence from the John Birch Society to the Promise Keepers* (Boston: Beacon Press, 1999). See also William Coons, *Sagebrush Rebellion: Legitimate Assertion of States' Rights or Retrograde Land Grab? A Selected Subject Bibliography and Resource Guide* (Monticello, IL: Vance Bibliographies, 1981).

3. Nathan Glazer and Danial Patrick Moynihan, *Beyond the Melting Pot* (Cambridge: MIT Press, 1963).

4. Louis Winnick, *Ford History*, Ch. II, pp. 44–45.

5. Ibid., pp. 99–100.

6. This was a report for the Coalition for a Livable Washington, c/o Institute for

Washington's Future, 1900 S. Puget Drive, Renton, WA 98055. Orfield at the time had recently published his first major book on the subject: *Metropolitics: A Regional Agenda for Community and Stability* (Washington, DC: Brookings Press, 1997). Brookings Press published his latest book, *American Metropolitics: The New Suburban Reality*, in 2002 and wrote that it "applies the next generation of cutting-edge research on a much broader scale than the earlier book. The book provides an eye-opening analysis of the economic, racial, environmental, and political trends of the 25 largest metropolitan regions in the United States—which contain more than 45 percent of the U.S. population."

7. After a lapse of two decades or more, attention is swinging back to the need for an overall federal policy concerning the American metropolis; an example is *Place Matters: Metropolitics for the Twenty-First Century*, by Peter Dreier, John Mollenkopf, and Todd Swanstrom (Lawrence: University Press of Kansas, 2001).

8. A prime source of data would have been the files of *Architectural Digest*, which, during the most active years of the urban renewal programs, published in-depth studies of many of the major redevelopment projects across the nation. At one point I proposed that the magazine let me use its files to compare the original plan with what actually transpired. I would have enjoyed seeing the result of such an analysis, but the idea was turned down by Time, Inc., the *Digest*'s owner. Maybe no one wanted to know.

9. But perhaps at a significant psychological cost as well, as suggested in Richard Sennett's *The Uses of Disorder: Personal Identity and City Life* (New York: Vintage/Random House, 1970).

10. The federal government's active interest in "the infrastructure problem," came in the mid-1980s. The "problem" was that states did not have the money they felt they needed to fix up crumbling bridges and aging central-city facilities. A number of studies were initiated. I found that local officials across the nation generally intended to use whatever federal funds might arrive to build facilities for growing suburban, even "exurban" populations, with not much left over for central cities. Activity in this area, at the moment, appears to be located in the U.S. Department of Transportation and, for Congress, in the House of Representatives' Committee on Transportation and Infrastructure.

11. The 2001 brochure, with headline "Still Getting Your Kicks on Oklahoma Route 66," comes from Oklahoma Route 66 Museum, 2229 Gary Freeway, Clinton, OK 73601–5304.

12. Data for the last quarter of the twentieth century concerning the amount of housing assisted by federal government programs are found in Cushing, Dolbeare and Sheila Crowley, *Changing Priorities: The Federal Budget and Housing Assistance, 1976–2007*, Washington, DC: National Low Income Housing Coalition, August 2002; information on mortgages during the period is to be found in Kent W. Colton, *Housing Finance in the U.S.: The Transformation of the U.S. Housing Finance System*, Cambridge Joint Center for Housing Studies, Harvard University, 2000, WO2–5. Also, "Public Housing at a Crossroads," Executive Director's Message, *NAHRO Monitor*, January 31, 2003, p. 3.

13. Alan Rabinowitz, Nestor Terleckyj, and Kerry Brooks, *Markets for New Construction 1980–87–95*, (Washington, DC: NPA Data Services, Inc. and Territory Research, Inc., 1988). Part I: Analysis of Construction Markets; Part II: Handbook of the U.S. Construction Markets 1980–87, with Trend Projections to 1995; Part III: Data Disks and Appendixes.

14. The major categories of data for the residential series were single family, multifamily, new two-unit, new three- or four-unit, and new five- or more units. For the nonresidential series, the categories were residential additions and alterations, office construction, industrial buildings, stores, nonresidential additions and alterations, hotel/motel/other housekeeping facilities, hospitals, etc., other nonresidential structures, structures other than buildings, church/religious buildings, private public-utility buildings, private school/education buildings, amusement/recreation buildings, parking garages, and service/repair garages.

15. Eventually we selected five variables to represent the variety of distinguishing features in each economic area: (1) per capita expenditures on residential structures, in constant 1982 dollars, summed for the six years 1980 to 1985 and divided by the 1980 population, (2) per capita expenditures on nonresidential structures, in constant 1982 dollars, summed for the six years 1980 to 1985 and divided by the 1980 population, (3) percent change in population, 1980 to 1985, (4) new residential units permitted 1980 to 1985 as a percentage of the stock of housing units in 1980, and (5) the total number of housing units in 1980. Many of these variables are highly correlated with one another, as might be expected, but on the basis of extensive simple correlation analysis, we selected what we deemed was the best set.

16. Kitty Calavita, Henry N. Pontell, and Robert H. Tillman, *Big Money Crime: Fraud and Politics in the Savings and Loan Crisis* (Berkeley: University of California Press, 1997).

17. Ibid., pp. 18, 21, and 24.

18. More on the Resolution Trust Corporation can be found in reports of congressional hearings held by the Senate Committee on Banking and Currency, June 1991; House Subcommittee on Financial Institutions Supervision, Regulation, and Insurance of the Committee on Banking, Finance and Urban Affairs, 1993; and the House Subcommittee on General Oversight and Investigations of the Committee on Banking and Financial Services, June 1995, (available from the Government Printing Office).

19. Alan Rabinowitz, *The Real Estate Gamble* (New York: Amacom, 1980).

20. David Bollier, *How Smart Growth Can Stop Sprawl*, obtainable from: sprawlwatch.org; smartgrowth.org; fundersnetwork.org. And see Linda A. Long, "Playing It Smart," *Foundation News*, March 2003, p. 13.

21. One of the most convincing of the early studies is by William L.C. Wheaton and Morton J. Schussheim, *The Cost of Municipal Services in Residential Areas* (Washington, DC: GPO, 1955). The best treatment of the subject, with an exceptionally comprehensive bibliography, is *The Fiscal Impact Guidebook: Estimating Local Costs and Revenues of Land Development*, compiled for the Department of Housing and Urban Development's Office of Policy Development and Research by Robert W. Burchell and David Listokin at the Center for Urban Policy Research at Rutgers University, New Brunswick, New Jersey, 1978.

22. Bollier, *How Smart Growth Can Stop Sprawl*, p. 3.

23. See, for instance, the many articles in the special issue on new urbanism, *Planners Network* 150 (Winter 2002).

24. See Neal R. Pierce, "Smart Growth Still a Movement With Legs," *Seattle Times*, March 3, 2003, p. B4. Pierce is perhaps the best (and best-known) syndicated columnist on urbanism at work in recent decades.

25. Available on-line www.cnu.org.

26. James Howard Kunstler, "Home From Nowhere," *Atlantic Monthly*, September 1996, p. 43ff.

27. See Lloyd Rodwin and Bishwaprya Sanyal, *The Profession of City Planning: Changes, Images, and Challenges: 1950–2000* (New Brunswick, NJ: Rutgers University, Center for Urban Policy Research, 2000), especially the essay by Michael B. Teitz, "Reflections and Research on the U.S. Experience," p. 275ff. I am also interested that Israel Stollman in his essay, "Looking Back, Looking Forward," says that "Peter Hall believes the gulf between practice and theory is increasing" (p. 105).

28. Kunstler, "Home From Nowhere," p. 44.

29. One of the American Planning Association's contributions here is the publication of Jonathan Barnett's *Redesigning Cities* (Chicago: Planners Press, 2003).

30. See, for instance, "Do the Voters Really Hate Sprawl?" by D.J. Waldie, *New York Times* op-ed page, March 3, 2000.

31. See Jonathan Barnett, ed., *Planning for a New Century: The Regional Agenda* (Washington, DC: Island Press, 2001).

32. The literature in the planning field is chock-full of theories as to how decisions are actually made or should be made. All that literature is beyond the scope of this book (although I once taught courses in it at the University of Washington); I will merely acknowledge the source of the term "disjointed incrementalism" as David Braybrooke and Charles E. Lindblom, *A Strategy of Decision: Policy Evaluation as a Social* Process (New York: Free Press of Glencoe, 1963), Chapter 5. See also the insightful book by Charles E. Lindblom and David K. Cohen, *Usable Knowledge* (New Haven: Yale University Press, 1979).

Chapter 13

1. See, for instance, Daniel Bell's *The Coming of Post-Industrial Society: A Venture in Social Forecasting* (New York: Basic Books, 1976).

2 Jane Jacobs, *Cities and the Wealth of Nations: Principles of Economic Life* (New York: Random House, 1984).

3. The eventual bibliography on this subject will contain hundreds of citations, for new articles appeared daily in the months after the attack, and, since then, after several cycles of architectural competitions to provide models for public inspection and comment (those competitions and public "participation" being something never tried before with respect to such a major land area), the press has been full of critiques of the implications and meaningfulness of the various architectural solutions proposed as redevelopment guides. Among the major critics of the physical design procedures during 2002 is Peter Marcuse, whose article, "The Ground Zero Architectural Competition: Designing Without a Plan," in *Planners Network*, no. 154 (Winter 2003), states:

> Whatever the merits of the nine proposals, the basic problem is that the program they [the internationally-renowned architects] were given by the LMDC (Lower Manhattan Development Corporation), developed without adequate public input, was the wrong program at the wrong time. The LMDC has set out a planning process that is hasty, undemocratic and evades the critical planning and policy questions.

Among the most interesting of the postattack publications are the compilation of essays in *Planning Network* 179 (September–December 2001), and Michael Tomasky's "The World Trade Center: Before, During, and After," *New York Review* 49(5), March 28, 2002, reviewing the Darnton book cited in footnote 6 below. William Langewiesche's articles in *Atlantic Monthly Magazine* in mid-2002 entitled "American Ground: Unbuilding the World Trade Center," since republished in book form, focus primarily on the human and technological stories in clearing the site for redevelopment rather than on the challenges to city form, function, and feelings being generated by new construction on the site.

4. For a famous study of Moses, see Robert A. Caro, *The Power Broker* (New York: Knopf, 1974).

5. C. Wright Mills, *The Power Elite* (New York: Oxford University Press, 1956); Robert Staughton Lynd and Helen Merrell Lynd, *Middletown: A Study in Contemporary American Culture* (New York: Harcourt Brace, 1929).

6. See Eric Darnton, *Divided We Stand: A Biography of New York's World Trade Center* (New York: Basic Books, 2002); also Angus K. Gillespie, *Twin Towers: The Life of New York City's World Trade Center* (New Brunswick, NJ: Rutgers University Press, 2002).

7. *Commissioner of Internal Revenue v. Shamberg's Estate (1944)*, 144 F. 2d. 998, majority opinion by Justice Augustus N. Hand, dissent by Justice Jerome Frank.

8. Chester Hartman in his *Between Eminence and Notoriety: Four Decades of Radical Urban Planning* (New Brunswick, NJ: Rutgers University, Center for Urban Policy Research, 2002), 47, p. 29, noted: "In June 1999, PEO's founder and guiding light, Walter Thabit, one of the original advocate planners, working in the Cooper Square neighborhood of New York City . . . produced 'A History of PEO' . . . which may evolve into a more elaborate project and publication on the role of progressive planning in the 1960s. . . . The history is available from Professor Kenneth Reardon, Department of City and Regional Planning, Cornell University, Ithaca, NY 14853."

9. Jane Jacobs, *The Life and Death of Great Cities* (New York: Random House, 1966).

10. For a fine op-ed article on how critical decisions to restore utilities and streets to an area tend to be made before any rebuilding plans are agreed upon thus foreclosing many options, see Witold Rybczynski, well-known professor of urbanism at the University of Pennsylvania, "How Quickly a City Can Grow," *New York Times*, March 25, 2002.

Chapter 14

1. Ayn Rand, *The Fountainhead* (New York: Bobbs Merrill, 1943).

2. Set design by Otto Hunte, Eric Kettlehut, and Karl Vollbrecht.

3. Leslie Halliwell, *The Filmgoers Companion*, 6th ed. (New York: Avon Books, 1977).

4. Unpublished transcript of the remarks of Robert Moses, chairman of the Triborough Bridge and Tunnel Authority, at a luncheon of the Joint Center for Urban Studies of the Massachusetts Institute of Technology and Harvard University, Cambridge, Massachusetts, November 15, 1966.

5. "Urban Processes as Viewed by the Social Sciences," a National Academy of Sciences Symposium organized by The Urban Institute and moderated by William Gorham, Washington, DC: The Urban Institute, 1972.

6. E.F. Schumacher, *Small Is Beautiful: A Study of Economics as If People Mattered* (London: Blond & Briggs, 1973; Sphere Books, 1974).

7. A galaxy of organizations in a variety of fields are interested in the principles of sustainability; much of the effort is in the context of the 1996 report of the President's Council on Sustainable Development, *Sustainable America*, with its ten goals relating to health and the environment, economic prosperity, equity, conservation of nature, stewardship, sustainable communities, civic engagement, population, international responsibility, and education. The council had been established by President Clinton in 1993.

8. Louis Winnick, et al., *Philanthropy's Adaptation to the Urban Crisis*, Unpublished Manuscript, 1987–1989, Ford Foundation Archives Report #012158, Ch. II, "Philanthropy's Housing Programs: Redevelopment or Conservation, p. 36.

9. Nico Calavita, "Smart Growth as a Trojan Horse," *Planners Network: The Magazine of Progressive Planning*, no. 150, Winter 2002, p. 26.

Index

Abercrombie, Patrick, 21
Adams, Thomas, 21
Addams, Jane, 65
Advisory Commission on Inter-
   governmental Relations, U.S., 186
AFL-CIO, 145
African-Americans, 139, 150
   civil rights and, 46, 51
   migration of, 118
   See also racism
After the Planners, 162
Alaska
   acquisition of, 44, 45
   construction and, 171
Albany, New York
   population shift and, 79
Alexander, Christopher, 176
Amalgamated Clothing Workers Union,
   101
Amalgamated Housing Corporation, 194,
   195, 227n22
America First, 127
American City Corporation, 152
American Civil Liberties Union,
   establishment of, 120
American Council to Improve Our
   Neighborhoods (A.C.T.I.O.N.), 142,
   143, 146, 194
*American Dilemma, An: The Negro
   Problem and Modern Democracy*,
   130, 139
American Economic Association, 57, 88
American Institute of Certified Planners
   (AICP), 221n18
American Institute of Planners, 221n18
American Institute of Real Estate
   Appraisers, 98
American Museum of Natural History,
   95

American Planning Association, 221n18
American Public Health Association
   (APHA), 89, 90, 93
American Revolution, 38, 67, 192
American Society of Planning Officials
   (ASPO), 221n18
Amtrak
   See transportation
Anderson, Martin, 144, 160
Appalachia, 188
Appalachian Mountains, 39, 44, 67
Appalachian Regional Development Act of
   1965, 150
architect-builders
   protection from, 198, 200
architects, 167
   development and, 19, 208
   garden cities and, 21, 24
   planning and, 25
   landscape, 95, 99
architecture
   sprawl and, 176
   new urbanism, 179
Area Redevelopment Act, 148
Arizona (admission to union), 42
Aronovici, Carol, 106
Arrow, Kenneth, 201
Arthur D. Little, Inc., 152, 195
Atlanta
   population density and, 79, 81
Augusta, Georgia Planning Area, 82, 83
automobiles
   See transportation

Babbitt, 6, 30
Babbitt, George, 6, 30
"Babbitts," 6, 14, 25, 26, 29, 30, 31, 34, 91,
   92, 98, 99, 113, 119, 137, 166, 199,
   211

About the Author

Alan Rabinowitz has worked and taught in the intersecting fields of urban land-use analysis, economic development, housing, city and regional planning, real estate investment, state-local finance, and community organizing for many decades. He holds a Ph.D. from MIT and an M.B.A. from Harvard. He has written a number of books and has worked in the United States and abroad for private consulting, financial and investing firms, and for governmental agencies. He currently lives with his wife in Seattle.